D0408408

Household Politics

✳ ✳ ✳

HOUSEHOLD POLITICS

Conflict in Early Modern England

Don Herzog

Yale
UNIVERSITY PRESS

NEW HAVEN & LONDON

Published with assistance from the Annie Burr Lewis Fund
and from the Louis Stern Memorial Fund.

Yale University Press books may be purchased in quantity for educational, business, or promotional use. For
information, please e-mail sales.press@yale.edu (U.S. office) or sales@yaleup.co.uk (U.K. office).

Set in Fournier type by Keystone Typesetting, Inc., Orwigsburg, Pennsylvania.
Printed in the United States of America.

ISBN: 978-0-300-18078-7 (cloth)

Catalogue records for this book are available from the British Library and from the Library of Congress..

This paper meets the requirements of ANSI / NISO Z39.48–1992 (Permanence of Paper).

10 9 8 7 6 5 4 3 2 1

for Isaac Kramnick

Contents

Preface

First licensed for production in 1626 and staged repeatedly over the
years, John Fletcher's *The Noble Gentleman*[1] isn't a magnificent literary
achievement. But it's plenty interesting for my purposes. Marine, the not-
quite-noble gentleman of the title, is tired of loitering at court, an activity his
wife adores. Listen to Marine's soliloquy as he screws up his courage to tell
his wife that they're abandoning city life:

> Why what an Asse was I that such a thing
> As a wife is could rule me? Know not I
> That woman was created for the man,
> That her desires, nay all her thoughts should be
> As his are? is my sense restor'd at length?
> Now she shall know, that which she should desire,
> She hath a husband that can govern her,
> If her desires leades me against my will.

Sounding in the book of Genesis, the passage asserts a classic justification for
male dominance. It's unblushing in describing that dominance as governance. Look what happens when his wife battles back.[2] Horrified, she insists

---

1. [John Fletcher], *The Noble Gentleman*, ed. L. A. Beaurline, in *The Dramatic Works in the
Beaumont and Fletcher Canon*, ed. Fredson Bowers et al., 10 vols. (Cambridge: Cambridge University
Press, 1966–96), 3:115.

2. Compare the trajectory of Lord Wronglove's blustering in Colley Cibber, *The Lady's Last Stake:
or, The Wife's Resentment*, 3rd ed. (London, 1736).

that he can't back out now, when all the work of cultivating the favor of the court is about to bear fruit. He's unmoved:

> *Gentleman.* Wife talke no more, your Retoricke comes too late,
>   I am inflixable; and how dere you
>   Adventure to direct my course of life?
>   Was not the husband made to rule the wife?
> *Lady.* 'Tis true, but where the man doth misse his way,
>   It is the womans part to set him right;
>   So Fathers have a power to guide their Sonnes
>   In all their courses, yet you oft have seene
>   Poore litle children that have both their eyes
>   Lead their blind Fathers.
> *Gentleman [aside].* She has a plaguy witt.—
>   I say you'r but a little piece of man.
> *Lady.* But such a peice, as being tane away,
>   Man cannot last: the fairest and tallest ship,
>   That ever saild, is by a little peice
>   Of the same wood, steerd right, and turnd about.
> *Gentleman [aside].* 'Tis true she sayes, her answers stand with reason.

That "little peice of man," Eve from Adam's rib, continues the appeal to Genesis. Not that his wife meekly submits to scripture's authority. Instead, she blithely swaps rudder for rib and plots to undo her husband's newfound resolution. Amusingly, she has her disguised confederates shower phony aristocratic titles on him. Stunned, in the midst of changing his "grave and thrifty habit" for clothes suiting his apparent new station as duke, Marine kneels to his wife:

> And here in token that all strife shall end
> 'Twixt thee and me, I let my drawers fall
> And to thy hands I do deliver them:
> From this time forth my wife shall wear the breeches.[3]

Her servant vigorously approves the ribald ceremony: "An honourable composition."

Ignominiously stripped of his fictive titles, the Gentleman addresses the

---

3. Compare the women's song, with men eavesdropping, in *The Woman's Prize* [1646], in Bowers et al., *Dramatic Works in the Beaumont and Fletcher Canon*, 4:54, and see in the same collection *Rule a Wife and Have a Wife* [1624], 6:521.

audience: "Be warned all ye Peers, and by my fall, / Hereafter learn to let your wives rule all."

Picture a 1626 audience chuckling at a clown of a husband who in winking asides assures them that women should rule. Should women wear the breeches? (The phrase appears in a book of sayings from the same year as Fletcher's play. It would still be ricocheting around England some two centuries later.)[4] I don't mean to suggest that Fletcher intends to press any such moral. Nor do I mean to suggest that he's endorsing male dominance. I'm concerned not with Fletcher's intentions, but with what contemporary audiences and readers could and would make of his work. Ponder the gentleman's asides, snipped out of the main line of dramatic action and presented as bracketed confidences. They're not bombshells of bold radicalism exploding on the playgoers' dazed imaginations. They're reminders of everyday platitudes, likely to provoke wry snickering and rueful wincing. The Gentleman may need to strike an imperious stance with his wife to propel the plot, but he acknowledges that she's got the better of the argument, indeed that she ought to rule. He knows his claims of authority ring hollow. If chortling, not chagrin, is in order, we have a husband puerile in his high-handed assertion of dominance, what helps make him the butt of an extended joke.

That's a glimpse of the sort of evidence I'll canvass in this book. I hope to conjure up a social world full of ornery, funny, sickening, and lethal controversies about gender, patriarchy, misogyny, public and private, and more. After visiting a character whose romantic fantasies are punctured and the ensuing spirited debate about sexual disgust, I cheerfully demolish two views that have enjoyed some currency. First: people back then imagined that male power was natural or necessary, part of the woodwork of the world, not a contingent social practice that could be reformed or even abolished. Second: the public / private distinction was gendered—so public man, private woman —and that explains the political subordination of women. Whether you believe these claims, put starkly or subtly, or already know they're patently misguided will depend in part on your disciplinary interests. Regardless, my demolition permits me also to sharpen some concepts. I want to clarify what we might mean in invoking *natural* or *essentialized*, *public* and *private*. Having cleared the ground, I move to my constructive agenda. I explain what we

4. H[enry] P[arrot], *Cvres for the Itch* (London, 1626), sig. E4 verso; Anna Clark, *The Struggle for the Breeches: Gender and the Making of the English Working Class* (Berkeley: University of California Press, 1995).

might mean—and what the early modern English did mean—in casting the household as political. I argue too that conflict isn't the opposite of social order. To cash out these abstract positions, I reconstruct contemporary struggles over domestic servants.

Throughout, I rely on long-standing convictions, which I'll put briefly and polemically. I'm heartened to know that these convictions are pedestrian in many fields. Not, alas, in political theory. So: beneath the austere vistas of the likes of Hobbes and Locke are plenty of smart and savvy sources of great interest in their own right, not simply for helping us get a fix on what is linguistically or conceptually innovative in canonical texts. I don't mean the allegedly lesser lights of, say, Mandeville or Swift. I mean popular songs, jokes, sermons, pamphlets, diaries, letters, and more. And only mischief follows in the wake of the distinction between social and intellectual history, a hangover of a bad nineteenth-century debate about the ideal and material aspects of social life. (There's still a lot to learn from Hegel and Marx, but not *that*.) The only decent argument for the primacy of either is the manifest inadequacy of the other. Then there are the endless refinements: so for instance should intellectual historians pursue concepts or ideas or texts or languages or discourses or epistemes or . . . ? But if these are refinements of an unhelpful distinction, they're not worth pursuing. We can strive for better than filigreed confusion. Imagine stumbling on a lost tribe of academics who'd adopted this peculiar division of labor: some studied objects smaller than six cubic inches, some larger. You'd act faintly embarrassed if someone demanded that you swear allegiance to one side and you'd try to change the subject. Our quaint divide between social and intellectual history deserves the same treatment.

Political theorists inherit a canon—the one that runs Plato, Aristotle, Augustine, Aquinas, Machiavelli, Hobbes, Locke, and so on, blithely skipping over centuries and continents—centered on abstract theoretical investigations of the ideal government. It's a mistake to enlist those sources as the distilled essence of their times and places. So we notice that Hobbes and Locke say little about gender and the family and we infer that back then people didn't understand how deeply political those matters were. But nothing follows about the salience or understanding of those issues in early modern England from what Hobbes and Locke happen not to say. Maybe noncanonical contemporaries had all kinds of interesting things to say about household politics. Maybe our vision has been occluded by the pinched criteria that shaped our traditional canon. Instead of detecting the subterranean influence of Hobbes's or Locke's commitments about gender and the family, we could shrug and admit that our canon has served as a straitjacket. I hereby shrug.

Worse, perhaps: too many political theorists blithely help themselves to views about modernization, state building, the rise of the bourgeoisie, patriarchy, and the like without bothering to learn any history. But these aren't just richly complex issues. They're also contingent and—relax, no appeals to barefoot positivism here—empirical. It behooves us to muck around in the evidence.

Most of my evidence is from England in the years 1650 to 1750. But I roam from the fifteenth century to the later eighteenth century, as the argument demands. Sometimes too I trespass over national boundaries and introduce tidbits from Scotland and Ireland. You can think of this time and place as roughly Charles I's execution to the last gasp of Jacobitism, or, more historiographically and less politically, a trespass over one wall of the so-called long eighteenth century. This panoramic a view invites the rejoinder that surely there was change worth noting. I note change only here and there: so, for instance, over time the law frowned increasingly, if never all that severely, at wife beating and skimmingtons. One could usefully chart variation or focus more narrowly. Still, the panoramic view is useful, too.

When academic exchange goes well, it's a model of conflict. I presented draft portions of this work at Harvard, Northwestern, NYU, Yale, and the Universities of Chicago, Michigan, North Carolina, Toronto, and Virginia. I happily profited from pointed questions. I'm also grateful to friends and colleagues who read earlier drafts: Liz Anderson, Laura Davulis, Mary Dietz, Katharine Gillespie, John Goldberg, Scott Hershovitz, Susan Juster, Ellen Katz, Val Kivelson, Daryl Levinson, Lori Marso, Peggy McCracken, Jane Metcalf, Bill Miller, Bill Novak, Jim Oakes, Adela Pinch, Gil Seinfeld, Kathrina Szymborski, David Velleman, Adrian Vermeule, Mark West, and Liz Wingrove. Thanks too to Colleen Manwell for checking citations, to Robin Du-Blanc for impeccable copyediting, and to Margaret Otzel for expert production editing.

I owe a different kind of debt. Thirty-some years ago, a wonderful teacher and remarkable scholar at Cornell was insanely generous. He super-vised me in three semesters of independent study: six credits a term, a ten-page paper due just about every week, densely scribbled and occasionally legible comments in return, exhilarating weekly meetings. I'll never forget the experience, which set me on this path. Dedicating this book to him is laughably inadequate recompense. But will he scribble in the margins?

CHAPTER I

A Tale of Two Poems

Wasn't the culture of early modern England chock-full of misogyny? You betcha. (What time and place hasn't been? Sorry, no points for suggesting today's United States.) *Mysogynus* versified such sentiments in 1682:

> Whate're was left unfit in the Creation
> To make a Toad, after its ugly fashion,
> Of scrapings from unfinished Creatures had,
> Sure was the body of a Woman made:
> Yet there's some finer Atoms daub'd upon,
> Which makes her seem so beauteous to look on.[1]

Consider the thought that misogyny reigned across the board, that everyday life was so drenched in it that people couldn't imagine or pursue alternatives, that men and women alike were blind to the suffering and injustice at stake. Let's call this thought the big sleep thesis. It's an ominous image of how ideology might work, in a way some call totalizing.[2]

---

1. *Mysogynus: or, A Satyr upon Women* (London, 1682), 2.

2. Such a view is staked out by Pierre Bourdieu, *Masculine Domination*, trans. Richard Nice (Cambridge: Polity, 2001), 1–2, 54, 88. See too for instance Catharine A. MacKinnon, *Toward a Feminist Theory of the State* (Cambridge, MA: Harvard University Press, 1989), 99–100; Judith Butler, *Gender Trouble: Feminism and the Subversion of Identity* (New York: Routledge, 1990), 8, 33. Similar theses surface in other domains. For instance Lucien Febvre, *The Problem of Unbelief in the Sixteenth Century: The Religion of Rabelais*, trans. Beatrice Gottlieb (Cambridge, MA: Harvard University Press, 1982), is probably right to argue that Rabelais was not an atheist. But I emphatically disagree with his further claim that atheism was unthinkable in the sixteenth century.

But the very appearance of such texts as *Mysogynus* counsels against the big sleep thesis. Why bother vehemently announcing something everyone takes for granted? Whenever we find people promulgating such a view, we should immediately infer that others doubted or denied it, or at least that the promulgators think such doubts and denials a real possibility. So supporters of the big sleep thesis should search for settings where no one mentions an issue. But early modern England turns out to be stuffed not only with misogyny, but also with spirited rejoinders. Conflict, not consensus, was the order of the day. No surprise that a year after *Mysogynus,* we find *Haec & Hic: or, The Feminine Gender More Worthy than the Masculine: Being a Vindication of That Ingenious and Innocent Sex from the Biting Sarcasms, Bitter Satyrs, and Opprobrious Calumnies, wherewith They Are Daily, tho Undeservedly, Aspers'd by the Virulent Tongues and Pens of Malevolent Men,* declaring that "those usual Satyrs and Invectives against that Sweetly-temper'd Sex, only Betray Men's greater Imbecility."[3] No surprise either that in 1697, Daniel Defoe proposed an "Academy for Women": "I Have often thought of it as one of the most barbarous Customs in the world, considering us as a Civiliz'd and a Christian Countrey, that we deny the advantages of Learning to Women. We reproach the Sex every day with Folly and Impertinence, while I am confident, had they the advantages of Education equal to us, they wou'd be guilty of less than our selves."[4] No surprise that we also find pithy assertions of natural equality: "Women are neither those Angels, nor those Devils we make 'em; for bating *Propagation,* they differ but little from Men in any thing."[5]

3. [James Norris], *Haec & Hic* (London, 1683), 4. See too James Hodges, *Essays on Several Subjects* (London, 1710), the Epistle Dedicatory, n.p., and 70–71; J[ames] Bland, *An Essay in Praise of Women; or, A Looking-glass for Ladies to See Their Perfections In* (London, 1733), 256.

4. [Daniel Defoe], *An Essay upon Projects* (London, 1697), 282. On the vexing matter of Defoe attributions, I have followed P. N. Furbank and W. R. Owens, *A Critical Bibliography of Daniel Defoe* (London: Pickering & Chatto, 1998). See too A Lover of Her Sex [Mary Astell], *A Serious Proposal to the Ladies, for the Advancement of Their True and Greatest Interest* (London, 1697), pt. 1; A Lady of Quality [Mary Lee Chudleigh], *The Female Advocate: or, A Plea for the Just Liberty of the Tender Sex, and Particularly of Married Women* (London, 1700), vii. Deriding the prospects for women's education, A Gentleman, *Man Superior to Woman; or, A Vindication of Man's Natural Right of Sovereign Authority over the Woman: Containing a Plain Confutation of the Fallacious Arguments of Sophia, in Her Late Treatise Intitled, Woman Not Inferior to Man* (London, 1739), 56. Saluting the progress of women's education, *Rambler,* no. 173 (12 November 1751), in *The Yale Edition of the Works of Samuel Johnson,* ed. W. J. Bate et al., 23 vols. to date (New Haven, CT: Yale University Press, 1958–), 5:152–53. On a journal with polite readers of both sexes swapping math riddles in verse, see Shelley Costa, "The *Ladies' Diary:* Gender, Mathematics, and Civil Society in Early-Eighteenth-Century England," *Osiris,* 2nd ser., 17 (2002): 49–73.

5. *The English Theophrastus: or, The Manners of the Age,* 2nd ed. (London, 1706), 35.

So too, with a normative spin, for the epilogue to *The Woman's Prize* of 1646: urging that men

> should not raign as Tyrants o'r their wives.
> Nor can the women from this president,
>> Insult, or triumph: it being aptly meant,
> To teach both Sexes due equality;
>> And as they stand bound, to love mutually.[6]

So too, finally, for the 1701 verse that teeters back toward female superiority:

> Stand up *Fair Ladies* and your Rights maintain,
> Heav'n gives you equal Liberty with *Man*,
> *Woman* is Born by nature full as free,
> And is, if learn'd, as wise and Brave as *He*.
> *Woman* in Beauty's far more perfect made,
> And rather than Obey should be Obey'd;
> For less Perfections doubtless should adore
> The worthy'r *Being*, which is Bless'd with more.[7]

I'll produce much more evidence of conflict and controversy. Keith Thomas once found in seventeenth-century England "a universal belief in [the] inferior capacity" of women, but that's a mirage.[8]

---

6. *The Woman's Prize* [1646], in *The Dramatic Works in the Beaumont and Fletcher Canon*, ed. Fredson Bowers et al., 10 vols. (Cambridge: Cambridge University Press, 1966–96), 4:117, italics reversed. Compare Scarborrow's and Clare's claims about marriage in George Wilkins, *The Miseries of Inforst Marriage* (London, 1607), sig. B2 verso.

7. *Wedlock a Paradice: or, A Defence of Woman's Liberty against Man's Tyranny* (London, 1701), 13. For man's power over woman as usurped and unnatural, see *An Epistle to Mr. Lyttleton* [1733], in Henry Fielding, *"The Journal of a Voyage to Lisbon," "Shamela," and Occasional Writings*, ed. Martin C. Battestin (Oxford: Clarendon, 2008), 92. See too C[hristopher] N[ewstead], *An Apology for VVomen: or, Womens Defence* (London, 1620).

8. Keith Thomas, "Women and the Civil War Sects," *Past & Present*, no. 13 (1958): 43. See too Susan Dwyer Amussen, *An Ordered Society: Gender and Class in Early Modern England* (Oxford: Basil Blackwell, 1988), 133 ("Everyone agreed that men were superior to women, that husbands ought to govern their households and that the household was the basis of order"), 182 ("although the gender order was challenged, that challenge was never explicit or direct. Women did not ask to govern, claim equality with their husbands or declare the family an irrelevant institution"). On the analytic front, see Lawrence Stone, *The Family, Sex and Marriage: In England, 1500–1800* (New York: Harper & Row, 1977), 151, glossing *patriarchy* as "the despotic authority of husband and father" and adding, "It survives and flourishes only so long as it is not questioned and challenged, so long as both the patriarchs and their subordinates fully accept the natural justice of the relationship and of the norms within which it is exercised." Close to my own view is Margaret J. M. Ezell, *The Patriarch's Wife: Literary Evidence and the History of the Family* (Chapel Hill: University of North Carolina Press, 1987), esp. chap. 2.

A society making a proverb out of "Better to be a shrew, then a sheepe" isn't all that docile about male dominance.[9] Mary More tried "to prove a greater equality between Husbands and Wives then is allowed and practiced in England" in an essay she wrote for her "little Daughter."[10] She must have had conceptual and cultural resources to draw on. The big sleep thesis requires ignoring the ample chorus sharply dissenting from the views *Mysogynus* dispenses. It might mean seeing misogyny when it isn't there. Here's one case.

Poem the First

The advertisement was stuck between two others. First came an announcement of the second edition of *Prosodia Chirurgica*. This "neat Pocket Volume" promised to teach new and seasoned surgeons alike the meanings and proper pronunciations of "all the Terms of Art." Last came Dr. R. Nelson's pitch for his "most Noble Cleaning and Strengthning ELIXIR," good for impotence and urinary problems alike. Nelson assured the newspaper's readers that he was "well known to have made the Cure of Seminal and Genital Imbecilities his chief Study and Practice for above 30 Years." The middle advertisement was cast in the usual unassuming form. "This Day is publish'd," it announced, "THE LADY'S DRESSING-ROOM . . . By the Rev. Dr. S——t."[11] The tantalizing abbreviation of the author's name offered only a sheen of implausible deniability. This, surely, was the latest by Jonathan Swift, then sixty-four years old. Indeed it was, so it was destined to outlive *Prosodia* and elixir alike.

Here it is:

> FIVE hours, (and who can do it less in?)
> By haughty *Celia* spent in Dressing;
> The Goddess from her Chamber issues,
> Array'd in Lace, Brocades, and Tissues.
> *Strephon*, who found the Room was void,
> And *Betty* otherwise employ'd;

---

9. [William Camden], *Remaines, concerning Britaine* (London, 1623), 272. See too G[eorge] Steevens, *A Pleasaunt Conceited Historie, Called The Taming of a Shrew* (London, 1607), sig. G2 recto; [John Taylor], *Divers Crabtree Lectures* (London, 1639), 148; J[ames] H[owell], *Proverbs: or, Old Sayed Sawes and Proverbs* (London, 1659), 8; *Grim, the Collier of Croydon* [1662], in *A Select Collection of Old Plays*, 12 vols. (London, 1744), 5:280.

10. Mary More, "The Womans Right," in Ezell, *Patriarch's Wife*, 193.

11. *Daily Post*, 16 June 1732, italics removed.

Stole in, and took a strict Survey,
Of all the Litter as it lay;
Whereof, to make the Matter clear,
An Inventory follows here.

    And first a dirty Smock appear'd,
Beneath the Arm-pits well besmear'd.
Strephon, the Rogue, display'd it wide,
And turn'd it round on every Side.
On such a Point few Words are best,
And *Strephon* bids us guess the rest;
But swears how damnably the Men lie,
In calling *Celia* sweet and cleanly.
Now listen while he next produces,
The various Combs for various uses,
Fill'd up with Dirt so closely fixt,
No Brush could force a way betwixt.
A Paste of Composition rare,
Sweat, Dandriff, Powder, Lead and Hair;
A Forehead Cloth with Oyl upon't
To smooth the Wrinkles on her Front;
Here Allum Flower to stop the Steams,
Exhal'd from sour unsavoury Streams,
There Night-gloves made of *Tripsy*'s Hide,
Bequeath'd by *Tripsy* when she dy'd,
With Puppy Water, Beauty's Help
Distill'd from *Tripsy*'s darling Whelp;
Here Gallypots and Vials plac'd,
Some fill'd with Washes, some with Paste,
Some with Pomatum, Paints and Slops,
And Ointments good for scabby Chops.
Hard by a filthy Bason stands,
Fowl'd with the Scouring of her Hands;
The Bason takes whatever comes
The Scrapings of her Teeth and Gums,
A nasty Compound of all Hues,
For here she spits, and here she spues.
But oh! it turn'd poor *Strephon*'s Bowels,
When he beheld and smelt the Towels,

Begumm'd, bematter'd, and beslim'd
With Dirt, and Sweat, and Ear-Wax grim'd.
No Object *Strephon*'s Eye escapes,
Here Pettycoats in frowzy Heaps;
Nor be the Handkerchiefs forgot
All varnish'd o'er with Snuff and Snot.
The Stockings, why shou'd I expose,
Stain'd with the Marks of stinking Toes;
Or greasy Coifs and Pinners reeking,
Which *Celia* slept at least a Week in?
A Pair of Tweezers next he found
To pluck her Brows in Arches round,
Or Hairs that sink the Forehead low,
Or on her Chin like Bristles grow.

   The Virtues we must not let pass,
Of *Celia*'s magnifying Glass.
When frighted *Strephon* cast his Eye on't
It shew'd the Visage of a Gyant.
A Glass that can to Sight disclose,
The smallest Worm in *Celia*'s Nose,
And faithfully direct her Nail
To squeeze it out from Head to Tail;
For catch it nicely by the Head,
It must come out alive or dead.

   Why *Strephon* will you tell the rest?
And must you needs describe the Chest?
That careless Wench! no Creature warn her
To move it out from yonder Corner;
But leave it standing full in Sight
For you to exercise your Spight.
In vain, the Workman shew'd his Wit
With Rings and Hinges counterfeit
To make it seem in this Disguise,
A Cabinet to vulgar Eyes;
For *Strephon* ventur'd to look in,
Resolv'd to go thro' thick and thin;
He lifts the Lid, there needs no more,

He smelt it all the Time before.
As from within *Pandora*'s Box,
When *Epimetheus* op'd the Locks,
A sudden universal Crew
Of humane Evils upwards flew;
He still was comforted to find
That *Hope* at last remain'd behind;
So *Strephon* lifting up the Lid,
To view what in the Chest was hid.
The Vapours flew from out the Vent,
But *Strephon* cautious never meant
The Bottom of the Pan to grope,
And fowl his Hands in Search of *Hope*.
O never may such vile Machine
Be once in *Celia*'s Chamber seen!
O may she better learn to keep
"Those Secrets of the hoary deep["]!

      As Mutton Cutlets, Prime of Meat,
Which tho' with Art you salt and beat,
As Laws of Cookery require,
And toast them at the clearest Fire;
If from adown the hopeful Chops
The Fat upon a Cinder drops,
To stinking Smoak it turns the Flame
Pois'ning the Flesh from whence it came;
And up exhales a greater Stench
For which you curse the careless Wench;
So Things, which must not be exprest,
When plumpt into the reeking Chest;
Send up an excremental Smell
To taint the Parts from whence they fell.
The Pettycoats and Gown perfume,
Which waft a Stink round every Room.

      Thus finishing his grand Survey,
Disgusted *Strephon* stole away
Repeating in his amorous Fits,
Oh! *Celia, Celia, Celia* shits!

But Vengeance, Goddess never sleeping
Soon punish'd *Strephon* for his Peeping;
His foul Imagination links
Each Dame he sees with all her Stinks:
And, if unsav'ry Odours fly,
Conceives a Lady standing by;
All Women his Description fits,
And both Idea's jump like Wits:
By vicious Fancy coupled fast,
And still appearing in Contrast.
I pity wretched *Strephon* blind
To all the Charms of Female Kind;
Should I the Queen of Love refuse,
Because she rose from stinking Ooze?
To him that looks behind the Scene,
Statira's but some pocky Queen.
When *Celia* in her Glory shows,
If *Strephon* would but stop his Nose;
(Who now so impiously blasphemes
Her Ointments, Daubs, and Paints and Creams,
Her Washes, Slops, and every Clout,
With which he makes so foul a Rout;)
He soon would learn to think like me,
And bless his ravisht Sight to see
Such Order from Confusion sprung,
Such gaudy Tulips rais'd from Dung.[12]

The second edition has two corrections worth noting. (I don't know whether Swift found compositor's errors or seized the chance to sharpen his work.) "And up exhales a greater Stench" yields to "And up exhales a greasy Stench": true, Celia's coifs and pinners (two kinds of caps) already have been branded greasy, but the change nicely finishes off the grilled mutton. And Statira becomes a "pockey Quean."[13] The *e* in *pocky* is an innocent variation

12. The Rev. Dr. S——t, *The Lady's Dressing Room: To Which Is Added, a Poem on Cutting Down the Old Thorn at Market Hill* (London, 1732).

13. The Rev. Dr. S——t, *The Lady's Dressing Room* . . . , 2nd ed. (London, 1732). The first two Dublin editions of 1732 have "pocky Quean" but not "greasy," and instead of "the Rev. Dr. S——t" on the title page an array of asterisks; the third Dublin edition of 1732, claiming on the title page to be "From the Original COPY," has "pocky Quean" and "greasy," and supplies the author as "D——n S——t." *Dean* was Swift's position in the church. The standard modern edition is in *The Poems of Jonathan Swift*, ed. Harold Williams, 2nd ed., 3 vols. (Oxford: Clarendon, 1958), 2:524–30.

in spelling, leaving her skin not so innocently speckled with the telltale signs of syphilis. Not so the *a* in *Quean,* which turns the word explicitly derogatory. The *OED* defines *quean* as "A bold, impudent, or ill-behaved woman; a jade, hussy; and spec. a harlot, strumpet."[14]

This—for now, let's call it the clinical dissection of a woman's private space and elaborate bodily rituals—wasn't virgin territory. Not even for poetry. Some four decades before Swift entered the lists came *The Ladies Dressing-Room Unlock'd, and Her Toilette Spread.*[15] A satirically detailed catalog of sumptuous clothing, jewelry, and makeup, it's edgy.[16] But it's discreet, delicate, dainty, compared to Swift's romp. There's nothing discreet, though, about *The Folly of Love,* also some four decades before Swift. It undresses a woman to mortify the flesh:

> Imagin now from Play-house just return'd
> A Lady, who when there, in fancy burn'd;
> Uneasy by some disappointments made,
> Preparing to undress her self for Bed;
> *Her* curled Locks (mistaken for her own)
> Are in confusion on her Toylet thrown;
> Next her Glass Eye put nicely in a Box,
> With Ivory Tooth, which never had the *Pox,*
> Her stiff *Steel-Bodies,* which her *Bunch* did hide,
> Are with her artificial *Buttocks* laid aside;
> Thus she who did but a small hour ago,
> Like *Angel* or *Terrestrial Goddess* show,
> Slides into loathsom sheets, where since we've fixther,
> Leave her, of *Pride* and *Lust,* an equal mixture.[17]

14. *The English Fortune-Teller* (London, [1675]) offers advice for choosing a wife: "'Tis a bad thing to meet with a scold, / 'tis a worse thing to meet with a Quean."

15. [Mary Evelyn?] *Mundus Muliebris: or, The Ladies Dressing Room Unlock'd, and Her Toilette Spread* (London, 1690).

16. *A Brief Anatomie of Women: Being an Invective against, and Apologie for the Bad and Good of the Sexe* (London, 1653), 2 indicts women with golden (dyed?) hair and makeup as satanic.

17. [Richard Ames], *The Folly of Love: or, An Essay upon Satyr against Woman* (London, 1691), 7. See too for instance "A Satyr upon a Woman," in [John Oldham], *Satyrs upon the Jesuits* (London, 1681), 149; *Spectator,* no. 41 (17 April 1711), in *The Spectator,* ed. Donald F. Bond, 5 vols. (Oxford: Clarendon, 1965), 1:173–77; *A Satyr upon Old Maids* (London, 1713), 7–8; *The Rape of the Lock* [1714], in [Alexander] Pope, *Poetical Works,* ed. Herbert Davis (London: Oxford University Press, 1966), 91–92. For later knockoffs with a lighter touch, see "A Beautiful Young Nymph at Her Toilet," in *The Bath, Bristol, Tunbridge and Epsom Miscellany* (London, 1735), 25–28; "A Letter to M——H——," in C. F., *The Merry Medley for Gay Gallants and Good Companions* (Dublin, 1748), 46–47.

Swift himself found this terrain irresistible. Two years later, he'd return with *A Beautiful Young Nymph Going to Bed*. Corinna, the alleged nymph, is really an old whore. Swift subjects the reader to a caustic account of her undoing one prop after another: "artificial Hair," "Crystal Eye," "Eye-Brows from a Mouse's Hyde," fake teeth, fake hips, rags "contriv'd to prop / Her flabby Dugs," and more. The narrator shrinks from describing Corinna reassembling herself in the morning:

> The bashful Muse will never bear
> In such a Scene to interfere.
> *Corinna* in the Morning dizen'd,
> Who sees, will spew; who smells, be poison'd.[18]

After the unrelenting catalog of her undressing, the self-restraint has to be facetious. But it acknowledges that this poetry is disgusting.

So too for the heroine of *The Lady's Dressing Room*. Streaming, steaming, seeming to slink off the page in stinking infamy, Celia never appears. But her body is appallingly present, thanks to its spewed discharges. Strephon is disgusted: who sees, and smells, shall spew here too. Many of Swift's readers were disgusted too, and not only by this work. Dyspeptic Dr. Johnson wondered "by what depravity of intellect he took delight in revolving ideas, from which almost every other mind shrinks with disgust."[19] Sir Walter Scott detected "the marks of an incipient disorder of the mind, which induced the author to dwell upon degrading and disgusting subjects, from which all men, in possession of healthful taste and sound faculties, turn with abhorrence."[20] Celia is disgusting. But so by disgust's magical contagion[21] is Swift's poem — the depiction itself, not just what it depicts. That suggests: who *reads* shall spew. Apparently one woman "instantly threw up her Dinner" on reading the poem.[22] So perhaps Swift himself is disgusting for writing it. (And me for

18. [Jonathan Swift], *A Beautiful Young Nymph Going to Bed: Written for the Honor of the Fair Sex* (Dublin, 1734), 7.

19. Samuel Johnson, *The Lives of the Most Eminent English Poets; with Critical Observations on Their Works*, ed. Roger Lonsdale, 4 vols. (Oxford: Clarendon, 2006), 3:213.

20. Walter Scott, *Memoirs of Jonathan Swift, D. D.*, 2 vols. (Paris, 1826), 2:84. See too "Swift," in Aldous Huxley, *Do What You Will* (Garden City, NY: Doubleday, Doran, 1929), 105; "Politics vs. Literature: An Examination of *Gulliver's Travels*," in *The Collected Essays, Journalism, and Letters of George Orwell*, ed. Sonia Orwell and Ian Angus, 4 vols. (New York: Harcourt Brace Jovanovich, 1968), 4:216–17.

21. William Ian Miller, *The Anatomy of Disgust* (Cambridge, MA: Harvard University Press, 1997), is invaluable.

22. *Memoirs of Mrs. Laetitia Pilkington*, 3 vols. (Dublin and London, 1748–54), 3:161.

quoting it?) I doubt, though, that the poem is evidence of insanity. I'll still doubt it even if you remind me of the debilitating mental affliction Swift suffered in his last years. Or, if you like, there's method in his madness—or there will be if we can find a way of approaching the poem that makes its outrageous immersion in disgust a sensible strategy.

We're up against disgust, even if we cheerfully agree that disgust has a history. Though that history might not be one of ever more severe disgust thresholds.[23] One anonymous defender of "those *fatal Verses* called the *Lady's Dressing Room*" insisted that Swift was not nearly as offensive as a famous Roman poet: "*Horace,* you see, makes Use of the plain slovenly Words, which our decent *Irish Poet* industriously avoids, and skips over a Hundred dirty places, without fouling his Shoes."[24] Nor is it that only decades later did people become polite enough to recoil from his parade of horribles. Decades before, some "General RULES for Behaviour and Genteel Conversation" warned, "we are to avoid all such things as annoy the Senses."[25] A year after Swift's poem was published, some "Rules of Civility and Decent Behaviour" insisted, "it is unbecoming to put another in Mind of any unclean or unsavoury thing," an injunction tailor-made for shrinking from Celia's— Swift's—"sour unsavoury Streams."[26] Perhaps the earlier writers wouldn't have judged Swift's poem unsavory, but reserved the category for fouler displays. But I doubt it. If we set aside talking about filth and consider filth itself, we find strictures on cleanliness centuries before Swift. A fifteenth-century *Book of Curtesye* instructed the reader to comb his head, keep it clean, "Purge your nose / lete noman in it see / The vile mater," and so on.[27] Celia's detritus is disgusting. So is Swift's meticulous inventory.

---

23. Compare Norbert Elias, *The History of Manners,* trans. Edmund Jephcott (New York: Urizen Books, 1978).

24. *A Modest Defence of a Late Poem by an Unknown Author, Call'd, "The Lady's Dressing Room"* ([London? 1732?]), n.p. The piece is reprinted in *The Prose Works of Jonathan Swift,* ed. Herbert Davis, 14 vols. (Oxford: Basil Blackwell, 1939–68), 5:337–40. The text of Horace at issue is the *Ars Poetica,* which figured frequently and with different force in discussion of these matters. Compare for instance *Of Dramatick Poesie, an Essay* [1668], in *The Works of John Dryden,* ed. Edward Niles Hooker et al., 20 vols. (Berkeley: University of California Press, 1956–94), 17:41.

25. *Wits Cabinet: or, A Companion for Young Men and Ladies,* 8th ed. (London, 1698), 153.

26. W[illiam] W[instanley], *The New Help to Discourse: or, Wit and Mirth, Intermix'd with More Serious Matters,* 9th ed. (London, 1733), 136. Editions of this work go back to 1672; this language seems to enter in the 8th edition of 1721, at 136.

27. *Explicit the Book of Curtesye,* 2nd ed. (Westminster, 1477–78), n.p. On the importance of cleanliness in a male lover, see *Ovid's Art of Love Paraphrased* [1747], in Fielding, *"The Journal of a Voyage to Lisbon,"* 435.

So maybe what's shocking in his poem isn't the news that women's bodies have any number of foul discharges. Everyone knows *that*. But no one talks or writes about it, at least not in full-frontal-assault detail. (Dr. Nelson may be teetering close to the line in invoking seminal and genital imbecilities, but his learned polysyllables maintain decorum and distance.) In a sense, no one thinks about it. Well, how could you not? You have to tend your own body and its foul ways. You might well be in close quarters with others tending theirs. (In Swift's day, the wealthy aside, architectural crowding was ordinary.) But at least today, barring, say, embarrassment at passed gas or a noisy belch, embarrassment which usually triggers a practiced ability to ignore what's just happened, we don't usually think about such issues. Swift forces us to.

To what end? We might take a cue from Swift's dotty friend, Laetitia Pilkington. She "imagined the Dean had only mustered up all the dirty Ideas in the World in one Piece, on Purpose to affront the Fair Sex, as he used humorously to stile old Beggar-women, and Cinder-Pickers." Nor did Swift reserve such affronts for print. Pilkington recalled supping at Swift's with some other women and his regaling them with a tale of "the nastiest, filthiest, most stinking old B——ch that ever was yet seen, except the Company, Ladies! except the Company! for that you know is but civil." The humor, if that's what it is, is eccentric, barbed, hateful. Funny, though, how firmly etiquette held the startled guests in its elegant coils even as their host reveled in his escape. "We all bowed," confessed Pilkington; "could we do less?"[28]

Why insult women? Writing to Katharine Richardson, Swift spat out, "when I see any of your sex, if they be worth mending, I beat them all, call them names, until they leave off their follies, and ask pardon."[29] Richardson responded that she'd be honored to be beaten, "but I fear you would find my faults so numerous, that you would think me one of those ladies that do not deserve to be mended."[30] Whatever one makes of these sadistic pedagogic techniques, we have a name for a man who revels in how nauseating women's bodies are and who coarsely insults his women guests. That name is *misogy-*

28. *Memoirs of Pilkington*, 2:144–45.

29. Swift to Katharine Richardson, 28 January 1738, in *The Correspondence of Jonathan Swift, D. D.*, ed. David Woolley, 4 vols. (Frankfurt: Peter Lang, 1999–2007), 4:493.

30. Katharine Richardson to Swift, 23 February 1738, in Swift, *Correspondence*, 4:498. Compare Thomas Sheridan, *The Life of the Rev. Dr. Jonathan Swift, Dean of St. Patrick's, Dublin* (London, 1784), 409.

nist.[31] (Despite *Mysogynus*, Swift's contemporaries were more likely to say *woman-hater.*) No wonder Swift's anonymous defender conceded that his verses "have so highly inflamed the whole sex (except a very few of better Judgment)."[32] What did he suppose that women allegedly of better judgment saw? That Swift was celebrating personal cleanliness. That line of defense is hopeless. At least some of Celia's foul rags betray not lackadaisical filthiness but studied hygiene: you don't get earwax on your towel if you're not bothering to clean out your ears.

And then why Celia? Why Corinna? Aren't men's bodies and their endless discharges disgusting, too? An anonymous poet seized on that helpful thought and offered *The Gentleman's Study in Answer to the Lady's Dressing-Room.* The opening sneers at Swift:

> SOME write of Angels, some of Goddess,
> But I of dirty human BODIES,
> And lowly I employ my Pen,
> To write of naught, but odious MEN.
> And Man I think, without a Jest,
> More nasty, than the nastiest Beast.

The awkward rhymes pale next to Swift's verse, but the substance is pretty much symmetrical. The man's wig is perfumed to mask the stench of sweat. His bedclothes are bloody from venereal disease, his breeches lined with feces. Even his room is filthy, "With Flegm and Vomit on the Walls," just another reminder of foul bodily eruptions that won't be contained. In this poem, the offending man finally makes an appearance. Strephon (who else?) burps, farts, pukes, and shits. Then he collapses into bed, where "He Turns, Farts, Hiccups, Groans and Snores." A didactic closing verse reveals that this bodily filth is the emblem of moral turpitude: "let them Dress the best they can, / They still are fulsome, wretched MAN."[33] No wonder another poet, commenting on this poem and Swift's original, wrote drily, "I find all the

31. For a mix of biographical and textual considerations appraising Swift here, see Margaret Anne Doody, "Swift among the Women," *Yearbook of English Studies* 18 (1988): 68–92, and Louise Barnett, *Jonathan Swift in the Company of Women* (Oxford: Oxford University Press, 2007). I have reservations about Barnett's account: see especially 170–72, issuing in this conclusion: "Where Swift most openly exhibits misogyny is in his tendency to make Strephon's mistake in *The Lady's Dressing Room* and imagine that *all* women are as dirty as Celia. . . . *The Lady's Dressing Room* does not suggest that [Strephon's] conclusion, that any woman is other than a gaudy tulip raised from dung, is wrong."

32. *A Modest Defence*, n.p.

33. [Miss W——], *The Gentleman's Study in Answer to the Lady's Dressing-Room* (Dublin, 1732).

Knowledge we have by what's writ / Is, that both, Male and Female, sweat, stink, fart, and sh——t."[34] But *The Gentleman's Study* doesn't establish a suitably malodorous equality, and no, I don't mean that actually women smell worse than men. Swift is up to some further mischief.

So what's the affront about? Not, surely, the revelation that lots of artifice goes into one's presentation as an attractive woman. Comic Roman playwright Plautus has Adelphasium fume that she and her sister labor endlessly in that cause.[35] It's the refrain of earnest moralists, stale by repetition by Swift's day. No wonder he wastes no time on his opening gambit, that Celia takes five hours to dress. Most women were "highly inflamed"—at what?

Poem the Second

The Dean's Provocation for Writing the Lady's Dressing-Room appeared anonymously in London in 1734, two years after Swift's original, but it was by the fiendishly talented Lady Mary Wortley Montagu. In a 1729 letter, Montagu declared, "I never had any acquaintance with Dr Swift, am an utter stranger to all his affairs, and even his person, which I never saw to my knowledge":[36] Swift's poem is the target of her searing attack, not a pretext for it. (Her passing swipe at Alexander Pope's *Essay on Man* is another matter.)[37] Still, there's no room here for any space between Jonathan Swift and the narrator of his poem:

> The Doctor, in a clean starch'd Band,
> A Golden Snuff-box in his Hand,
> With Care his Diamond Ring displays,
> And artful shows its various Rays;
> While grave, he stalks down —— street
> His dearest —— to meet.

34. "Thoughts upon Reading the *Lady's Dressing-Room* and the *Gentleman's Study*," in *Chloe Surpriz'd: or, The Second Part of the Lady's Dressing-Room* (London, 1732), 7.

35. *Poenulus*, act 1, sc. 2.

36. Lady Mary Wortley Montagu to John Arbuthnot, [October 1729], in *The Complete Letters of Lady Mary Wortley Montagu*, ed. Robert Halsband, 3 vols. (Oxford: Clarendon, 1965–67), 2:92. This is fully consistent with "Biographical Anecdotes of Lady M. W. Montagu," in Lady Mary Wortley Montagu, *Essays and Poems and Simplicity, a Comedy,* ed. Robert Halsband and Isobel Grundy (Oxford: Clarendon, 1977), 23: Lady Mary "abhorred the very name of Dean Swift."

37. The cause of Pope's fury with Montagu remains unclear. For some of his swipes, see Isobel Grundy, *Lady Mary Wortley Montagu* (Oxford: Oxford University Press, 1999), chaps. 16, 19.

Long had he waited for this Hour,
Nor gain'd Admittance to the Bow'r,
Had jok'd, and punn'd, and swore, and writ,
Try'd all his Gallantry and Wit;
Had told her oft what part he bore
In OXFORD's Schemes in Days of yore;
But Bawdy, Politicks, nor Satyr,
Could touch this dull hard-hearted Creature.

JENNY, her Maid, could taste a Rhyme,
And griev'd to see him lose his time,
Had kindly whisper'd in his Ear,
For twice two Pounds you enter here;
My Lady vows without that Sum,
It is in vain you write or come.

The destin'd Off'ring now he brought,
And in a Paradise of Thought;
With a low Bow approach'd the Dame,
Who smiling heard him preach his Flame.
His Gold she took (such Proofs as these
Convince most unbelieving Shees)
And in her Trunk rose up to lock it,
(Too wise to trust it in her Pocket)
And then return'd with blushing Grace,
Expects the Doctor's warm Embrace.

And now this is the proper Place,
Where Morals stare me in the Face;
And for the sake of fine Expression,
I'm forc'd to make a small Digression.

Alas! for wretched Human-kind,
With Wisdom mad, with Learning blind,
The Ox thinks he's for Saddle fit,
(As long ago Friend *Horace* writ;)
And Men their Talents still mistaking,
The Stutterer fancys his is speaking.

With Admiration oft we see,
Hard features heighten'd by Toupet;
The Beau affects the Politician,
Wit is the Citizen's Ambition;
Poor P— philosophy displays on,
With so much Rhyme and little Reason;
But tho' he preaches ne'er so long,
That *all is right,* his Head is wrong.
None strive to know their proper Merit
But strain for Wisdom, Beauty, Spirit.

Nature to ev'ry thing alive,
Points out the Path to shine or thrive,
But Man, vain Man, who grasps the whole,
Shows in all Heads a Touch of Fool;
Who lose the Praise that is their due,
While they've th' Impossible in view.

[So have I seen the injudicious Heir,
To add one Window, the whole House impair.]³⁸

Instinct the Hound does better teach,
Who never undertook to preach;
The frighted Hare from Dogs does run
But not attempts to bear a gun—

Here many noble thoughts occur
But I Prolixity abhor,
And will pursue th' instructive Tale,
To show the Wise in some things fail.

The Rev'rend Lover, with surprise,
Peeps in her Bubbies and her Eyes,
And kisses both—and tries—and tries—
The Ev'ning in this hellish Play,
Besides his Guineas thrown away;
Provok'd the Priest to that degree
He swore, *The fault is not in me.*

---

38. These square brackets, unlike the others, are in the original.

Your damn'd Close-stool so near my Nose,
Your dirty Smock, and stinking Toes,
Would make a *Hercules* as tame,
As any Beau that you can name.

    The Nymph grown furious, roar'd, by G——d,
The blame lies all in Sixty odd;
And scornful, pointing to the Door,
Sai'd, "*Fumbler see my face no more.*["]
With all my Heart, I'll go away,
But nothing done, I'll nothing pay;
Give back the money—how, cry'd she,
Would you palm such a cheat on me?
For poor four Pounds to roar and bellow,
Why sure you want some new Prunella?
What if your Verses have not sold,
Must therefore I return your Gold?
Perhaps you have no better Luck in
The Knack of Rhyming than of —
I won't give back one single Crown,
To wash your Band, or turn your Gown.

    I'll be reveng'd, you saucy Quean,
(Replys the disapointed Dean)
I'll so describe your *Dressing-Room*
The very *Irish* shall not come;
She answer'd short, I'm glad you'll write,
You'll furnish Paper when I Sh——e.[39]

Poor pathetic Swift, impotent with a prostitute, blaming it on her smells, having the effrontery to demand a refund, and vowing to write a poem, his *Lady's Dressing Room*, suitable for use as toilet paper. Adolescent or not, "Perhaps you have no better Luck in / The Knack of Rhyming than of Fucking" is a delicious couplet. Montagu's *Provocation* is better poetry than

---

39. *The Dean's Provocation for Writing the "Lady's Dressing-Room": A Poem* (London, 1734). For the modern edition, *Essays and Poems and Simplicity*, 273–76. I wonder if Lady Mary knew the closing couplet of "Verses to Be Prefix'd before Bernard Lintot's New Miscellany" [1727–28], in Pope, *Poetical Works*, 668: "*Lintot*'s for gen'ral Use are fit; / For some Folks read, but all Folks sh——." See too the closing couplet of "Epigrams Occasioned by Cibber's Verse in Praise of Nash," in Pope, *Poetical Works*, 703, not published until 1954.

The Gentleman's Study—and it gets in focus something about what Swift is up to, something distinct from the misogyny of dwelling on what's oozing, lousy, crappy in the female body.

Not to be coy: Montagu gives us male impotence in the presence of an actual woman. More humiliating yet, that actual woman is a prostitute, her sexual availability guaranteed for a mere £4. So why impotent? Is it that she hasn't emptied and cleaned the chamber pot? that she hasn't washed her clothes and feet? Or is he too old for the job?

Montagu's Swift, like Swift's Strephon, is revolted when confronted with the concrete reality of what he longed for. Remember, by the poem's end Strephon can't look at a woman without summoning up "all her Stinks." The narrator comments,

> I pity wretched *Strephon* blind
> To all the Charms of Female Kind;
> Should I the Queen of Love refuse,
> Because she rose from stinking Ooze?

If he'd just "stop his Nose," Strephon would learn to rejoice in "gaudy Tulips rais'd from Dung" or female beauty emerging when Celia leaves behind her disgusting discharges. The sentiment reverses a proverb recorded the same year as Swift's poem: "Beauty is but Skin deep; within is Filth and Putrefaction."[40] That proverb tilts toward a Christian renunciation of the body and sexuality. Less stern was *Female Policy Detected:* "If you like a Woman, and would discover if she be in Nature, what perhaps she may seem by Art, surprize her in a Morning undrest, and it is Ten to One, but you will find your Goddess hath shifted off her Divinity, and the Angel you so much admired turn'd into a *Magmallion*."[41] So women's wiles extend to dress and makeup. Even that might horrify Strephon. Swift's narrator takes far more forbidding revelations in stride.

I wouldn't claim that the *I* of Swift's poem is the innocent mouthpiece of Swift's own thoughts. But I do want to suggest that Strephon, not Celia, is the object of the poem's mockery. "*Celia, Celia, Celia* shits!" Well, of *course* she

---

40. Thomas Fuller, *Gnomologia: Adagies and Proverbs; Wise Sentences and Witty Sayings, Ancient and Modern, Foreign and British* (London, 1732), 35, no. 950.

41. [Edward Ward], *Female Policy Detected: or, The Arts of a Designing Woman Laid Open* (London, 1695), 2–3.

does. How does male sexual desire shrivel and die in the face of that completely obvious fact? How ridiculous, how contemptible, is Strephon, anyway? Has he been lusting after an actual woman or a fantasy? Does he want a human body in his arms or not?

Strephon had appeared as a lovelorn shepherd in that perennial best seller from the sixteenth century, Sir Philip Sidney's *Arcadia*. The name became a staple of pastoral verse—and parodies of it.[42] As a precocious teenager, Montagu herself penned a romance starring Strephon and even adopted Strephon as her alias.[43] The *Tatler* lampooned a lover named Strephon and his vacuously poetic language.[44] But two prior Strephons, one in and one not quite in the giggle-worthy priapic corpus of the Earl of Rochester, are of special interest. In one of his odes, a condescending Strephon, about to jilt Daphne, explains loftily that fidelity is the enemy of love. She plays along awhile but then reveals that he's a chump:

> Silly *Swain*, I'll have you know,
> 'Twas my practice long ago:
> Whilst you Vainly thought me true,
> I was false in scorn of you.
> By my Tears, my Heart's disguise,
> I thy Love and thee despise.
> Woman-kind more Joy discovers
> Making Fools, than keeping Lovers.[45]

42. [Nicholas Amhurst], *Strephon's Revenge: A Satire on the Oxford Toasts* (London, 1718), 27–28, has a Celia in passing; *Celia's New Garland: Compos'd of Eight New Songs* (London, [1728?]), 4 has a Strephon, too. "The Delights of Marriage," in *The Art of Courtship: or, The School of Delight* (London, 1686), n.p., also has a Strephon and a Celia. I owe that last reference to Margaret Spufford, *Small Books and Pleasant Histories: Popular Fiction and Its Readership in Seventeenth-Century England* (Cambridge: Cambridge University Press, 1981), 159–60.

43. Grundy, *Montagu*, 19, 20. At sixteen, Pope wrote "Spring: The First Pastoral of Damon," in Pope, *Poetical Works*, 14–19, starring Strephon and Delia.

44. *Tatler*, no. 60 (27 August 1709), in *The Tatler*, ed. Donald F. Bond, 3 vols. (Oxford: Clarendon, 1987), 1:415–17. In *Celias Answer to the Lover's Complaint* ([London, 1694–1700]), Strephon complains that he will die because Celia's heart is made of stone; she responds that she will love him if his love is true. See too *The Enchanted Lover: or, Celia Triumphant* (West Smithfield, [1672]), for another smitten Strephon, and *Loves Triumph over Bashfulness: or, The Pleas of Honour and Chastity Over-ruled* ([London, 1670–96]): "And after some strugling she yielded to bliss"; [Thomas D'Urfey], *The Constant Lover: or, Celia's Glory Express to the Life* ([London, 1682–88]). In [Charles Johnson], *Caelia: or, The Perjur'd Lover* (London, 1733), 25, Strephon "corrects his passion" when he learns sex would require marriage.

45. "A Dialogue between Strephon and Daphne," in *The Poems of John Wilmot, Earl of Rochester*, ed. Keith Walker (Oxford: Basil Blackwell for the Shakespeare Head Press, 1984), 14.

In another, Rochester rattled off some conditions for his happy sexual performance. The flowers of the first stanza are a euphemism for menstruation, but
otherwise he pulls no punches:

> By all *Loves* soft, yet mighty *Pow'rs*,
> It is a thing unfit,
> That *Men* shou'd Fuck in time of *Flow'rs*,
> Or when the *Smock's* beshit.
>
> Fair nasty *Nymph*, be clean and kind,
> And all my joys restore;
> By using Paper still behind,
> And Spunges for before.
>
> My spotless *Flames* can ne're decay,
> If after ev'ry close,
> My smoking *Prick* escape the *Fray*,
> Without a Bloody *Nose;*
>
> If thou wou'dst have me true, be wise,
> And take to cleanly sinning;
> None but fresh *Lovers Pricks* can rise,
> At *Phillis* in foul linnen.[46]

Now there's a man ready to refuse the queen of love rising from stinking
ooze. No Strephon appears in that verse. But when Rochester died at thirty-
three, probably of venereal disease, Aphra Behn saluted him with unutterably
cheesy bombast—and the refrain "the charming *Strephon* is no more."[47] I
don't know if Swift knew Rochester's poem or Behn's tribute. But readers
familiar with both would sensibly connect them in reading Swift's poem.
They'd already met a Strephon turned off by an unclean woman's body.[48]

46. "Song," in *Poems of Wilmot*, 45–46.
47. "On the Death of the Late Earl of Rochester," in *The Works of Aphra Behn*, ed. Janet Todd, 7
vols. (Columbus: Ohio State University Press, 1992–96), 1:161–63.
48. Rochester's poems have a complicated publication history. The one I've quoted does not appear
in *The Works of the Earls of Rochester, Roscomon, Dorset, &c.,* 2 vols. (London, 1718), though Behn's
tribute does (1:lxii–lxvi). But Rochester's poems, including the one at issue, were long available and
recognized as his when Behn and Swift wrote: see *Poems on Several Occasions by the Right Honourable, the
E. of R——* (Antwerp, [1680?]), 72. Contrast "The Question," in *Miscellanies by Henry Fielding, Esq.,* ed.
Henry Knight Miller et al., 3 vols. (Middletown, CT and Oxford: Wesleyan University Press and Oxford
University Press, 1972–97), 1:62–63, where stammering Strephon's erection assures Celia how well he

I suggested that there might be some reason for Swift to dwell on the female body, that the riposte of *The Gentleman's Study*, exploring the smelly and disgusting male body, didn't quite work. Now we can see a reason: if or insofar as one thinks there is something distinct about (straight) male sexual desire, so that men but not women long for bodies that somehow won't have the ineluctable characteristics of actual bodies, then the way is clear to explore Strephon's plight by rejoicing in Celia's discharges. One might think just that—if the local culture equates femininity with daintiness and refinement, masculinity with robust bodily strength or energy. That suggests that any such picture of femininity doesn't somehow undercut disgust at women's bodies, but undergirds it. Not for the first time,[49] we can see a familiar pedestal as complicit in contempt. But the contempt in question is that of Strephon and his ilk, not yet at least that of Swift.

One omission in the poem tilts against seeing it as a misogynist tirade. Unlike Rochester, nowhere does Swift even tiptoe toward menstruation. It seems implausible that Swift, no halfhearted iconoclast, would have found menstrual blood more revolting than the rest of what he cheerfully tramps through. Even the lesser poets in this discussion don't shrink from what we might imagine unspeakable in their day. *The Gentleman's Study* offers an explicit homoerotic episode. Strephon's male servant comes to "undress" him, and Strephon coos, "Come hither *Tom*, and Kiss your Master, / Oons to my groin, come put a *Plaister*." (*Oons* is a further abbreviation of *Zounds*, the oath for *God's wounds*.) Tom doesn't shrink from the task or from Strephon's genital lymph nodes, swollen from infection—"To touch his BUBO's not afraid"—before the poet plunges into more of Strephon's stinking discharges. So too *The Ladies Dressing-Room Unlock'd* triggered a derisive riposte urging that its misogyny was a cover for repulsive homosexuality:

> For who that loves as Nature teaches,
> That had rather not kiss the Breeches
> Of Twenty Women, than to lick
> The Bristles of one Male dear Dick?[50]

---

loves her. Harry M. Solomon, "'Difficult Beauty': Tom D'Urfey and the Context of Swift's *The Lady's Dressing Room*," *SEL* 19, no. 3 (1979): 431–44, suggests a different target.

49. See my *Poisoning the Minds of the Lower Orders* (Princeton, NJ: Princeton University Press, 1998), 264–71.

50. *Mundus Foppensis: or, The Fop Display'd: Being the Ladies Vindication, in Answer to a Late Pamphlet, Entituled, "Mundus Muoliebris"* (London, 1691), 13.

True, Swift's omission of menstruation might counsel against seeing his Strephon as Rochester. But it also counsels against seeing Swift as dishing out a contempt specially focused on women's bodies.

Swift liked his triumphant repetition—"Oh! *Celia, Celia, Celia* shits"— well enough to recycle it as the closing line of "Cassinus and Peter," published two years after *The Lady's Dressing Room.*[51] Finding Cassinus in agony, Peter wants to know what's wrong. Cassinus "Cry'd, *Caelia!* thrice, and sigh'd the rest"—unintelligibly, apparently. Peter asks if she's died, if she's "play'd the Whore," caught "the small or greater Pox" (smallpox or syphilis) and so lost her looks. Cassinus rejects each suggestion and rounds on him.

> But, oh! how ill hast thou divin'd
> A Crime that shocks all human Kind;
> A Deed unknown to Female Race,
> At which the Sun should hide his Face.
> Advice in vain you would apply—
> Then, leave me to despair and dye.

His language ever more florid and preposterous, Cassinus prepares to die, but agrees to whisper Celia's dread misdeed to Peter. If Peter ever repeats it, he warns, Cassinus's ghost will plague him. The awful secret? The closing line, of course. There's no way to read "Cassinus and Peter" as a misogynist assault on Celia. The point must be that Cassinus is a dolt. Granted, the shared line doesn't mandate the same reading of *The Lady's Dressing Room.* Maybe Swift is playing virtuoso, showing to what different uses he can put the same line. But I don't think so. I think Strephon's agonies are like Cassinus's.

Strephon reappears in yet another of Swift's poems, "Strephon and Chloe." Chloe is quite the paramour: "So beautiful a Nymph appears / But once in Twenty Thousand Years." Unlike Celia, Chloe is the soul of implausible cleanliness. Apparently she doesn't smell or sweat, urinate or excrete. Strephon marries her, but he's confounded by wedding-night tradition. How can he possibly climb in bed with such a refined creature? He might smell and sweat; his "prickled Beard, and hairy Breast" might offend. He strips and creeps into bed, but keeps his distance. And then? Chloe's had twelve cups of tea. She "brings a Vessel into Bed" and urinates.[52]

---

51. *Poems of Swift,* 2:593–97.

52. And I wonder if Swift knew "On a Lady Who P——st at the Tragedy of Cato" [1727–28], in Pope, *Poetical Works,* 677, with a Celia who pisses. Compare Pope to Teresa and Martha Blount,

Even if this is some different Strephon, he's as amusingly naïve as his counterpart. He "Cry'd out, ye Gods, what Sound is this? / Can *Chloe*, heav'nly *Chloe* — ?" Indeed she can. And as he demonstrates, he can join in — and fart in her face while he's at it. If you're guessing that this time, Strephon finds himself at peace with sex and effluvia alike, guess again. Instead the moment marks the end of "ravishing Delights, / High Raptures, and romantick Flights," and the comfort they gain in one another's frankly bodily presence is purchased at the price of her beauty and desirability. Once again, male sexual desire can't survive the presence of the object of desire. Nor is this narrator ready to embrace the queen of love as she rises from stinking ooze. Instead he sternly instructs Strephon,

> Had you but through a Cranny spy'd
> On House of Ease your future Bride,
> In all the Postures of her Face,
> Which Nature gives in such a Case;
> Distortions, Groanings, Strainings, Heavings;
> 'Twere better you had lickt her Leavings,
> Than from Experience find too late
> Your Goddess grown a filthy Mate.
> Your Fancy then had always dwelt
> On what you saw, and what you smelt;
> Would still the same Ideas give ye,
> As when you spy'd her on the Privy.
> And, spight of *Chloe*'s Charms divine,
> Your Heart had been as whole as mine.[53]

Celia shits, Chloe strains: both kill sexual passion. This narrator is unlike that of *The Lady's Dressing Room*. (Unless Swift changed his mind within two years, at least one narrator can't be his mouthpiece.) This one waxes on, sententiously explaining that women can't sustain their sexual allure, so they adopt one mad strategy after another to hold their men.

I use the language of power and possession because Swift does. "UN-JUSTLY all our Nymphs complain, Their Empire holds so short a Reign": and then again,

---

8 October 1718, in *The Correspondence of Alexander Pope*, ed. George Sherburn, 5 vols. (Oxford: Clarendon, 1956), 1:516.

53. "Strephon and Chloe," in *Beautiful Young Nymph*, 8–24.

They take Possession of the Crown,
And then throw all their Weapons down;
Though by the Politicians Scheme
Whoe'er arrives at Pow'r supreme,
Those Arts by which at first they gain it,
They still must practice to maintain it.

Resist the impulse to evade the language. Sure, there is something familiar, fatigued, fatiguing about the suggestion that wives rule husbands, if only for the instant they're still sexually attractive. But the cogency of that judgment isn't yet the point. "Our Nymphs" and Swift's narrator agree that marriage is a matter of politics. The narrator adds that sexual desire is a tool of power and conquest. These claims don't seem to require any special defense. The poem's blithe recital suggests they're uncontroversially true.

We were on a quest to nail down the affront at *The Lady's Dressing Room*, a quest underwritten by a contemporary claim that all but a few women were highly inflamed. But now we have Swift and Montagu crossing swords over male impotence. So what happened to the affront? It's not obvious how much there was. (Swift's cousin and loyal housekeeper, Mrs. Whiteway, assured him that *The Lady's Dressing Room* and "Strephon and Chloe" "gained the hearts of the whole sex."[54] Maybe this is pious flattery. Maybe not.) Nor is it obvious how much there should have been. But what happened to the insult Swift hurled at Pilkington and his other women guests, the belligerence he conveyed to Richardson? It's not obvious what they could have to do with anxieties about male impotence.

It's easy to indict *The Lady's Dressing Room* as a misogynist rant. I don't think that's right, but I don't want to engage in any special pleading for Swift's poem, either. It's prickly and offensive no matter what else it turns out to be.[55] It's fine with me if we see Swift's celebrated irony not, as one distinguished literary critic astonishingly has it, as saying the opposite of what he means;[56] but rather as advancing a number of possibilities, including

---

54. Mrs. Whiteway to Swift, 2 December 1735, in Swift, *Correspondence*, 4:243.

55. Still instructive is this exchange: Susan Gubar, "The Female Monster in Augustan Satire," *Signs* 3, no. 2 (1977): 380–94; Ellen Pollak, "Comment on Susan Gubar's 'The Female Monster in Augustan Satire,'" *Signs* 3, no. 3 (1978): 728–32; Susan Gubar, "Reply to Pollak," *Signs* 3, no. 3 (1978): 732–33.

56. Ian Watt, "The Ironic Tradition in Augustan Prose from Swift to Johnson," in *Stuart and Georgian Moments*, ed. Earl Miner (Berkeley: University of California Press, 1972), 166: "If a sentence is to be susceptible of two contrary interpretations, the simplest kind of predication will be best: to get the opposite we only have to supply a 'not' for the verb, or an antonym for the noun." Watt's suggestion that Swift uses irony, so understood, to send different messages to two different audiences, mob and elite,

if you like unvarnished misogyny, and refusing to stand authoritatively behind any of them.

But consider finally one bit of indirect evidence that Swift was lampooning Strephon, not Celia, or at least that contemporaries reasonably saw his work that way. In 1748, Mary Leapor published "St[r]ephon to Celia: A Modern Love Letter." This Strephon, too, is in paroxysms over how Celia's is not any ordinary human body, as if all the overheated hyperbole of lovers is literally true in her case:

> Your Breast so mighty cold I trow,
> Is made of nothing else but Snow:
> Your Hands (no wonder they have Charms)
> Are made of Iv'ry like your Arms.
> Your Cheeks that look as if they bled,
> Are nothing else but Roses red.
> Your Lips are Coral very bright,
> Your Teeth—tho' Numbers out of spite,
> May say they're Bones—yet 'twill appear
> They're Rows of Pearls exceeding dear.[57]

All this sighing and swooning gets punctured, but not in Swift's way. Strephon is gunning for Celia's considerable wealth and he must be hoping that she can be suckered because of her own romantic illusions. Still, Leapor agrees with Swift that the stylized sentiments we call *romantic* are pernicious nonsense. Leapor isn't piling on after Swift—she's tweaking his take—but I think her decision to deploy the same old pair of names is a bid to count as co-conspirator in demystification.

Enough of Swift's literary antics. I worry that one way of deploying *misogyny*—and *patriarchy* and *essentialism* and . . . —is an obstacle to serious

---

raises further difficulties I shan't pursue here; but see my *Poisoning*, 176–79 and chap. 12, on eavesdropping. F. R. Leavis, "The Irony of Swift," *Scrutiny* 2, no. 4 (1934): 364–78, is *much* better, but I don't share Leavis's assessment of that irony.

57. Mrs. [Mary] Leapor, *Poems upon Several Occasions* (London, 1748), 105. The table of contents and the poem's title both have "Stephon," but the letter-cum-poem is signed "*Strephon.*" For canned lavish compliments to women, see [Charles Sackville, Earl of Dorset], *The New Academy of Complements* (London, 1669), 13–25; "Complemental Expressions, and Love Posies," in *The Art of Courtship: or, The School of Delight* ([London], 1688), n.p.; "Amorous Expressions of Gentlemen to Ladies, Gentlewomen and Maides, &c.," in *The Theatre of Complements: or, A Compleat New Academy* (London, 1689), 17–24; "The Art of Complementing and Wooing," in *Wits Cabinet*, 49–53; *The Compleat Academy of Complements* (London, 1705), 91–96; *Wits Secretary: or, The Lovers Magazine* (London, [1720?]), 15–22.

thought. Labeling something, as if that's the end of the matter, doesn't orient us to the intricate complexities of the social landscape. Instead it papers them over with complacencies. So used, the abstractions permit us, invite us, propel us to take up inane roles in musty morality plays while congratulating ourselves on our sophistication. So you can say that Swift's poem is patriarchal or that Montagu's is counterhegemonic. But you may be missing the stakes and getting the scorecard wrong to boot. Better to take such abstract categories, especially ones so politically loaded, as the names of the questions, not the names of the answers.[58]

Last word to Lady Mary, who decades later staged another collision between the distressing discharges of a woman's body and the lofty literature of her opponents. She built a commode backed with the works of Pope, Bolingbroke, and Swift and enjoyed "the satisfaction of shitting on them every day."[59]

---

58. For recent examples of invigorating and intelligent criticism putting pressure on the cogency of our conceptual frames and commitments, see Valerie Traub, *The Renaissance of Lesbianism in Early Modern England* (Cambridge: Cambridge University Press, 2002); Erica Longfellow, *Women and Religious Writing in Early Modern England* (Cambridge: Cambridge University Press, 2004); and Katharine Gillespie, *Domesticity and Dissent in the Seventeenth Century: English Women Writers and the Public Sphere* (Cambridge: Cambridge University Press, 2004).

59. Robert Halsband, "New Anecdotes of Lady Mary Wortley Montagu," in *Evidence in Literary Scholarship: Essays in Memory of James Marshall Osborn*, ed. René Wellek and Alvaro Ribeiro (Oxford: Clarendon, 1979), 245.

CHAPTER 2

Husbands and Wives, Gender and Genre

You might be willing to concede that the big sleep thesis invites a lazy reliance on such prefabricated abstractions as misogyny, that those loyal to it are prone to misread Swift's poem and miss the stakes of Montagu's sizzling response. But my skepticism about the big sleep thesis is bolder than that. I will argue that the early modern English, to use some recently fashionable jargon, didn't "naturalize" or "essentialize" patriarchal authority.[1] I don't think, that is, that they misunderstood contingency as necessity.

Oh, I know: the sources insist that patriarchal authority is natural. It's their ceaseless refrain. Usually they're serene, sometimes with the smug and bloated complacency of people confident in the conventional wisdom, often anyway without the skittish or hysterical energy of conservatives who know they're losing. I don't want to sweep this evidence under the rug. I want to linger over it.

From 1597, Hooker's *Laws of Ecclesiastical Polity:*

> So that woman being created for mans sake to be his helper in regard of the
> end before mentioned namlie the havinge and the bringing up of children,
> whereunto it was not possible they should concurre unless there were
> subalternation between them, which subalternation is naturallie grounded
> upon inequalitie, because things equall in everie respect are never willinglie

---

1. For an instance of this usage, see Slavoj Žižek, "Against Human Rights," *New Left Review* 34 (July–August 2005): 115–31.

directed one by another, woman therefore was even in hir first estat framed by nature not onlie after in time but inferior in excellencie also unto man.[2]

As so often, invoking nature here already means invoking scripture: Eve came from Adam's rib "after in time." God is author of the book of nature, His general revelation.[3] So we will also have to consider the thought that patriarchal authority is divinely mandated.

Whatever his differences with "the Judicious *Hooker,*" John Locke took a similar line. True, he demurred that *paternal power* was misnamed. It should be *parental power,* since children are in fact equally obliged to both parents. But he also held that providence, law, and custom dictated that a woman "be subject to her husband"—and, he added, "there is, I grant, a Foundation in Nature for it." There's no contradiction here. The obligations of children to parents are independent of the obligations of wives to husbands. Those obligations were profound in everyday life as well as Locke's political theory. Writing to his "Most deare and ever loveing father," the young John Locke wrote, "Pray remembr my humble duty to my mother" and signed, "Tuus obedientissimus filius."[4] Nor is there any contradiction with Locke's claim that the state of nature is one of "perfect freedom" and equality:

> Creatures of the same species and rank promiscuously born to all the same advantages of Nature, and the use of the same faculties, should also be equal one amongst another without Subordination or Subjection, unless the Lord and Master of them all, should by any manifest Declaration of his Will set one above another, and confer on him by an evident and clear appointment an undoubted Right to Dominion and Sovereignty.[5]

These creatures are men. For all his vaunted individualism, Locke thinks that the state rules over male heads of households, not individuals as such. Not

---

2. Richard Hooker, *Of the Laws of Ecclesiastical Polity,* ed. W. Speed Hill, 4 vols. (Cambridge, MA: Belknap Press, Harvard University Press, 1977–82), 2:402.

3. See especially John Edwards, *A Demonstration of the Existence and Providence of* GOD, *from the Contemplation of the Visible Structure of the Greater and the Lesser World* (London, 1696). For more instances of this usage, see for instance Thomas Cranmer, *A Confutation of Vnwritten Verities,* trans. E. P. (n.p., [1556]), n.p.; John Doue, *The Confvtation of Atheisme* (London, 1605), 19–20, 41, 86; Thomas Fuller, *Two Sermons* (London, 1654), pt. 1, p. 53; James Tyrrell, *A Brief Disquisition of the Law of Nature,* 2nd ed. corr. and enlarged (London, 1701), 104; Joseph Collet, *The Unsearchable Depths of God's Judgments Considered* (London, 1742), 14.

4. John Locke to John Locke, sen., 11 May 1652, in *The Correspondence of John Locke,* ed. E. S. de Beer, 8 vols. (Oxford: Clarendon, 1976–89), 1:7–8.

5. John Locke, *Two Treatises of Government,* bk. 2, §§ 5, 52; bk. 1, § 47; bk. 2, § 4.

only other political theorists, but also political actors, even radical ones, agreed: the French revolutionary assembly held that only men could be active citizens. After the Terror, it pulled back from earlier projects intended to make the oppression of women and children politically and legally visible, so paving the way for Napoleon's notoriously patriarchal Civil Code.[6] *Fraternité* indeed.

From 1655—this is not a debate where reactionary men line up against (proto)feminist women—Lady Margaret Cavendish:

> True it is, our Sex make great complaints, that men from their first Creation usurped a Supremacy to themselves, although we were made equal by Nature, which Tyrannical Government they have kept ever since, so that we could never come to be free, but rather more and more enslaved, using as either like Children, Fools, or Subjects, that is, to flatter or threaten us, to allure or force us to obey, and will not let us divide the World equally with them, as to Govern and Command, to direct and Dispose as they do; which Slavery hath so dejected our spirits, as we are become so stupid, that Beasts are but a Degree below us, and Men use us but a Degree above Beasts; whereas in Nature we have as clear a understanding as Men, if we were bred in Schools to mature our Brains, and to manure our Understandings, that we might bring forth the Fruits of Knowledge. But to speak truth, Men have great Reason not to let us in to their Governments, for there is great difference betwixt the Masculine Brain and the Feminine, the Masculine Strength and the Feminine; For could we choose out of the World two of the ablest Brain and strongest Body of each Sex, there would be great difference in the Understanding and Strength; for Nature hath made Mans Body more able to endure Labour, and Mans Brain more clear to understand and contrive than Womans.[7]

One wonders if women's complaints about male tyranny are themselves supposed to be evidence of women's stupidity. How could equality be sensible when men are naturally gifted with splendidly superior bodies and brains?

From 1688, Halifax's advice to his daughter:

6. William H. Sewell Jr., *Work and Revolution in France: The Language of Labor from the Old Regime to 1848* (Cambridge: Cambridge University Press, 1980), 136–37; Suzanne Desan, *The Family on Trial in Revolutionary France* (Berkeley: University of California Press, 2004), chap. 8. On the predecessor regime, consider Sarah Hanley, "Engendering the State: Family Formation and State Building in Early Modern France," *French Historical Studies* 16, no. 1 (1989): 4–27.

7. Lady Margaret Newcastle [Cavendish], *The Worlds Olio* (London, 1655), preface, n.p., italics reversed.

You must first lay it down for a Foundation in general, That there is *Inequality* in the *Sexes*, and that for the better Oeconomy of the World, the *Men*, who were to be the Law-givers, had the larger share of *Reason* bestow'd upon them; by which means your Sex is the better prepar'd for the *Compliance* that is necessary for the better performance of those *Duties* which seem'd to be most properly assign'd to it. This looks a little uncourtly at the first appearance; but upon examination it will be found, that *Nature* is so far being unjust to you, that she is partial on your side: She hath made you such large *Amends* by other Advantages, for the seeming *Injustice* of the first Distribution, that the Right of Complaining is come over to our Sex; you have it in your power not only to free your selves, but to subdue your Masters, and without violence throw both their *Natural* and *Legal* *Authority* at your Feet.[8]

Gallant or not, nature here has purposes: she hands out different capacities to men and women to secure "the better Oeconomy" or organization "of the World." But her purposes, or anyway accomplishments, are also complicated. Halifax's tone is arch in concluding that women can overthrow male authority: not that he thinks it's false, but that he is sardonic about its truth, even if it will enable his daughter to fight rearguard actions. But he wasn't alone in finding it tricky to decipher the book of nature—or, better, in reading the book effortlessly and finding its messages contradictory.

From 1697, *The Character of a Good Woman:*

A Man is the Head of the Wife, and from the Head are to come those Influences, and that Guidance which may be serviceable to all the other parts, and for their common good. It would be an Head extremely Empty that should only be solicitous for its own Wellfare, neglecting all the parts of the Body besides, in as much as by their Illness it will be at length incommoded. A Man is to *rule his Wife*, but then he must govern by *Law*, for else his Empire is *Tyrannical*. He must remember whilst he commands her, he is God's Subject, and accountable to him for his Administration. He may expect that the Obedience of his Wife should be free and unconstrained, but he must abhor the thought of using her like a slave.[9]

8. [George Savile, Marquis of Halifax], *The Lady's New-Years Gift: or, Advice to a Daughter*, 3rd ed. corr. (London, 1688), 26–27. On the power of women in the face of the authority of men, compare Wetenhall Wilkes, *A Letter of Genteel and Moral Advice to a Young Lady* (Dublin, 1740), 117.

9. Timothy Rogers, *The Character of a Good Woman, Both in a Single and Marry'd State* (London, 1697), 54–55. Compare the inflection of this trope in *Basilikon Doron* [1599], in *The Political Works of James I*, ed. C. H. McIlwain (Cambridge, MA: Harvard University Press, 1918), 36; Rachel Speght, *A*

There's no explicit invocation of nature here, but we're looking for a kind of argument, not a word. This passage has the same logic as some of the others, moving from claims about natural facts—here, the organization of a body—to normative conclusions. It's a variant on the more familiar body politic, representing the whole realm. (A 1612 dialog offered the same variant and made it more explicit. "I set my selfe before my houshold," declares Joshua, "because the head leadeth first the body, before the body can mooue by the members to performe any office. So it is in the naturall constitution of a body, so in the politicall gouerment of the common wealth . . . from the head commeth life & motion to the body. And the same order is to bee obserued in well guiding of a family.")[10] This time the married couple is itself a body. Then the metaphor grinds inexorably to the usual conclusion: the head must govern in the interests of the whole.

A 1705 sermon adduced three reasons wives must submit to husbands. Subordination was underwritten second by universal "Use and Custom," third by "the Laws of God." First came this homework assignment for wives.

> They are to consider where *Nature* has design'd this Sovereignty, and that we may well presume to be, where she has given the greatest strength and abilities; where she has made the body and the mind fittest to undergo the toils and labours that are absolutely necessary to the being and well-being of the World, to the carrying on business at home, and trade abroad, to the defending ones Country from foreign Foes, and to the administring Justice to one another; now where we perceive Nature has best qualified her Creatures for performance of these functions, that are so necessary, that the World cannot subsist in peace and order without them, we may very safely conclude she design'd to place the Superiority.[11]

Here again nature has purposes. But the sermon ratchets up Halifax's "better Oeconomy of the World." Now men are "best qualified" to perform abso-

Moʒvell for Melastomvs (London, 1617), 16–18; Immanuel Bourne, *A Gold Chain of Directions, with Twenty Gold-Linkes of Love, to Preserve Love Firm between Husband and Wife* (London, 1669), 71–76.

10. Richard Bernard, *Iosvahs Godly Resolution in Conference with Caleb, Touching Houshold Gouernment for Well Ordering a Familie* (London, 1612), 24. Sam[uel] Slater, *The Protectors Protection: or, The Pious Prince Guarded by a Praying People* (London, 1659), 38, is eccentric in urging the duty of the members to "act for the good and welfare of the Head" in family and nation alike.

11. W[illiam] Fleetwood, *The Relative Duties of Parents and Children, Husbands and Wives, Masters and Servants, Consider'd in Sixteen Sermons* (London, 1705), 168–69.

lutely necessary work. Don't let women do that work, lest the world's "peace and order" collapse.

There's lots more, but that will do. Nature underwrites the authority of husbands over wives: so that authority is naturalized, right? Not so fast. We don't know yet that contemporaries' sense of *nature* in such passages maps neatly onto our talk of what's *naturalized*. Surely we've known for a very long time that the concept of nature is complex—or better, perhaps, that the word is a homonym.[12] So let's pause to ask how the invocation of nature works in these passages. I'll start with a simple distinction and then complicate it.

That something is natural might mean that in fact it's how things (necessarily) are. That picture removes whatever's in question from the realm of criticism and justification. There's no point asking whether it's good or bad, right or wrong, just or unjust if it's how things are, period. We don't worry about whether gravity is good and we don't argue about whether humans should be silicon-based.

Or the claim that something is natural—or unnatural—might be a move in a legitimation game, not an announcement that it's not the right occasion to play the game. So let's play fill in the blank:

_____ is natural and therefore right; or

_____ is unnatural and therefore wrong.

The skeptical view—it's mine—is that there is no sound way to fill in the blank, gloss *natural* or *unnatural*, and explain how the inference marked by *therefore* follows. Even today, people try all the time. (Familiar contenders for the second blank include gay sex and gay marriage.) Skepticism here is not skepticism across the board about normative argument. So those of us grimacing when people rhapsodize about natural law or the like might not be philistines refusing to engage profound questions. On the contrary, we might be eager to engage those questions and distressed by the equivocations looming before us.

Recall the thesis that patriarchal authority was naturalized or essentialized. The most straightforward rendition of that thesis is that contemporaries took the first view of what it means to call something natural: it's how

12. Canonically, David Hume, *A Treatise of Human Nature*, ed. L. A. Selby-Bigge, rev. P. H. Nidditch, 2nd ed. (Oxford: Clarendon, 1978), 473–75; John Stuart Mill, "Nature," in *Three Essays on Religion*, in his *Essays on Ethics, Religion and Society*, ed. J. M. Robson (Toronto: University of Toronto Press, 1969), 373–402.

things are, like it or not. That would explain the view that they didn't see that authority as politically controversial or that they found it invisible or part of the woodwork of the world. It would explain the tight association between *naturalized* or *essentialized* and the big sleep thesis. But in these sources—I didn't sneakily choose them for this reason—talk of nature works the second way. It's a move in a legitimation game. These sources offer reasons that husbands ought to rule, wives to submit. You might think that the essentialism thesis requires only that more or less everyone agreed with a particular view of legitimacy. But then you have to wonder why so many repeated that view. What were they worried about? Again, doesn't the mere fact that some people doggedly insisted that patriarchal authority is justified suggest that others doubted or disputed it?

Now it's time to complicate this simple distinction. Is it possible to run together these two modes of argument? Not coherently. Either we're stuck with some feature of the world or we could change it. But people can equivocate between these two claims, not simply because the word *nature* appears in both, but because of lingering affection for teleology. To see all kinds of organisms as striving to flourish, to realize their natural ends, is—in a confused way—to see empirical necessity or anyway regularity *and* desirability. Aristotle himself knew that nature doesn't always realize her ends. Most acorns don't become majestic oak trees. They get eaten or they rot. You can think it's illuminating to see a rotting acorn as suffering arrested development. There will still be an explanatory account of why it's rotting—one of Aristotle's four causes is the efficient cause—and still an independent question of how to identify its natural end.

The passages I've quoted are saturated with teleology. But we can make sense of them without any appeal to nature's purposes. Suppose that we take some end—social order or the Oeconomy of the World—as given or uncontroversial. We might imagine that there are different ways of securing that end. But once we focus on how men and women differ, we realize that the best (Halifax) or only (1705 sermon) way is for men to rule. That too complicates the simple distinction I began with. If or insofar as everyone does (shades of Kant's assertoric hypothetical imperative) or should share the end, and if or insofar as the story of factual constraint is right, then once again we're stuck with patriarchal authority. There's nothing invalid about this line of argument. That doesn't mean it's sound—or that many contemporaries embraced it.

What changes if we shift the argument into the register of providence or divine command? *The Character of a Good Woman* also offers this reminder: *"This Vertuous Woman shews her Goodness by her dutiful behaviour to her Husband.* She remembers the order in which her Creation has placed her. She is a Companion, but a Subject, *Eph.* 5. 24. 1 *Cor.* 7. 34. 1 *Pet.* 3. 5, 6 *Tit.* 2. 4. *Est.* 1. 22."[13] (String citations to scripture are endemic in early modern sources, not just those by churchmen. We do ourselves no interpretive favors if we ignore them.)[14] If God commands the subordination of women, does that naturalize or essentialize it? The options look much as they did before. It's tempting to conflate empirical and moral necessity—one thinks here of Hobbes's enlisting "no kicking against the pricks" in his early account of divine sovereignty[15] and, from after my period here, William Paley's curious account of *obligation* as being "urged by a violent motive resulting from the command of another"[16] —but easy enough to pry them apart. God leaves it up to us to decide whether to follow His commands and the world is drenched in sin. One can think that we ought to submit to God's will and that He wills patriarchy. ("AND since Gods assignation has thus determined subjection to be the womens lot, there needs no other argument of its fitness, or for their acquiescence.")[17] There's one crucial further move in this tradition, not routinely made when people invoke nature, and that's invoking the prospects of heaven and hell. Here too we can always distinguish the causal thesis that those prospects will make believers do as God wills from the justificatory thesis that it gives them good reason to. No doubt the logical distinction doesn't settle what to do. But it has to be an open question how many contemporaries thought in these ways about God's will. Plenty didn't, and I don't have in mind the occasional raucous village atheist.

So far, it looks like there was room for contemporaries to have (what we call) a naturalized view. In fact, if you will, there were four rooms. They could have thought patriarchal authority a necessary fact, beyond the scope of criticism and justification. Or they could have entertained some characteristic confusions surrounding teleology. Or they could have thought patri-

---

13. Rogers, *Character*, 17.

14. Moses à Vauts, *The Husband's Authority Unvail'd* (London, 1650), is spectacularly dense with marginal references to scripture: see his postscript, 101, for a vigorous defense.

15. *De Cive*, chap. 15. But see Hobbes's distinction between "being obliged" and "being tied being obliged" in *De Cive*, chap. 14, n*.

16. *The Principles of Moral and Political Philosophy*, bk. 2, chap. 2.

17. [Richard Allestree], *The Ladies Calling in Two Parts* (Oxford, 1673), pt. 1, p. 40. See, more colloquially, A True-born English Man, *The Prerogative of the Breeches, in a Letter to the Sons of Men: Being an Answer to Petticoat-Government* (London, 1702), 34–35.

archy the best or only way of securing social order or some other obviously attractive or mandatory end. Or they could have submitted to what they took to be God's will.

They could have; doubtless some did. In challenging the claim that the early modern English naturalized or essentialized patriarchal authority, I don't mean that nobody did. I mean that so many didn't that it's wrong to describe the whole society that way. I don't want to bicker about the numbers: we don't have them. But here's the crux: even defenders of nature weren't blind to deep controversies about authority in the family. There's nothing placid or mind numbing about holding a naturalized view when you know all too well that plenty of others reject it.

No wonder participants in this debate found it very easy—easier than we do—to invoke household government. Martin Luther's injunction appeared in English in 1577:

> For when the house is wel gouerned, then shal it go well with the common wealth. For houshold gouernment is the founteyne of ye common wealth. If father, mother, husband & wife be lacking which should bring forth children, nourish them and bring them vp, there can be no common wealth. Of a house therefore is made a citie, which is nothing els but many houses & families, of cities is made a dukedom or a shire: of dukedoms or shires is made a kingdom, which ioyneth all these in one. Of all these houshold gouernment is the founteyne & headspring.[18]

From 1584: "Those which gouerne the familie, are those Superiours who have authoritie in the same." Exquisite judgments had to be made about treating women, children, and servants; secular and religious affairs; and so on. "For all these haue not one and the same Rule of decencie." But maintaining "rule" and "subiection" with what scripture calls "comeliness" was the "generall rule in euerie parte of householde gouernment."[19] A 1610 writer chimed in, saluting "*Houshold Gouernment*, I say, the Parent & first beginner of Common-wealthes, the Seminary of Kingdoms, & Counsels; the discerner of naturall wisedome, the Architect of honour, and Disciplinarie school of a wise, vertuous, and happy life."[20] A 1637 commentary on scripture yields this parallel: "Unto order in a Common wealth belongs the duty of Subjects: and

---

18. Martin Luther, *A Commentarie vpon the Fiftene Psalmes*, trans. Henry Bvll (London, 1577), 129.

19. [Dudley Fenner], *The Artes of Logike and Rethorike* (n.p., 1584), n.p.; the same in *The Order of Hovsholde*, in Dudley Fenner, *Certain Godly and Learned Treatises* (Edinburgh, 1591), 2.

20. Ed[ward] Topsell, *The House-Holder: or, Perfect Man* (n.p., 1610), Epistle Dedicatorie, n.p.

unto household government belongs the duty of Servants, Wives, and Husbands."[21] "Domesticall government is the very Image and modell of Soveraignty in a Common-weale," offered a 1642 writer entering the torrid debate about King Charles I.[22] Here's the entry for *servitude* in *A Complete Christian Dictionary* of 1661:

> *Politicall* is threefold:
>   1. Civill,
>   2. Filial,
>   3. Servile.
> *Civill,* is of the Subject unto the Magistrate.
> *Filiall,* of the Childe to the Parents.
> *Servile,* of the Servant to his Master.

The authority of husband over wife isn't on the list. But elsewhere the *Dictionary* refers to the husband's "authority over [the wife] in governing her."[23] "If thou art a Wife, and would'st preserve fervent conjugal love between thee and thy Husband, live in a voluntary obedience and subjection to him," counseled one 1685 writer. Even if "his softness or yieldingness cause him to relinquish his Authority . . . do not deceive thy self to think it enough to give the bare title of Government to thy Husband, when yet thou wilt in all things have thine own will, for this is but mockery, and not obedience; and self-willedness is contrary to subjection and obedience."[24] So too a 1747 pamphlet, *The Art of Governing a Wife; with Rules for Batchelors,* offers a blunt statement of a gendered division of labor: "it is the Husband's Duty to furnish Money, and the Wives to govern the Family. That House in which each does his Duty, may be called a well-governed Monastery; and that where every one draws a different way, is a meer Hell." The wife is governing the family—the children

---

21. Nicholas Byfield, *A Commentary vpon the First Three Chapters of the First Epistle Generall of S^t. Peter* (London, 1637), 422.

22. [John Spelman], *A View of a Printed Book Intituled Observations upon His Majesties Late Answers and Expresses* (Oxford, 1642), 9. I owe the reference to Gordon J. Schochet, *The Authoritarian Family and Political Attitudes in 17th-Century England: Patriarchalism in Political Thought* (New Brunswick, NJ: Transaction Books, 1988), 100.

23. Thomas Wilson, *A Complete Christian Dictionary* (London, 1661), 574 s.v. *servitude,* 126 s.v. *covering;* and see p. 37 s.v. *authority.* On the "Soveraign authority of Fathers over their Children," see *The Batchelor's Directory: Being a Treatise of the Excellence of Marriage,* 2nd ed. (London, 1696), 48–49, 251; see too Richard Whytforde, *A Werke for Housholders* (n.p., [1530]), sig. Bii verso.

24. [J. R.], *The Honourable State of Matrimony Made Comfortable: or, An Antidote against Discord betwixt Man and Wife* (London, 1685), 97–98, italics reversed. See too E[dward] B[ury], *A Looking-Glass for the Unmarried* (London, 1697), 25, 35; [Richard] Steele, *What Are the Duties of Man and Wife towards Each Other* (Exon, 1711), 6.

and servants, or, as the pamphleteer has it, "Diet and Cloathing"[25]—but the husband is still governing her. All these writers agreed that authority was central in the household. Quaker William Penn was breathtakingly radical in rejecting one authority relationship, but even he didn't reject household government across the board: "Between a Man and his Wife nothing ought to rule but *Love*. Authority is for Children and Servants; Yet not without Sweetness."[26] So too for the 1640 author who offered a case of marital discord arising from the husband's efforts to dominate—"The more he labored to soveraignize; the quarrel ever became more implacable"—but still thought husbands were "Princes in their owne Families."[27]

No wonder Katherine Fox uttered the words she did. Her family was so poor that their "young Babes" were famished, but her husband sailed off to the tavern. When she showed up "to seek Relief from his hands, for her, and her poor Children," he beat her so badly "that as he thought, he had left her Dead, and past Recovery." "So pressed by these Miseries, and brought to . . . Despair," Fox killed her children. When her husband staggered home drunk and fell asleep, she killed him too: "Thou shalt die, thou negligent Man, since thy ill Government hath been the Ruine of me and my Children."[28] No wonder Lady Sarah Cowper, a Tory miserable in her marriage to leading Whig politician William, fumed in her diary when he scolded her for removing a table from a crowded room: "'Tis mervellous to hear him talk how much he is for Liberty . . . when at the same time there is not a more absolute Tyrant, where he hath power (which indeed he has not over any one but me) than himself."[29] I'll recur to such language, which doesn't obscure authority. People who don't stumble over talk of household government are not snoring in a moribund big sleep, not waiting to be awakened by the pinprick of ideological critique.

Many of these textual snippets invoke the natural authority of husbands

25. *The Art of Governing a Wife; with Rules for Batchelors* (London, 1747), 29, 113. For the complaint that "Household Affaires are the Opium of the Soul," from a woman who must have meant governing the servants, see Lady Masham to John Locke, 14 November [1685], in *Correspondence of Locke*, 2:757.

26. [William Penn], *Some Fruits of Solitude: In Reflections and Maxims Relating to the Conduct of Human Life* (London, 1693), 36.

27. Philogenes Panedonius [Richard Brathwaite], *Ar't Asleepe Husband?* (London, 1640), 113, 199.

28. *The Distressed Mother: or, Sorrowful Wife in Tears* (London, [1690]), n.p. For a servant murdering his wife and baby after her gentle reproach, see *A Full and True Account of a Horrid, Barbarous and Bloody Murder Committed by One Thomas Hide, Servant to Mr. Robert Allen a Maulster Near Finchly, on the Body of His Own Wife and Child* (London, 1709). See too *Anne Wallens Lamentation* (London, 1616).

29. Anne Kugler, *Errant Plagiary: The Life and Writing of Lady Sarah Cowper, 1644–1720* (Stanford, CA: Stanford University Press, 2002), 49 (1701).

and household government. They cohere readily. The discussions of household government tilt toward seeing the passages on natural authority as moves in a legitimation game. The latter are typical but not alone: other players make other moves. And there's a crucial sense in which they *aren't* broadly representative. These sources are all lofty, impartial, austere: conduct manuals, some highly abstract and some painfully concrete. They are not innocent snapshots of the social world. (*No* kind of source is that: not diary entries, not newspaper stories, not portraits, not engravings.) We might wonder how the manuals were received. Did people follow them? Unthinkingly? Did they mock them? Subvert them? Roll their eyes and ignore them? Use and abuse them? Hug and discard them? We need to get a more vivid sense of what people made of such conduct manuals.

To do that, I'm going to turn to genres far removed from the learned abstractions that engage political theorists.[30] Perusing the likes of Hooker, Hobbes, and Locke; pondering the philosophical merits of sermons on the dictates of nature; thinking about the integrity of the body politic metaphor: these are fine activities. But we might also see the views articulated in such sources as blather. I don't mean that they're nonsense. I don't mean that they can or should be surgically snipped out of the historical record so we can lay bare material reality. The wisdom of the conduct manuals circulated widely, even among those who never read a word of them: indeed some manuals are at least as much crystallizations of already circulating views as progenitors. But it's an open question how people used and abused that wisdom. Calling it blather is uncharitable. But it will remind us that maybe some people rolled their eyes at it.[31]

John Dunton had the curious if instructive habit of publishing accounts of his marital difficulties. Upon reconciling with his wife in 1701, he wrote, "my Dear, as much as I love thee, my *Affection must not lessen my Authority over thee*—: I ought to take into my Hands that Power, with which both God and Nature has invested me. *I would be Lord at home,* and rule there as I

---

30. This isn't virgin territory: see especially Pamela Allen Brown, *Better a Shrew than a Sheep: Women, Drama, and the Culture of Jest in Early Modern England* (Ithaca, NY: Cornell University Press, 2003).

31. Contrast the treatment of Athens and Aristotle in Alasdair MacIntyre, *After Virtue: A Study in Moral Theory,* 2nd ed. (Notre Dame, IN: University of Notre Dame Press, 1984), chaps. 11–12. MacIntyre's odd comments about Aristotle on conflict (157, 163–64) make one wonder why bk. 5 of the *Politics* is missing, let alone other kinds of sources.

please."[32] Well, he says he wrote that to her. I'm inclined to believe him, but maybe the sheer eccentricity of publishing such accounts makes him an unreliable narrator. But suppose he did just that. I don't know what Mrs. Dunton made of it. But contrast the conduct manual with the husband addressing his wife. There's a difference that matters. Or so I'll now argue.

I want to exploit the space opened by this proverb—you might initially find it baffling—from 1617: "He that hath no wife beateth her often."[33] I take it the thought is that single men learn a script about marriage casting husbands as using brute physical force to maintain authority.[34] Once married, though, they learn better. Not because they realize triumphantly that they can maintain their authority without such beatings, that women are already putty in their hands. Rather because the script is defective. Can I prove that that's what the proverb means? No. But I will canvass plenty of other sources suggesting that people were skeptical of blather: that they mocked, defied, subverted, smirked at it. Not always: sometimes they rallied to it. I'm happy to include evidence of the latter motif, too. Remember that my central negative thesis is that the vision of the conduct manuals was controversial, not that no one believed it or that it was universally flouted, still less that early modern England was a feminist or egalitarian society. I may be wrong, but I'm not crazy.

To defend that thesis, it's not enough to adduce disorderly women. On the contrary, some of them count as support for the prevalence of patriarchal authority: sometimes the putative disorder is defying fathers or husbands.

32. [John Dunton], *The Case Is Alter'd: or, Dunton's Re-marriage to the Same Wife: Being the First Instance of That Nature That Has Been in England* (London, 1701), 47. See too *The Case of John Dunton, Citizen of London: With Respect to His Mother-in-Law, Madam Jane Nicholas, of St. Albans; and Her Only Child, Sarah Dunton* (London, 1700); *Reflections on Mr. Dunton's Leaving His Wife: In a Letter to Himself* ([London, 1700]). For difficulties with a mother-in-law voiced privately, see Samuel Hyland to Nathaniel Collyer, [1682?], in Mary Adelaide, Lady Jennings, *A Kentish Country House: or, Records of the Hall House, Hawkhurst, and Its Inhabitants, from the Great Plague of London to the Jubilee of Queen Victoria, 1665–1887* (Guildford, 1894), 28–29.

33. "Choice and Witty Proverbs," in *The Booke o Merrie Riddles* (London, 1617), no. 79, n.p. Compare [William Camden], *Remaines, concerning Britaine* (London, 1623), 266: "Batchellers wiues, and maides children be well taught," echoed in J[ames] H[owell], *Proverbs: or, Old Sayed Sawes and Proverbs* (London, 1659), 7.

34. Compare Toby's vision of marriage in Tho[mas] Durfey, *Madam Fickle: or, The Witty False One* (London, 1677), 5: "Yes! Hang't I will marry—I fancy there's a great deal of pleasure in't. First to command a Family, and sit at the upper end of the Table. Then to make my Wife serve instead of a *Vallet de Chambre*, and never pay her no Wages neither: Then to command her this way; that way, t'other way, and every way; for this thing, that thing, t'other thing, and every thing: Udshash 'tis very pretty—"

But sometimes we find sympathy for the allegedly disorderly woman, and I don't mean sympathy of the form, "Oh, poor thing, this is hard on her, but she must submit." Sometimes the sources are explicit that the problem is the claim of patriarchal authority, not resistance to it. That comes in weaker and stronger forms. The weaker form: this particular bid to or use of authority is overweening, excessive, unjust. The stronger form: patriarchal authority itself is wrong. Both forms are common. That fact reflects back on other tales of disorderly women. It means we should beware the ready inference that their disorder testifies to the power of patriarchy.

Comedies

"Our Comedies are the best Representations of Life," announced a correspondent to *Mist's Weekly Journal* in the 1720s.[35] That sounds like the snapshot view I've already disavowed. But with a more capacious account of *representations*, we can redeem this claim. The period's comedies are chockfull of scenes of marriages, families, household government. Over the decades, from playwright to playwright, the tableaux on offer are strikingly similar.[36] No play should be read as a stenographic report of exchanges in any actual household. But to work, these plays have to comment on everyday life. They may echo or spoof or caricature dynamics their audiences are painfully familiar with. I would not underplay how differently plays can comment on society. But to elicit laughs—and paying audiences—plays can't swoop off into fancies only tenuously related to everyday life. The general point holds outside the comic theater, too. Take the whimsical tale of complaining men who bring their wives to a miller who grinds and cures them.[37] It doesn't make us wonder whether men pulverized their wives with windmills. It makes us reflect on the hankering for violence as a recipe for submission.

35. *A Collection of Miscellany Letters, Selected out of "Mist's Weekly Journal,"* 4 vols. (London, 1722–27), 3:131. Consider too *Rambler*, no. 4 (31 March 1750), in *The Yale Edition of the Works of Samuel Johnson*, ed. W. J. Bate et al., 23 vols. to date (New Haven, CT: Yale University Press, 1958–), 3:20. For evidence of popular attendance at plays, see Martin Butler, *Theatre and Crisis, 1632–1642* (Cambridge: Cambridge University Press, 1984), chap. 6 and app. II.

36. Compare Keith Thomas, *History and Literature* (Swansea: University College of Swansea, 1988); William Ian Miller, *Bloodtaking and Peacemaking: Feud, Law, and Society in Saga Iceland* (Chicago: University of Chicago Press, 1990), 43–51; Elizabeth A. Foyster, *Manhood in Early Modern England: Honour, Sex and Marriage* (London: Longman, 1999), 16–22.

37. *The Merry Dutch Miller: And New Invented Windmill* (London, 1672); see too *The New German Doctor: or, An Infallible Cure for a Scolding Wife* ([London, 1688–92]).

Comedy after comedy portrays husbands striving to act out time-honored profiles of patriarchal authority and failing miserably. Not because they can't live up to the strenuous demands of the role, but because the role itself is ludicrous. The more assiduously they insist on their rights, the more wives run circles around them and the more third parties censure, mock, snicker at the witless husbands. Many of these comedies suggest that recitations of male dominance may be dandy when you're sitting in church or reading a treatise of political theory, but not in daily life. Nor is it just that they should remain unspoken because it's brutal to insist on a dominance that everyone understands. In some of these comedies, it's ridiculous even to try to follow them. To emphasize that the plays can comment on everyday life without echoing it, I'll start with a comic portrait of an extraordinary husband.

Meet Carizales, the, um, protagonist? of Charles Johnson's *Generous Husband*—the title is scathingly facetious—of 1711.[38] Carizales is smitten with the categories of property. The comedy is a critique of commodification from a period full of them. ("It is a Stock-jobbing age," sighs Fielding's Mr. Bellamant; "ev'ry thing has its Price; Marriage is Traffick throughout.")[39] Back from "30 years Toil in the *Indies*," sixty-year-old Carizales has purchased fifteen-year-old Lucy as his wife, or at least he thinks he has. "I have given a Sum of Money for her, not receiv'd one with her"—no dowry for him—"and made her a Settlement likewise Equivalent to the Money I gave. It seems to me therefore she is by so much the more my Property—she is indeed my Chattel real, upon no account to be alienated." "She is a Jewel that I have purchas'd at a costly Price; and being so . . . have I not a Right to lock it up in my Casket, or wear it abroad on Holidays, as I think fit?" Carizales pursues a relentless campaign of control. Lucy's apartment is surrounded by high walls, with no windows that might display an ogling young man.[40] "Who then can call me jealous?" demands our valiant husband. "Who suspicious? I am free from all suspicion, by knowing I have prevented the Occasion of it.—We Husbands live in a world of licens'd Thieves; a Fellow that steals your Handkerchief shall be hang'd by the Law, but he may run away with your

<hr>

38. Charles Johnson, *The Generous Husband: or, The Coffee House Politician* (London, 1711).

39. *The Modern Husband* [1732], in Henry Fielding, *Plays*, ed. Thomas Lockwood, 2 vols. to date (Oxford: Clarendon, 2004–), 2:237.

40. See too William Wycherley, *The Country-Wife, a Comedy, Acted at the Theatre Royal* (London, 1675), 32, where jealous Mr. Pinchwife's wife sighs to her sister, "Wou'd it not make any one melancholy, to see you go every day fluttering about abroad, whil'st I must stay at home like a poor lonely, sullen Bird in a cage?"

Wife, and you must put your Horns in your Pocket," that is, live quietly as a cuckold.

Lucy appears onstage to report, "I have a mind to go abroad." She doesn't mean to another country. She just wants to go outside. Lucy assures an alarmed Carizales that he can join her. Unmoved, he disgorges this nugget of patriarchal wisdom: "Did I not tell you at first, Chuck, that one of the chief Articles of a Wife's Duty was not to dispute the absolute Will of her Husband, or ask Questions?" She uses the same pet name for him, but she isn't deferring. "You say you will give me every thing that I want, and yet forbid me to ask Questions; indeed, Chuck, I cannot tell you my mind without speaking." This exchange kicks off careening plots of deception and seduction. Carizales wrongly believes that Lucy has been philandering. But eventually she does say she will steal gold from Carizales and run off with her would-be lover, who's actually her sister in disguise. This is funny, perhaps, but it also makes the flirtation safe for the audience, in on the deception.

Finally, a chastened Carizales promises vengeance—against himself. "I ought, Fool that I was, to have consider'd how inconsistent the 15 Years of this Girl were with the threescore of mine; like the Silk-worm, I have wrought my own Tomb, and I lie down in it in peace." All shall dance, he agrees—his resignation is a triumph—and he unfurls a moral of the story. "I have learnt, that 'tis as possible to imprison Air or Fire, as to keep a Woman from her Will. I know too that Jealousy is an ungovernable Passion. If I suspect my Servant to be a Thief, he thinks he has a Right to rob me; and if I am jealous of my Wife, do I wonder if it piques her to Revenge? Henceforth, my Dear, thou sha't be as free as my Thoughts, which shall never any more be violated with base and unjust Fears."[41]

Husbands can't treat wives as property: or anyway sixty-year-old husbands can't treat teenaged wives that way. Veramant promptly follows up Carivales's ruminations with a moral of his own. "Why should you pretend to lock up a Treasure to which all Mankind have a Key?" he wonders. "No, rather take the Instructions of the Poet." He quotes the closing couplet of Matthew Prior's "English Padlock":

41. See too Charles Johnson, *The Wife's Relief: or, The Husband's Cure* (London, 1736), epilogue. So too, in *Female Innocence: or, A School for a Wife* (Southwark, [1732?]), old Mr. Porter has been bringing up Nanny to be his perfect wife. She can rehearse a catechism of wifely duties and sins. But she's been flirting with others. After huffing and puffing about "thy treason against thy lord and master" and setting up a staged beating, he relinquishes her.

> Let all her Ways be unconfin'd:
> And clap your PADLOCK—on her Mind.[42]

Carizales disavows the quest for dominance; Veramant suggests that the problem was only his tactics. It's not a particularly funny or happy note to close on, but comedies needn't be formulaic. The one-two punch leaves the audience plenty to think about.

Property claims and a husband squirreling away his wife also animate a 1706 comedy,[43] but to different effect. This comedy was enough of a crowd-pleaser to go through multiple editions for over sixty years—and this first printing announces on the title page that it's already been popular onstage "for many years." Barnaby Brittle forbids his wife to go see a play: "I say, No." Women in the audience are on notice. Brittle, they must realize—so must any husbands accompanying them—would likely not let them attend this play, either.[44] Saucy Mrs. Brittle shoots back, "But, I say, Yes. Do you think you shall keep me always stifling within Doors, where there's no body to be seen but your old fusty self?" She protests being "shut up in a Nunnery" and being married to an older man. "And I wou'd have you to know, tho' you have forc'd me to Wed my self with old Age and ill Humours, I am not wedded to my Grave!—'tis time enough Forty Years hence to think of that, and I have a great deal to do before that time comes; therefore I must, and I will go abroad."

Brittle does what many another jittery authority does in the face of insubordination. His name has warned us what to expect: he threatens her with force. "Stir one step if you dare," he sputters, and "*Spits in his Fist.*"

> If you go to that: I'll try who wears the Breeches, you or I. You shall stay at home and keep me company; I'll spoil your going to Plays, your Appointments and your Intrigues—I'll make you know that I am your Husband, and that you shall do what I please. Sdslife, What's here to do! What, have you forgot your Marriage Vows already? Pray, who am I? Am I not your Husband? Are you not married to me?

---

42. "An English Padlock" [1704], in *The Literary Works of Matthew Prior*, ed. H. Bunker Wright and Monroe K. Sears, 2 vols. (Oxford: Clarendon, 1959), 1:229. I've used this typography; that of the play is italicized and varies some.

43. [Thomas Betterton], *The Amorous Widow: or, The Wanton Wife: A Comedy* (London, 1706).

44. [John Tatham], *Knavery in All Trades: or, The Coffee-House* (London, 1664), exploits the same motif in the exchange between Mrs. Olive and Fraile at sig. C3 verso.

"No," his wife spits back, "you forc'd me: I never gave you my Consent, in Word or in Deed. Cou'd you think I was in Love with Avarice, with Age and Impotence?" Brittle stammers incredulously. "Give me Patience! How! How!" "No," she continues implacably, "you basely bought me of my Father and Mother." "Wou'd I cou'd sell thee again," he fumes. "Like a Slave you bought me," she perseveres, "and so you intend to use me, were I fool enough; but I'll see you hang'd first."

She is the daughter of the genteel Prides, she announces, and rues the day she married a lowly tradesman. The Prides, dutifully appearing onstage, are hilariously pompous and the play now recycles a gag. Brittle keeps trying to show the Prides that his wife is flirting and worse with Lovemore, but every time she runs circles around him. The Prides force him to apologize to Lovemore even as she's professing her love for Lovemore right over unwitting Brittle's shoulder. She even thrashes Brittle with a cane to show him what she'd do to Lovemore if he attempted her honor. No wonder Brittle spits in his hand again when his wife proclaims, "I'm resolv'd to encourage every Man that makes Love to me. . . . I can't find a Name bad enough for thee." "Odd, I've a great mind to spoil that handsome Face," he muses. But he thinks better of it.

Finally, Mrs. Brittle overhears Lovemore admit that he is fickle, so she reconciles with her husband. If nothing else, the play gives us another husband whose bid to wear the breeches is foiled. And it creates yet another audience invited to rejoice in his errant wife's rollicking triumphs. It's a relatively harmless pleasure for patriarchs, you might think, since the Brittles do reconcile. Yet one wonders how the quarrelling couple will do after the curtain falls.

Eliza Haywood tried her hand at the same formula, wife as property, with *A Wife to Be Lett*.[45] Mr. Graspall has agreed to rent his wife to Harry Beaumont for £2,000. Beaumont has sent the cash in a locked chest; he's keeping the key until Graspall delivers his wife. Unmoved by her irate recriminations, Graspall coos, "Now, *Pudsy*, if thou hast any Love for thy old Hubby, never let such a Sum depart the House, by a foolish Denial." Mrs. Graspall pretends to be having another affair and to have made off with the money, all to jolt him out of his "covetous, sordid Disposition." In John Gay's rollicking *Beggar's Opera*, Peachum is appalled that his daughter is thinking of marriage. "Married! If the

---

45. Eliza Haywood, *A Wife to Be Lett: A Comedy* (London, 1724).

Wench does not know her own Profit, sure she knows her own Pleasure better than to make herself a Property!"[46] In Fielding's *Love in Several Masques*, Helena is aghast at her impending marriage: "To be sold! to be put up at Auction! to be disposed of, as a piece of Goods, by way of Bargain and Sale!"[47]

What are these plays worrying about? After all, the conduct manuals don't urge that the husband *own* his wife. Contemporary practices illuminate the worry. Take the negotiations over dowry and jointure surrounding marriages among the elite. Despondent over such protracted negotiations, Lady Mary wrote to Wortley—before eloping with him against her father's will— "People in my way are sold like slaves, and I cannot tell what price my Master will put on me."[48] The scandal surrounding Theophilus Cibber's broken marriage included the allegation that he took money to let another man sleep with his wife.[49] For centuries, kings and other great men routinely paid off husbands for the privilege of sleeping with their wives.[50] Also—the backstory here is the complex history of writs and pleadings—a cuckold filing a tort action for "criminal conversation" or adultery would be claiming trespass *vi et armis*. The Latin means *with violence*, but what's salient is the idea of a wrongful invasion of a property right.[51] Later I'll turn to wife sales.

But the comic probing of property outruns such practices. Maybe these comedies are lampooning everyday possessiveness, but not exactly male sovereignty. Then again it's easy to glide from sovereignty to property or even to

46. [John] Gay, *The Beggar's Opera*, 2nd ed. (London, 1728), 7.

47. *Love in Several Masques* [1728], in Fielding, *Plays*, 1:41.

48. Lady Mary Pierrepont to Wortley, [14 November 1710], in *The Complete Letters of Lady Mary Wortley Montagu*, ed. Robert Halsband, 3 vols. (Oxford: Clarendon, 1965–67), 1:64. See too Lady Mary to Wortley, [11 June 1712], in *Letters*, 1:123. For an interlude on women as "*the property of your Husbands*," Henry Fielding, *Amelia* [1751], ed. Martin C. Battestin (Middletown, CT: Wesleyan University Press, 1983), 413–15. For a wife protesting to her abusive husband that he's putting her up for sale "like a piece of silk in your shop," see *The Memoirs of Mrs. Catherine Jemmat*, 2nd ed., 2 vols. (London, 1765), 2:93.

49. [Francis Truelove], *The Comforts of Matrimony; Exemplified in the Memorable Case and Trial, Lately Had upon an Action Brought by Theo——s C——r against S—— Esq; for Criminal Conversation with the Plaintiff's Wife*, 6th ed. (London, 1739), 15, 35–36; *The Tryals of Two Causes, between Theophilus Cibber, Gent. Plaintiff, and William Sloper, Esq; Defendant* (London, 1740), 12.

50. Compare [Edward Ward], *A Dialogue, between a Depending Courtier, Who Would Have Sacrificed the Chastity of His Wife to a Certain Great Man, in Hopes of Preferment, and His Virtuous Lady, Who Was Avers'd to a Compliance* (Dublin, 1735); and see *The Tryal between Sir W——m M——rr——s, Baronet, Plaintiff, and Lord A——gst——s F——tʒ-R——y, Defendant, for Criminal Conversation* (London, 1742), 23, on "that sacred Property which every Man ought to have in his Wife."

51. William Blackstone, *Commentaries on the Laws of England*, 4 vols. (Oxford: Clarendon, 1765–69), 3:139. Keith Thomas, "The Double Standard," *Journal of the History of Ideas* 20, no. 2 (1959): 195–216, centers his explanation on "the desire of men for absolute property in women" (216).

conflate them—or to argue that property is delegated sovereignty, as legal realist Morris Cohen famously did.[52] Blackstone understood the allure of thinking of property as "that sole and despotic dominion, which one man claims and exercises over the external things of the world, in total exclusion of the right of any other individual in the universe."[53] (Contrary to mythology, Blackstone didn't himself champion this conception.) Sarah Chapone's petition to Parliament, complaining "That the Estate of Wives is more disadvantagious than *Slavery* itself,"[54] echoes Lady Mary's complaint, invoking a category merging property and government and making it sweepingly radical. So it's fair to enlist these comedies as commentaries on the conduct manuals. Casting wives as property brings into ominous focus what lofty talk of governance might amount to on the ground—and how it might be challenged.

Enough of property. Let's ponder *The Devil of a Wife* from 1686.[55] Nell's husband, Jobson the cobbler, likes to drink. The play opens with what must be a tired old argument. "GOOD Husband stay with me to Night and make an end of the Holiday at home," pleads Nell. Jobson will have none of it: "Peace, peace, and go Spin, for if I want any Thread for my stitching, I will punish you by virtue of my Sovereign Authority." "I warrant you," Nell responds glumly—she means, I bet you will—"But you'l go to the Ale-house, spend your Money, and get drunk, and come home like *Old Nick*," or Satan, "and use one like a Dog." That is, he'll abuse her—or have anal sex with her.[56]

Jobson is irate. "How now Brazen-Face do you speak ill of the *Government?* I am King in my own House, and this is Treason against my Majesty." "I don't understand your stuff," sniffs Nell. Her incomprehension of his majestic blather already speaks volumes, yet there's more: "but prithee don't go to the Ale-house." "Well then," concedes Jobson, "I will not go to the Ale-house." Small consolation: instead he'll get drunk at Sir Richard Lovemore's

52. Morris Cohen, "Property and Sovereignty," *Cornell Law Quarterly* 13 (1927): 8–30.

53. Blackstone, *Commentaries*, 2:2.

54. [Sarah Chapone], *The Hardships of the English Laws: In Relation to Wives* (London, 1735), 4. "Under what tyranny are women born!" cries a despondent Althea in Sir Charles Sedley, *The Mulberry Garden: A Comedy* (London, 1668), 23.

55. [Thomas Jevon], *The Devil of a Wife: or, A Comical Transformation* (London, 1686).

56. R. W. Dent, *Shakespeare's Proverbial Language: An Index* (Berkeley: University of California Press, 1981), 94, D514; R. W. Dent, *Proverbial Language in English Drama Exclusive of Shakespeare, 1495–1616: An Index* (Berkeley: University of California Press, 1984), 300, D514; Gordon Williams, *A Dictionary of Sexual Language and Imagery in Shakespearean and Stuart Literature*, 2 vols. (London: Athlone, 1994), 2:1462–63 s.v. *use*. Compare Henry Fielding, *Pasquin: A Dramatic Satire on the Times* (London, 1736), 27.

estate with the butler. She wants to join him. "No, you Jade," he scoffs. "I will be no Cuckold." Apparently he suspects that her chastity is soluble in alcohol.

So the cobbler would be king. He indignantly denies that he beats his wife and insists he will safeguard her sexual fidelity. But we watch this pompous costume unravel, as if it weren't obscenely threadbare as soon as he assumed it. Nell continues to plead and Jobson indulges in the very threat he just disavowed. "Why thou most audacious Strumpet, darst thou Dipute with me? go home and Spin, or else my Strap will wind about thy Ribs." To mollify her, on his way out he hands her some money: "here's six pence for you, get Ale and Apples, stretch and puff thy self up with Lambs Wool, rejoyce and revel by thy self, be drunk and wallow in thy own Stye like a Sow as thou art." But he can't even stick to this insulting generosity. Scant minutes later, believing Nell is drunk, Jobson beats her.

His proud boast that he won't be a cuckold gets shredded, too, with the help of a bedtrick orchestrated by a cunning man. Lovemore's shrewish wife and Nell change places: only they know what's going on. The shrew learns what it's like to have an abusive boor for a husband. Contrite, she pledges to mend her ways. Nell, let's say, enjoys her time away from home well enough. When she returns, Jobson vows never to beat her again. He worries too that the lord has cuckolded him. The lord denies it, but offers him £500. Johnson's gleeful response doesn't mean he believes the denial. The sorry king of this pathetic household hasn't been deposed, but his authority has taken a drubbing. Some audience members will celebrate Nell's triumph. Refractory husbands can morosely endure the travesty unfolding before them—or contemplate their own household government.

The gulf between Jobson's haughty claims and his ignoble actions motor the action: puncturing hypocritical pretensions is a foolproof recipe for comedy. A 1677 comedy[57] deploys the same tactics with Tom Essence, introduced in the cast of characters as "A Iealous Coxcomb of his Wife." The play opens with a distraught Theodocia studying a picture of Loveall, whom her father, Old Monylove, has ordered her to marry. (The cast of characters is helpful with Loveall, too. He's "a wilde Debaucht Blade.") Then she fondly turns to a picture of her beloved servant Courtly and swoons.

Another servant cries out for help and Tom appears: "She's cold—I'le try if she has life—(kisses her) Amber, Musk, and Civit!—I protest I know not

---

57. [Thomas Rawlins], *Tom Essence: or, The Modish Wife* (London, 1677).

whether she breaths or no—(kisses her again) she's *Essence* of Violets from head to foot—what a ravishing lip is here!" Tom hasn't noticed, but another woman glares from a window as he feasts on this unconscious morsel of perfumed splendor. It's his wife and she's no gem, either: the cast of characters labels her "very Impertinent and Iealous of her Husband." She rushes to the scene and is instantly smitten with Courtly's picture, which Tom sees her kissing. "S'life," he mutters, "she'l Fornicate with the Picture!" Then he has to listen to her gush: "Ah Mrs. *Essence,* what wou'd become of thee, had'st thou the addresses made thee by such a comely Person; that Woman were a Beast that cou'd deny the kindness he shou'd sue for," she soliloquizes. "A Goat wou'd to satisfie your Appetite," growls Tom, annoyed by her frank sexual desire. He grabs the picture and accosts her. "How now Madam *Flippant,* have I caught you traducing the Honour of your Lawful Sovereign, your Husband—" The two swap accusations in a rapid-fire call-and-response judicial indictment, each demanding how the other will plead.

This comedy doesn't portray a sympathetic wife stuck with a lout of a husband. If Tom's huffing and puffing about his sovereign authority is ridiculous, so are his wife's pretensions. Nor does the play invite the thought that he at least is entitled to talk and act this way. Later, Tom soliloquizes in his perfume shop about his lawsuit against Courtly for "violently assaulting the body of *Dorothy Essence,* my Wife." Customers enter and Tom shifts into lecherous salesman mode, fawning over and fondling them. ("*Pats their Breasts with Essences,*" says one stage direction.) One woman punches Tom in the head. He feels sorry for himself and never notices the disjuncture between his righteous indignation against Courtly, who actually hasn't raped his wife, and his own groping. But the audience has to notice.

Even the genuinely devoted *Artful Wife* of a 1718 comedy[58] subverts the high-minded wisdom of the conduct manuals as she endorses it. Lady Absent bemoans conflict with her husband:

> How delightful is the Matrimonial State, when two Minds have but one Desire! What Harmony does it produce, inspir'd with Friendship, Love and Generosity! The meanest Condition may thus be made most happy. Methinks there should be but few bad Women, Virtue is so delightful.—There can be no just Provocation why a Wife should use a Husband ill: Pride and Folly cry for Revenge.—Perhaps he likes another,—neglects her for his

---

58. [William] Taverner, *The Artful Wife: A Comedy* (London, 1718).

Bottle, or some other worthless Toy. — But of whom will she be reveng'd? — Upon her self: — Can his want of Honour be a Reason why she should sacrifice her own? No. The Men by Custom regain their Reputation when they but seem to mend: Woman's once lost is never to be found again, it dies for ever.

Lord Absent believes that Lady Absent is carrying on with his friend Sir Francis. She's not, though Sir Francis is interested. So she invites her husband to snoop. We watch Sir Francis's panting soliloquy. He might as well be rubbing his hands or, better, licking his lips: "She'll meet me in a Quarter of an Hour in the Summer House. — A convenient Place; and in the Dark. Modestly contriv'd to hide her Blushes. — She's a fine Woman; and who would not sacrifise a hundred Friends to obtain her? What Joy, what Raptures will she give! O Extasy!" With Lord Absent eavesdropping, Lady Absent reveals that she knows that Sir Francis has seduced her niece by promising her marriage. Sir Francis abuses Lord Absent — and keeps pressing himself on Lady Absent. She keeps demurring. Finally he snarls, "A little Force will break the Curb of Modesty." She cries for help and her husband and the servants rush in.

Lady Absent turns to her husband:

> I beg your Pardon, my Lord, for the Uneasiness I have occasion'd you; but you must now believe I meant no Ill; for all that I design'd was only to raise your Jealousy, by which means I hop'd to cure your Absent, Indolent, Unthinking Temper, expose a Villain, and prevent the Ruin of your Family. — It startles me to think what Hazards I have run; for had I not prevail'd on you to meet him here with me in the Dark, and given me that Opportunity to lay him open to your View, I might have forfeited your Esteem for ever, which I value more than all Things under Heaven.[59]

She's the soul of devotion and duty. "With what Delight I shall obey when you command," she exclaims: "Hours, Days, and Years shall glide away, in one continu'd Course of Constancy and Love." Ecstatic obedience and constant love: these are not antithetical, not anyway for Lady Absent.[60] But who's in charge of the Absents' marriage? And what about the impending marriage be-

---

59. Contrast the more docile methods Lady Easy uses to recall her straying husband to fidelity in C[olley] Cibber, *The Careless Husband: A Comedy* (London, 1705).

60. Compare *The Memoirs of Anne, Lady Halkett and Ann, Lady Fanshawe*, ed. John Loftis (Oxford: Clarendon, 1979), 103.

tween Sir Francis and Lady Absent's niece, into which the Absents promptly bully the reluctant groom? So honor dictates, as Lord Absent stubbornly maintains, even though he's already branded Sir Francis "the greatest Villain Nature ever form'd." Who will rule in *that* household? How happy will it be? Recall the language of the 1705 sermon: has nature really designed Sir Francis to be sovereign of his household? (That sermon, too, was popular enough to keep new editions rolling off the presses, including in 1716 and 1722. Its sentiments were surely in the air when this comedy was staged. Not because the sermon was deeply original and causally powerful, but because it was a rivulet of broader currents.) Audience members might not have entertained any such mordant thoughts about this bit of the happy ending. But I suspect some did.

   The Modern Wife[61] from 1744 is more programmatic. As the curtain opens, Sir George Modern basks in melancholy. Lady Modern has demanded the eye-popping sum of 100 guineas to play quadrille, a fashionable card game. If he doesn't supply her, she says, "a Gentleman, who would take it as a particular Favour to supply all her Wants," will. But she too wants to show her husband that his friend is trying to seduce her. Lest the ensuing she-nanigans make the audience approve her gallivanting ways, Lady Modern herself comes out to deliver the epilogue. Here's its opening:

> WELL!—tho' I've played To-night the MODERN WIFE,
> No *Woman* that is wise would lead my Life;
> Would e'er affect my *arbitrary Rule*,
> And make her *Spouse* such a tame, easy Tool;
> Would range, like me, without Controul, all Day,
> And, to indulge her boundless Thirst for Play,
> Throw, in one Night, her Wealth and Fame away.

I don't suppose the playwright intended these reassuring words ironically. Nor do I suppose many in the audience took them that way. But it would be odd to imagine the audience so slack-jawed that they gulped down this moral of the story and ignored the more mischievous strands of the play.

   One last comedy, *The Wedding* of 1734, merrily turns the world upside down.[62] (This one is subtitled *A Ballad Opera* because it's interspersed with

---

61. [John Stevens], *The Modern Wife; or, The Virgin Her Own Rival* (London, 1744). I've reversed the italics in the passage from the epilogue.
   62. *The Wedding: or, The Country House-Wife* (London, 1734).

songs. Today we'd call it a musical comedy.) Mrs. Squeesall warns her daughter Blouzella, "you shall find, to your Cost, that Women were born to live in continual Subjection, first to their Parents, and, all their Lives after, to their Husbands, Hussy." Blouzella is surprisingly nonchalant in the face of this deflating news. "If that be the Case," she retorts, "I have been mightily mistaken in my Notions of Matrimony; I vow I always thought, it was the Wife's Business to command, and the Husband's to obey." Her mother recoils: "Fine Doctrine truly! Pray what could put such a ridiculous Notion in your Head?" "Example, Madam," her daughter responds drily. "I am sure it is, and always has been the Fashion in our House; and it would be a Fault in me, if I should not endeavour to tread in your Steps."

Mrs. Squeesall comes clean. "Thou art a wicked Girl," she sighs, "and yet I cannot find in my heart to be angry with thee. What I said was with Design to try thy Temper; and, since I find thou hast a becoming Spirit, if you punctually observe the Rules I shall set you, I'll engage you shall be able to govern your Husband, without Controul." As a newlywed, she was naïve enough to think "that *Honey-moon* would last for ever, that my Commands would be obey'd, with as much Submission, as they had been, during the Time of Courtship." Alas, "My Humble Slave turn'd an absolute Tyrant" and her whimpering and "downright Scolding" only drove him away. He "corrupted two or three of his Tenants Daughters." She'd spare her daughter these gyrations, so she's ready to teach her the real arts of household government, ones the conduct manuals would brand unnatural. Her daughter's all ears: the father she knows never dares to dispute her mother's dictates.

Mrs. Squeesall knows that her husband is sleeping with the widow Saunter, but she chooses to ignore it. She realized long ago that she had to safeguard the family finances. So she stopped crying and chiding. Her husband "made me absolute Mistress of every Thing but his Person." She was sure to be charming to each new mistress. Her husband was moved enough to promise fidelity, but he never could keep that promise. Mistresses came and went until he fixed on the widow. She was past childbearing age, so no illegitimate child would muscle in on the Squeesall children's claims to the estate. This bleak tale is the prelude to the promised rules for governing a husband. Prelude is all we get: the dramatic action goes careening off into tangled romances and weddings. Along the way, though, we get another glimpse of what a wretch Mr. Squeesall is and what earns him his name: he's intent on screwing everything he can out of his tenants, partly for the money and partly to keep them from being impudent. (Here again is the marriage of property and government.) Did nature design him to govern? Or did the audience rally to the verve and, yes, authority with which Mrs. Squeesall has navigated an unhappy situation? It's hard to imagine that they blanched in uncomprehending outrage when she invoked her "command" and promised Blouzella she'd teach her how to "govern" her husband.

None of these comedies is a literary masterpiece. Yes, they were popular enough for someone to decide they were worth publishing. Some were reprinted. Still, they are basically forgotten texts by forgettable authors: nondescript, even nonexistent, from a literary point of view. That hack writers' debunking treatment of patriarchy is commonplace, even rote, suggests a perspective on early modern England unlike the blather of the conduct manuals. Sir Solomon Empty haughtily addresses his wife, who hates him: "Looky' Wife, I wou'd be mistaken in some things, a good States Man, like a good Wrestler, conceals his strength for an opportunity, and my Capacity is a Secret—but you are Women and don't understand things."[63] His name underlines the obvious: the audience isn't poised to root for him or unthinkingly assent to his contemptuous embrace of her political subjection. Congreve offered a comic negotiation of a marriage's terms far removed from blather—in a play tellingly called *The Way of the World*.[64]

Popular Songs and Doggerel Verse

Better yet are popular songs. Many seem to be folk songs. I presume they circulated by word of mouth, a sign of their popularity. Happily, contemporaries memorialized them in anthologies. I'll also include here what may well be such songs published under individual titles, frequently as single-sheet broadsides, but what might instead be solo-authored poetry or would-be song lyric. Only occasionally were songs published with sheet music: probably their simple stock melodies were familiar. Then too, many enthusiastic singers couldn't have read sheet music anyway. But you can today sing "A Farewell to Wives"[65]—"Once in our lives let us drink to our Wives, tho' the number of them is but small; God take the best, and the Dev'l take the rest,

63. [William Burnaby], *The Reform'd Wife: A Comedy* (London, 1700), 3.

64. [William] Congreve, *The Way of the World: A Comedy* (London, 1700), 56–59.

65. "A Farewell to Wives," in [John Hilton], *Catch That Catch Can: or, The Second Part of the Musical Companion* (London, 1685), sig. C recto.

and so we shall be rid of 'em all"—with the original 1685 melody. These sources, too, supply glimpses of married life that remind us not to mistake blather for reality.

Some are homespun vignettes of what we unthinkingly describe as the battle of the sexes.[66] 1714 gives us "The Good House-wife: or, A Tydy One":

> Not long ago I marry'd a Wife,
>   A tydy Huswife, a tydy one,
> She makes me weary of my Life,
>   And I think she proves a tydy one.
> I sent her to Market to buy me a Hen, &c.
> She lies a Bed till the Clock strikes Ten, &c.
> She well may be counted the Queen of Sluts, &c.
> She roasted a Hen both Feathers and Guts, &c.
> She meant to fill my Belly full, &c.
> She drest a Sheep's-head both Horns and Wool, &c.
> I went to make my Pudding of Fat, &c.
> And in it she let her Nose to drop, &c.
> She laid the Cheese upon the Shelf, &c.
> She let it alone till it turned it self, &c.
> She hung on the Kettle without any Water, &c.
> The Bottom fell out, and the Sides came after, &c.
> She sweeps the House but once a Year, &c.
> And then she tells me Brooms are dear, &c.
> For Cleanliness she will not fail, &c.
> Instead of the Vault makes use of a Pail, &c.
> For mending of Cloaths I had like to forgot, &c.
> Instead of Patches she tyes them in Knots, &c.
> At the Ale-house she loves to tipple and funk, &c.
> She seldom comes home until she be drunk, &c.
> For Scolding her Part it good she did make, &c.
> With any one of *Billinsgate, &c.*
> A beautious Creature she is without doubt,
>   A tydy Huswife, a tydy one.
> For her tawny Face is as round as a Colt,

---

66. "*Each Woman Wise her Husband* Rules; / Passive Obedience *is for* Fools," says one woman in "Conjugal Obedience: A Tale," in [Eustace Budgell], *The Bee: or, Universal Weekly Pamphlet,* 9 vols. (London, 1733), 2:1065–70, offering a series of women defiantly spurning instructions from their husbands to boil a pig. In concluding, the narrator disagrees. For an extraordinary collection of women haranguing their husbands, see [John Taylor], *Divers Crabtree Lectures* (London, 1639).

Which makes her look like a tydy one.
Besides she has gotten a fine beetle Brow,
      a tydy Huswife, a tydy one,
With a delicate Snout much like a Sow,
      which makes her look like a tydy one.

That's how he sees it. But don't bother figuring out the oral or aural equivalent of the male gaze. The same anthology immediately provides her counter:

My Husband of his Wife does cry,
A tydy Huswife a tydy one,
And he has as many Faults as I,
And I think he proves a tydy one.
Good People mind and you shall hear,
Of a careful Husband a careful one,
He paid for Water instead of Small beer,
And I think he proves a careful one.
Men came for Taxes for the King, &c.
Instead of two Groats a Crown he did fling, &c.
At the Tavern all Night he will be, &c.
He drinks till he can neither go, speak nor see, &c.
When all his Money is spent and gone, &c.
He reels home by the Light of the Sun, &c.
And when he to his Wife does come, &c.
He thumps her Bones for what he hath done, &c.
To save the Sheets from being tore, &c.
He makes his Wife lie on the Floor, &c.
Her squinting Eyes and his drivilling Chin, &c.
With a Pair of Breeches bepist within, &c.
Besides his Cleanliness is such, &c.
He'll scarce out of his Bed to ease his Breech, &c.
Each Day that he goes to work, &c.
The Money he gets, he spends with a Jirk, &c.
Oh! Women take care of Marrying with a Sot, &c.
You've heard by this Song what has been my Lot.[67]

Talk about unhappy equality! How might these songs be sung? Each by men and women together? With men singing the first, women singing the

---

67. [Henry Scougal], *The Compleat English Secretary, and Newest Academy of Complements* (London, 1714), 167–68, italics removed. Compare Mrs. Sullen's lament in [George] Farquhar, *The Beaux Stratagem: A Comedy* (London, [1707]), 12.

second? With gatherings of men singing only the first, women the second? Wouldn't the singers of one song likely know the other? Doubtless some singers imagined that one song captured something real and important and the other was frivolous. But I suspect most singers were not so provincial and boorish. Whatever one makes of the conduct manuals' affection for male dominance, this careful husband and his tidy wife unveil the all too human scenes of bickering and grievances, with neither spouse enjoying the upper hand and neither song intimating that either should.

1682 gives us "The Ranting City Dame: A Song Much in Use," the subtitle already an invitation to figure out what made it so popular. It's hard to construe the song as an indictment of urban vice or the freedom claimed by prosperous women:

> Ha now I am Married, let others take care,
> I've one to provide for me, and I'le not spare,
> I'le take me a Coach, and away to *Hide* Park,
> There I'le be Corted by every spark,
> There's none shall go finer whilst that it does hold,
> My Gown shall be *Tissue*, all spangl'd with Gold.
>
> My Jewels and Rings, and whatever beside,
> I will have, that may but conduce to my Pride,
> If Husband dare Grumble, I'le graft such a Crest,
> As it shall soon make him be known from the rest,
> Whilst I with fine Gallants do take my delight,
> We'l Revel all day, and we'l sport it all Night.[68]

The offstage husband probably submits rather than wear a cuckold's horns. His job seems to be to pay the bills and shut his mouth, not to rule for the better economy of the world. Is it even barely plausible that this song was sung in tones of abject horror, the singers sternly distancing themselves from such unnatural disorder? Are the only choices that they either emulated or renounced her actions? Couldn't they have embraced more or less of her stance? Couldn't they have seen what was choiceworthy about it, what lacking in feminine deference, and where those descriptions might overlap instead of diverge?

In summoning up complaint and disobedience, these songs must depend

---

68. "The Ranting City Dame: A Song Much in Use," in *A Collection of the Choicest Songs, as They Are Sung at Court, Both the Theaters, the Musick-Schools and Academies, &c.* (London, 1682), sig. E2 verso.

on standards for good behavior, standards that might not be followed and might not be justifiable—not only in our eyes, but in some of theirs. Other songs are politically invested in more explicit ways. Here's "A Psalm of Mercy," recorded after the interregnum:

> We will not be Wives
> And tye up our Lives
> To Villanous slavery.[69]

Or take "The Ladies Case," from the 1735 *Collection of Above One Hundred and Fifty Choice Songs and Ballads:*

> How hard is the fortune of all womankind,
> For ever subjected, for ever confin'd;
> The parent controuls us until we are wives,
> The husband enslaves us the rest of our lives.[70]

That's polite compared to the searing indictment of one of *A New Collection of the Choicest Songs* from 1676:

> *Woman who is by nature wild,*
> > *dull-bearded man incloses,*
> *Of natures freedom we'r beguil'd,*
> > *By Laws which man imposes,*
> *who still himself continues free,*
> *Yet we poor slaves must fettered be.*
> *Chorus:*
> > A shame and a Curse,
> > Of for better, for worse,
> 'Tis a vile imposition on Nature,
> > For women shou'd change,
> > and have freedom to range,
> Like to every other wild creature.[71]

---

69. "A Psalm of Mercy," in [Alexander Brome], *Rump: or, An Exact Collection of the Choycest Poems and Songs Relating to the Late Times* (London, 1662), pt. 2, p. 196.

70. "The Ladies Case," in *A Collection of Above One Hundred and Fifty Choice Songs and Ballads,* 2nd ed. (London, 1735), 105. See too *Women Will Have Their Will: or, Give Christmas His Due* (London, 1649), 9.

71. "Song," in *A New Collection of the Choicest Songs: Now in Esteem in Town or Court* (n.p., 1676), sig. C3 recto. This song, here with mostly incidental variations, is from Tho[mas] Shadwell, *The Libertine: A Tragedy* (London, 1676), 46–47 (or at least that seems likelier than that Shadwell lifted it from the songbook); the play was reprinted steadily through 1736. Compare William Hyland, *The Ship-Wreck: A Dramatick Piece* (London, 1746), 27–28.

"*Let us resume our ancient right,*" the song adds. It sounds curiously like a late-feminist variant on the intoxicated work of the radical Digger, Gerrard Winstanley. Here male dominance is unnatural in as blunt a rejection of patriarchal wisdom as we can imagine.

This dour view of the plight of women was met by laments for the plight of husbands, some of whom seem not to have found themselves natural sovereigns in their households. This bouncy verse, the sort of thing W. S. Gilbert and Dr. Seuss would specialize in, is humorously incongruous with the dreary substance it retails:

> Suppose a Man
> Do's all he can
> T'unslave himself from a scolding Wife,
> He can't get out,
> But hopps about,
> Like a marry'd Bird in the Cage of Life.
> She on Mischief bent
> Is never content,
> But makes the poor Man cry out,
> Rigid Fate,
> Marriage State;
> No Reprieve,
> But the Grave:
> Oh! hard Condition.

The song advises the husband to "let her squall, / And tear and bawl, / And with Whining cry her Eyes out." He should ignore her and seek consolation in his flask. Better yet, apparently, this tactic will "quickly bring her to her last."[72]

And what of the plight of this poor henpecked fellow?

> I Every morning make a fire,
>   all which is done to ease her,
> I get a Nut-meg, make a toast,
>   in hope therewith to please her:
> Of a Cup of nappy ale and spice,
>   of which she is first taster.

---

72. "Suppose a Man," in *The Nightingale* (London, 1738), 72–73. On meter and substance, compare the song of the beleaguered husband in [Braithwait], *Ar't Asleepe*, 108–10.

And yet this cros-grain'd quean will scold,
        and strive to be my master.[73]

Or this one:

My Wife doth tug me by the ears
        if I but ask for Bacon,
And flouts and taunts and scolds and jears,
        but she must have her Capon:
She kicks me up and down the house,
        and roars as loud as Thunder,
While I am silent as a Mouse,
        hold up my hands and wonder.[74]

Or this one, grimly convinced that whatever he does, he'll end up a cuckold:

What euer I doe say
        Shee will haue her owne way;
Shee scorneth to obey;
        Shee'll take time while she may;
And if I beate her backe and side,
        In spight I shall be hornify'd.[75]

Or the one who moans, "She will be so angry at me, I swear, / That I am ready to bepiss my Breaches for fear."[76] Or the one who confesses, "I dare not speak nor look awry / For fear of her severity."[77] Or the desperate wretch who frets, "I can't please her do all that I can," who bemoans his wife's heading "To the Tavern night and day; / with her Gallent to drink wine," and who finally implores, "Pray come old death, / And stop her breath."[78]

One dyer's "handsome wife" likes to "roam" with her "Gallant." She re-

---

73. *My Wife Will Be My Master: or, The Married-mans Complaint against His Unruly Wife* ([London, 1678–80]).

74. *Poor Anthony's Complaint and Lamentation against His Miseries of Marriage, Meeting with a Scolding Wife* ([London, 1662–88]), n.p.

75. *Cuckold's Haven: or, The Marry'd Man's Miserie* (London, n.d.), in *The Roxburghe Ballads*, ed. William Chappell et al., 8 vols. (New York: AMS, 1966), 1:148.

76. *The Cuckold's Lamentation of a Bad Wife* ([London, 1670–96]), n.p.

77. *The Invincible Pride of Women: or, The London Tradesman's Lamentation* ([London, 1670]), n.p.

78. *Weary Anthony: or, The Loving Husband and Scolding Wife* ([London? 1750?]); see too *Any Thing for a Quiet Life: or, The Married Mans Bondage to a Curst Wife* (London, [1620]). For high-minded cautions against scolding, see G[ervase] Markham, *The English House-Wife, Containing the Inward and Outward Vertues Which Ought to Be in a Compleat Woman* (London, 1683), 2–3. For the lament of yet another henpecked husband, see *Advice to Batchelors: or, The Married Man's Lamentation* (n.p., n.d.), in Chappell et al., *Roxburghe Ballads*, 3:376–79.

peatedly taunts her husband, "Thou art a Cuckold and so thou shalt dye." She boasts too that she redeemed their pawned clothes with her illicit earnings.

> Pray now did you e're flourish in all your Life,
> As now you do by the help of your Wife,
> Therefore my Crime you may well very well here excuse,
> Tell me I pray, do you ever want shooes?
> Yet know you not the price of those you wear,
> I get them by my industrious care,
> The truth of this sure you cannot deny,
> As you are a Cuckold and so you shall dye.[79]

The audience has to suspect that the conduct manuals haven't noticed the exigencies a loving wife might face—or how she might meet them.

No surprise that some songs celebrate the virtues of women and others condemn their vices.[80] No surprise either that some songs give voice to women arguing that their husbands' vices justify their own disobedience.[81] Yet other songs are frank, sometimes downright jovial, about violence. *Bang Her Well, Peter*[82] launches this way:

> I shall sing you a song to please you all well,
> Of a loving couple in this town did dwell,
> They had not been married a fortnight you hear,
> Before they fell out who the breeches should wear.

She's been guilty of adultery. Repeatedly. The two come to blows:

> She up with ladle, struck him on the crown,
> Which made the blood run trickling down;
> He took up a stick of noble black-thorn,
> And bang'd her hide like threshing of corn.

---

79. *The Dyers Destiny: or, The Loving Wife's Help in Time of Need* (London, [1685–88]). Compare the relaxed tone of "A Woman's Reason for Cuckoldom," in A Society of Gentlemen, *The Honey-Suckle* (London, 1734), 43–44.

80. Compare for instance "A Song in Praise of Women," in *Loves School: or, A New Merry Book of Complements* ([London], 1674), n.p., and "A Rhodomontade on His Cruel Mistress," in A Person of Quality, *Westminster-Drollery: or, A Choice Collection of the Newest Songs & Poems Both at Court and Theaters*, with additions (London, 1671), 14. Or compare "Against Women" and "Answer in Defence of Women," both in *Melpomene: or, The Muses Delight* (London, 1678), 99–107.

81. See for instance *The Duty of a Husband: or, The Lady's Answer to the Duty of a Wife* ([London, 1707?]).

82. *Bang Her Well, Peter* (London, n.d.), in *Madden Ballads*, reel 03, frame 2181.

By banging her well (*bang* comes to mean *fuck* only in the twentieth century, or so the *OED* reports, if more decorously), he prevails: "No more will I cuckold or strike you, my dear," she promises; "Come, give me a kiss, and a glass of good beer." That's the tale the narrator promises "will please you all well." The imagined audience rallies to a man brutal enough to thrash a wayward wife until she capitulates. Here is a vigorous defense of male dominance, if a more unabashed appreciation than the conduct manuals ever offer of the tactics it might take to secure it.[83]

This approach to wife beating isn't alone,[84] but it's also contested. Sometimes sweetly, as in suggesting that treating a bad wife well will make her good.[85] But sometimes rival views are more arresting. Another song celebrates a woman who beats her husband, a jealous "aged Miser" who'd been beating her. She narrates the tale with pride and even glee. Once again the ladle is the woman's weapon of choice, no doubt because she presides over the kitchen.

> His bitter blows I could not bear,
> Therefore next morning, I declare,
> While he was sleeping fast in bed,
> I with a ladle broke his head.
>
> With that he starts and stares about,
> I stood courageous, fierce and stout,
> Crying, I'll never be your Slave;
> With that another bang I gave.
>
> He with a cudgel run at me,
> I took a club as well as he,

83. Battering aside, for a song affirming patriarchal authority to be sung by men and to men, see "Women Are Wanton, &c.," in *The Lark* (London, 1740), 139–40. For a rueful rehearsal of numerous ways wives misbehave, with a plea "Hoping all women will amend," see "A Ballad of a Good Wife and a Bad," in J. P., *An Antidote against Melancholy, Made up in Pills* (London, 1669), 58–59, reprinted with trifling variation in W. N., *Merry Drollery Complete* (London, 1670), 302–4. For a vicious beating administered to cure a scold deemed "Mad," see *The Scolding Wife* (London, [1670]). For a poetic narrator approving a husband's beating a wife who hit him and said, "I set not by thee a stinking torde," see *Here Begynneth a Merry Ieste of a Shrewde and Crste Wyfe, Lapped in Morrelles Skin, for Her Good Behauyour* (London, [1580]), n.p.

84. See for instance the stanza on the crab in "The Twelve Signs of the Zodiac," in *Poor Robin, 1683* (London, 1683), n.p.

85. J. R., *The Taming of a Shrew: or, The Onely Way to Make a Bad Wife Good* (London, [1670?]).

Crying, I am resolv'd to try
Who shall be Master you or I.

I gave him not a minute's rest,
But round the room the Rogue I drest,
At length I brought him to his knees,
Henceforth I'll never you displease.

This was his cry, still o're and o're:
Quoth I, VVill you be jealous more?
No, no, I wont, sweet loving VVife,
If thou'lt be pleas'd to spare my life.

Pray keep your word, I then reply'd,
Or else, adsfoot, I'll thrash your hide;
You must not think that I'll be fool'd,
Or in the least be over-rul'd.

Thus I my Husband did subdue,
I'faith I made him buckle too,
Now ever since the truth to tell,
VVith him I live exceeding well.

He never offers now to fight,
But calls me love and hearts delight;
Thus, loving Neighbours, you may see,
I cur'd him of his jealousie.[86]

The loving neighbors summoned up, like those beckoned to be well pleased in *Bang Her Well, Peter,* make the song rejoice in what it describes. A misbehaving husband who's subdued, who buckles, who's punished by a valiant wife who won't "in the least be over-rul'd": what's not to like? Once again the conduct manuals have it all wrong.

The barber's wife of a 1690 verse pummels her husband with, you guessed it, a ladle[87]—and almost kills him:

---

86. *The Woman's Victory: or, The Conceited Cuckold Cudgel'd into Good Qualities, by His Fair and Vertuous Wife* (London, [1684–95]).

87. For yet another woman threatening her drunkard of a husband with a ladle, see [Taylor], *Crabtree Lectures,* 141.

> She with the Ladle broke his head,
>> and down the blood did trickle,
> He looked then as almost dead,
>> in this most fearful pickle:
> When falling down upon his knees,
>> said he, my dearest jewel,
> I never more will thee displease,
>> Sweet Wife be not so cruel.

She agrees to pardon him if he'll buy her "A Suit of new Apparel"; "cringing," he submits. But this song's scornful narrator accosts the audience:

> Pray was she not a loving Wife,
>> of tender pure affection,
> Who caused him to mend his life,
>> by giving him correction?
> Now she has brought him to her bow,
>> to him a place is given,
> And in the Hen-peck'd Frigat go,
>> to sail to Cucolds-Haven.[88]

Though it appears in a volume promising the *Most Delightful Mirth and Merriment*, I doubt this verse made anyone double over laughing. But a 1673 tale in verse of a hapless farmer married to a beauty is decidedly jolly about husband beating.[89] And a 1616 collection of proverbs with sharp responses includes this gem: "*P*. A Woman is the weaker vessel. / *C*. Not when a Curst Wife beates her husband."[90]

In the face of such instantly recognizable scenes of domestic disharmony, men and women alike were advised not to marry.[91] Take this wry counter-

---

88. "The Fearful Combat between the Barber and His Wife, after They Came Home Together," in *The Golden Garland of Most Delightful Mirth and Merriment* ([London, 1690]), n.p.

89. Abraham Miles, *Mirth for Citizens: or, A Comedy for the Country* (London, 1673). See too *A General Summons for Those Belonging to the Hen-Peckt Frigat, to Appear at Cuckolds' Point* ([London, 1688–95]).

90. B. N. [Nicholas Breton], *Crossing of Proverbs: Crosse-Answeres and Cross-Humours* (London, 1616), n.p.

91. See for instance *The Bachelor's Triumph: or, The Single-Man's Happiness* ([London, 1675]); *Good Advice to the Ladies: Shewing, That as the World Goes, and Is Like to Go, the Best Way for Them Is to Keep Unmarried* (London, 1702). The latter, reprinted as *Matrimony: or, Good Advice to the Ladies to Keep Single* (London, 1739), triggered *Celibacy: or, Good Advice to Young Fellows to Keep Single* (London, 1739). For an earlier exchange, see *Joy and Happiness to Youth: or, The Young Men and Maidens Encouragement to Speedy Marriage* (London, 1700), which recycles A Country Gentleman, *Marriage Asserted: In*

punch from 1546: "Be it far or ny, weddyng is desteny, / And hangyng lykewise, sayth that prouerbe, sayd I."[92] Marriages seemed not always to work out as splendidly as the harmonious prospects of male dominance touted by the conduct manuals would suggest. Indeed, some marriages didn't work out well *because of* visions of male dominance, which filled men's heads with noxious nonsense and led them to abusive behavior.[93] We catch a chilling glimpse of this dynamic in Matthias Brinsden's gallows speech, not repentant in the usual way.[94] After beating her many times, Brinsden finally murdered his wife, Hannah.

> And I believe we lov'd each other dearly; but often quareled and fought. Pray good People mind, I had no Malice against her, nor thought to kill her 2 Minutes before the Deed; but I design'd only to make her obey me thoroughly, which the *Scripture* says, *all Wives should do:* This I thought I had done, when I cut her Skull on *Monday,* but she was the same again by *Tuesday.*[95]

Answer to a Book Entitled "Conjugium Conjurgium" (London, 1674), defending marriage against William Seymar, *Conjugium Conjurgium: or, Some Serious Considerations on Marriage* (London, 1673). For a dispute about whether marriage is financially prudent, see [Edward Ward], *The Batchelor's Estimate of the Expences of a Married Life,* 3rd ed. (London, 1729); *The Woman's Advocate: or, The Baudy Batchelor out in His Calculation* (London, 1729); [Edward Ward], *None but Fools Marry: or, A Vindication of the Batchelor's Estimate* (London, 1730); and see the later *Fore-warn'd, Fore-arm'd: or, The Batchelor's Monitor: Being a Modest Estimate of the Expences Attending the Married Life* (London, 1741). Wryly taking stock of the flurry of debate about the merits of marrying and claims of male superiority, see *Champion,* 1 January 1740, in Henry Fielding, *Contributions to the "Champion" and Related Writings,* ed. W. B. Coley (Oxford: Clarendon, 2003), 99–103; and compare for instance "To a Friend on the Choice of a Wife," in *Miscellanies by Henry Fielding, Esq.,* ed. Henry Knight Miller et al., 3 vols. (Middletown, CT and Oxford: Wesleyan University Press and Oxford University Press, 1972–97), 1:42–50. Warning of various hazards—"a scolding wife," "a drunken wife," and "he that with a Slut doth meet / hath the worst luck of all"—and urging the merits of "a Countrey lass," see *The Politick Countreyman* ([London, 1681–84]).

92. John Heywood, *A Dialogue Conteinyng the Nomber in Effect of All the Prouerbes in the English Tongue, Compacte in a Matter concernyng Two Maner of Mariages* (London, 1546), chap. 3.

93. For emphatic egalitarianism about marriage, see [Daniel Defoe], *A Treatise concerning the Use and Abuse of the Marriage Bed* (London, 1727), 26.

94. For a sample of the usual repentance, see *The Wicked Husband, and Unnatural Father: Being a Sad and Deplorable Relation of One William Gilbert, a Farmer of Toddington Near Lynn in Norfolk, Who Coming Home Drunk Late in the Evening, on Tuesday the 7th of August, Did in a Most Barbarous and Inhumane Manner, Cut His Own Wife's Throat from Ear to Ear (Being Big with Child) without Any Provocation, and Murthered His Young Daughter of 12 Years of Age, by Beating out Her Brains with a Hammer* (London, 1705), 7–8.

95. *The Ordinary of Newgate's, Account of the Behaviour, Confession, and Last Dying Speech of Matthias Brinsden, Who Was Executed at Tyburn, on Monday, the 24th of September, 1722* (London, 1722), 6, italics reversed.

So blather about harmonious submission produces repulsive violence. Let's dub this motif the Brinsden effect. Its charming mouthpiece aside, even less radical songs supply glances, okay, more than glances, searching views of married life that tweak and mock and subvert the claim that patriarchal authority is natural.

Again, my claim is not that men and women enjoyed equality. I don't think for a moment that husband beating was nearly as common or effective as wife beating. But it did happen. Margaret Cavendish reports one case—"she beat him in a Publick Assembly, nay, being a woman of none of the least Sizes, but one of the largest, and having Anger added to her Strength, she did beat him Soundly, and it is said, that he did not resist her, but endured Patiently"—and gravely condemns it as "unnatural." "For a VVife to strike her Husband, is as much, if not more, as for a Child to strike his Father; besides, it is a breach of Matrimonial Government, not to Obey all their Husbands Commands." Husband beaters, she urged, "ought to be banished from their Husbands Bed, House, Family" and adulteresses "ought to suffer Death"—at the hands of their husbands.[96]

My claim instead is that patriarchal authority was intensely controversial. Scholars looking for historical evidence of feminism sometimes squint to find nonfiction writers saying things we expect feminists to say. (Does Mary Astell qualify?) But when we find popular songs championing the natural equality of women, ridiculing men as tinpot dictators, admiring women who resist and rebel to improve their lots, is there any question about whether any feminism was on offer? And if there's no question about that, is there any case for the thesis that patriarchal authority was naturalized or essentialized? or that the early modern English slumbered, blissfully unaware that patriarchy might be thought controversial?

Jokes and Proverbs

Let's turn to anthologies of jokes and proverbs. That a joke or proverb is published is no guarantee that it's widely recited. Maybe these anthologists smuggle in their own coinages to pad their pages or try to get their own *bons mots* in circulation. So too, republication is no guarantee of ongoing popu-

96. [Margaret Cavendish], Lady Marchioness of Newcastle, *CCXI Sociable Letters* (London, 1664), 49.

larity. Maybe later anthologists are lazily scouring and plagiarizing out-of-print predecessor volumes. But with some of these jokes and proverbs, the sheer frequency of variants, coupled with how they hook up with other sources, is telling evidence of popular circulation. Some anthologists advertise the popularity of their jokes. Consider for instance *Polly Peachum's Jests: In Which Are Comprised Most of the Witty Apothegms, Diverting Tales, and Smart Repartees That Have Been Used for Many Years Last Past, Either at St. James's or St. Giles's: Suited Alike to the Capacities of the Peer, and the Porter.* (Here's one: "You are a Whore, said Captain *P——n* to his Wife; you are a Cuckold, answer'd Madam, and a Lyar; but if one of us must prove our Words, I could produce an Evidence, and that's more than you can.")[97] There are other evidentiary obstacles. When an old joke doesn't seem funny, is it because we don't know some fragment of historical context? or because people's senses of humor vary and anyway not all jokes are funny?[98] Then too, it's a further question in what moods or to what effects they circulated. But there's no call for extravagant skepticism here, just the usual judicious caution.

Many jokes poke fun at men naïve enough to believe in their wives' innocence.

> A young man in Antwerp married a pretty bucksome young Woman, and being in Bed, the first Night let a rousing Fart. His Bride very much displeased thereat, asked him why he would be so unmannerly? Alas, Sweet-heart, said he, don't you know, when a Fortress is besieged, in making a Breach the Canon will roar? In troth, Husband, said [s]he, you need not have put your self to that trouble, for the Breach was made long since, wide enough for a whole Army to enter, two in a Breast.[99]

The man in this next joke isn't married. But one offstage is about to be.

> A Gentleman Riding on the Road, overtook a young brisk Countrey Lass, who after some time Travelling together, consented to his Amours; the Man being conscious of what he had done, and how Prejudicial it might prove to the Maid; told her, if any thing came of their Endeavours, she

97. *Polly Peachum's Jests* (London, 1728), 18. The original title reads "Aliked" rather than "Alike."

98. But desperately unfunny jokes get published, too, maybe because they're so bad: see for instance Dr. S——t [Thomas Sheridan?], *The Wonderful Wonder of Wonders: or, The Hole-History of the Life and Actions of Mr. Breech, the Eighth Wonder of the World*, 6th ed. (London, 1722).

99. *The Universal Jester: or, A Compleat Book of Jests* (London, 1668 [1718?]), 6.

should hear of him at a certain place in *London:* '*Tis no matter Sir,* said she, *I am to be married on* Monday.[100]

This conscientious fellow may be relieved, but what about newlywed men hearing the joke? What about women smugly in on the joke? Yes, the women in both jokes count as sexually licentious, officially to be reviled. But the jokes are unruffled by their easygoing sexuality. The butt of each joke is the man vacant or daffy enough to mistake blather for life.

But here's a 1733 joke affirming male solidarity and dominance. The title of the volume it's in, *Coffee-House Jests,* surely claims that people lounging in coffeehouses told the joke.

> A young Man married a cross Piece of Flesh, who not contented, tho' her Husband was very kind, made continual Complaints to her Father, to the great Grief of both Families: The Husband being no longer able to endure this Scurvy Humour, banged her soundly. Hereupon she complained to her Father, who understanding well the Perverseness of her Humour, took her to Task, and laced her Sides soundly too: saying, Go, and commend me to your Husband, and tell him, I am now even with him, for I have cudgell'd his Wife, as well as he hath beaten my Daughter.[101]

The humor, such as it is, arises this way. The daughter appeals to her father as her ally against her husband, who's her rival. Her father beats her too, because he's on his son-in-law's side, but finds a verbal formula pretending that he too is his son-in-law's rival.

The same anthologist offers a scatological joke with a political point:

> One who loved himself better than his Wife, used to make her go to Bed first in the Winter-time, to warm the same until he came: Then he would make her remove, and lie in her Place: And for this cause, he used commonly to call her his *Warming-pan.* She vexed hereat, resolved to fit him; and accordingly one Night, when he was ready to come, she (Sir-reverence) shit in his Place. He going to Bed, and smelling what was done; Wife, said he, I think the Bed is beshit. *No Husband,* said she, *it is only a Coal dropt out of your Warming-pan.*[102]

The *OED* defines *fit:* "To visit (a person) with a fit penalty; to punish." Now the stricture from *The Character of a Good Woman*—"*This Vertuous Woman*

100. [Humphrey Crouch], *England's Jests Refin'd and Improv'd,* 3rd ed. with additions (London, 1693), 52.

101. [William Hicks], *Coffee-House Jests* (London, 1733), 109–10.

102. W[illiam] Hicks, *Oxford Jests, Refined and Enlarged,* 13th ed. corr. (London, [1720?]), 137–38.

shews her Goodness by her dutiful behaviour to her Husband" —looks risibly abstract, overdrawn, stupid. Like the father of the previous joke, this warming pan of a wife has wittily opened an ironic gap between her speech and her action. This joke is told at her husband's expense, with an implicit suggestion that he gets what's coming to him. Again we have a bracing challenge to wife as property, even as implement. If she can't properly be required to do this, what can she?

Some jokes are more explicitly political. "ONE ask'd why Ladies called their Husband, Master such a one, and Master such a one, and Master such a one, and not by their Titles of Knighthood, as, Sir *Thomas,* Sir *Richard,* Sir *William,* &c. It was answer'd, That tho' others call'd 'em, by their right Titles, as Sir *William,* Sir *Thomas,* &c. *yet it was fit their Wives should master 'em.*"[103] Or again: "At a Feast, where many Citizens and their Wives were met, the chief of their discourse asking about Cuckolds; one asked the reason why the men wore the horns, when the women only were in fault? *That is,* said another, *because the man is the head, and where would you have the horns grow else?*"[104] Like the other sources I'm quoting, this joke is not a "hidden transcript," not "the privileged site for nonhegemonic, contrapuntal, dissident, subversive discourse."[105] The joke's humor lies in redeploying the hoary image of the man as head of his family and exploiting the tie between head and horns. (Here's the kind of condensation Freud thought the essence of wit.) A head turns out not to be austerely dignified. It's a fitting receptacle for humiliation and disgrace.

I want to contrast two sets of jokes and proverbs, everyday commentary on the law and social practices of wife beating and coverture. A 1632 hornbook affirmed that "if a man beat . . . his wife it is dispunishable, because by the Law Common these persons can haue no action: God send Gentlewomen

103. *The Merry Medley: or, A Christmas-Box, for Gay Gallants, and Good Companions,* 2 vols. (London, 1745), 2:51.

104. A Lover of Ha, Ha, He, *Cambridge Jests: or, Witty Alarums for Melancholy Spirits* (London, 1721), 69. For a whimsical sketch of a cuckolded husband who literally has horns, see *The London Cuckold: or, An Antient Citizens Head Well Fitted with a Flourishing Pair of Fashionable Horns, by His Buxome Young Wife, Who Was Well Back'd by a Coltish Spark, in the Time of Her Husbands Absence at the Campaign on Hounslow-Heath* ([London, 1688]).

105. James C. Scott, *Domination and the Arts of Resistance* (New Haven, CT: Yale University Press, 1990), 25. In the background here is Gramsci's tendency to think that different groups of intellectuals speak for different social groupings: see Antonio Gramsci, *Prison Notebooks,* ed. Joseph A. Buttigieg, trans. Joseph A. Buttigieg and Antonio Callari, 3 vols. (New York: Columbia University Press, 1992– 2007), esp. 2:199–203. I'm skeptical of any linear mapping of this sort, though a Gramscian could have profitable fun thinking about the role of the church in my period.

better sport, or better companie." The husband was free to beat his wife only "for lawfull and reasonable correction." Should he exceed the rightful boundaries of such discipline, his wife could sue for "surety of honest behauiour toward her." Surety of the peace and recognizances were legal devices requiring that the man forfeit money if he continue to misbehave and that he show up at the court's next sessions with the threat of punishment for continued misbehavior hanging over him.[106] This book, sympathetic to the plight of women,[107] added a poignant observation: "the actionlesse woman beaten by her Husband," that is, the woman with no lawsuit available, "hath retaliation left to beat him againe, if she dare." The language of *if she dare* made clear that the author had no illusions about the plight of battered women.

Later I'll touch on the unabashed controversy about the legitimacy of wife beating. There's no legal controversy: that a husband enjoys a legal privilege to beat his wife for reasonable correction remained settled law through my period.[108] By the 1760s, William Blackstone was suggesting that while wife beating itself had become illegal, "the lower rank of people, who were always fond of the old common law, still claim and exert their antient privilege."[109] There's a pamphlet controversy, itself a sign of broader controversies. But I've found no controversy in the proverbs. "A spaniel, a woman and a walnut tree, / The more they're beaten the better still they be."[110] That 1670 version cheerfully dismisses women's welfare, not least in lumping the woman together with dog and tree. (Compare this one: "The Bitch that I mean, is not a Dog.")[111] Flip the placement of *woman* and *spaniel* and you find the same proverb recorded in 1732.[112] One joke, too, is serene about wife beating:

---

106. On recognizances, see Bernard Capp, *When Gossips Meet: Women, Family, and Neighborhood in Early Modern England* (Oxford: Oxford University Press, 2003), 110–14.

107. [Thomas Edgar], *The Lavves Resolutions of Womens Rights: or, The Lavves Provision for Woemen* (London, 1632), 128–29 on wife beating, and see 377 on rape.

108. Thomas Wood, *An Institute of the Laws of England*, 2 vols. ([London], 1720), 2:728, echoed almost verbatim in T. S., *A Dissertation concerning the Evil Nature and Fatal Consequence of Immoderate Anger and Revenge* (London, 1725), 76. See too *The Student's Law-Dictionary* (London, 1740), s.v. *battery*; Giles Jacob, *The New Law-Dictionary* (London, 1743), s.v. *battery*.

109. Blackstone, *Commentaries*, 1:432–33.

110. J[ohn] Ray, *A Collection of English Proverbs* (Cambridge, 1670), 50.

111. Thomas Fuller, *Gnomologia: Adagies and Proverbs; Wise Sentences and Witty Sayings, Ancient and Modern, Foreign and British* (London, 1732), 189, no. 4426. The volume's subtitle of course requires caution about whether any particular entry in it was in fact in current use in Britain.

112. Fuller, *Gnomologia*, 290, no. 6404. From the dramatic stage, compare [William Burnaby], *The Lady's Visiting-Day: A Comedy* (London, 1701), 18; E. Dower, *The Salopian Esquire: or, The Joyous Miller* (London, 1739), 38.

> A Country Fellow that had married an idle House wife, upon a time coming
> from his Labour, and finding her sit lazing by the Fire, as her Custom was,
> betook a Holly-wand, and began to cudgel her soundly: the Woman cry'd
> out aloud, and said, Alas, Husband, what do you mean? you see I do
> nothing, I do nothing. Ah marry Wife, saith he, I know it very well, and *for
> that reason I beat thee*.[113]

But I haven't found many jokes about wife beating. It can't be because that's
no laughing matter.[114] The jokes we do have are perfectly calm; plenty of
others are unruffled in plumbing difficult topics; and as we've seen, popular
songs delight in the topic. I'm unsure what to make of the paucity of jokes and
I'm inclined to make nothing of it: it might be no more than an accident of
what was recorded and what records have survived.

The law of coverture, by contrast, gets copious attention. Women's legal
personality disappeared into that of their husbands upon marriage.[115] That
had far-reaching ramifications, but I'll focus on this one: husbands would
own their wives' property. This facet of coverture was what modern lawyers
call a default rule. It was possible to contract around it, but people rarely
did.[116] An Irish writer summarized the implications:

> By the common Law, Women, with all their moveable goods, so soon as
> they are married, are wholly *sub potestate Viri*, at the will and disposition of
> the Husband: He being *caput Mulieris* [head of the woman]. If any goods or
> chattels are given to a married Woman, they all immediately become her
> Husband's. She can't let, set, sell, contract, give away or alienate any thing
> without her Husband's consent.
>
> All the chattels personal the Wife had at the marriage, are so much her
> Husband's, that, after his death, they shall not return to his Wife, but go to
> the Husband's Executors or Administrators, as his other goods and chat-
> tels, except only her *paraphernalia* or *prater dotalia*, which are her necessary
> apparel, which, with her Husband's consent, she may dispose by Will, not

---

113. *Ornatissimus Joculator: or, The Compleat Jester* (London, 1703), 24. The same joke with less
detail is in Hicks, *Oxford Jests*, 19, and with minor variants in *Merry Medley*, 2:36.

114. [Susanna Centlivre,] *A Wife Well Manag'd* (London, 1715), features wife beating and is still
subtitled *A Farce*.

115. Garthine Walker, *Crime, Gender and Social Order in Early Modern England* (Cambridge:
Cambridge University Press, 2003), 201–9, corrects some misconceptions about coverture and criminal
responsibility.

116. For a sample of such contracting, see Elizabeth Foyster, *Marital Violence: An English Family
History, 1660–1857* (Cambridge: Cambridge University Press, 2005), 52. See generally Amy Louise
Erickson, *Women and Property in Early Modern England* (London: Routledge, 1993), chap. 8.

otherwise by our Law, because the property and possession even of the *paraphernalia* are in him.[117]

This regime was a nightmare, especially for women separated from their husbands. Divorce was available only by private act of Parliament, so only to powerful or wealthy couples.[118] But some unhappy marriages led to formal deeds of separation.[119] Elizabeth Freke's father sent her a gift of £100 and warned her "that if Mr Frek medled with itt itt should be lost." He warned in vain: her husband took it.[120] The day after their wedding, Alice Cleter's husband regaled her with this revelation: "Thinkst thou that I can love such a mustie rustie widdow as thou art thou hast a face that loketh like the back of a tode I married the[e] but to be mayntayned like a man and so I will be."[121] Jane Jepson had kept her own estate on marrying. She improved its value to £500 and drafted a will leaving some to relatives, some to a charitable trust for schools, and just £5 to her husband. Her executor tried to buy him off with an extra £20, but he wrote a will disposing of her estate, igniting protracted litigation.[122] Separated, opening a shop, Charlotte Charke was "horribly puzzled for the Means of securing my Effects from the Power of my Husband," who might swoop down at any moment and grab everything she had. She conducted transactions in the name of a widow who boarded with her.[123] That left her at the mercy of the widow.

One 1617 traveler thought Englishmen far more forbearing with their wives than these laws might suggest.[124] Still, imagine needing your husband's

---

117. Matt[hew] Dutton, *The Law of Masters and Servants in Ireland* (Dublin, 1723), 152. See Christine Peters, *Women in Early Modern Britain, 1450–1640* (Houndmills, Basingstoke: Palgrave Macmillan, 2004), 42–44.

118. Lawrence Stone, *Road to Divorce: England, 1530–1987* (New York: Oxford University Press, 1990), is wonderfully rich. Tim Stretton, "Marriage, Separation and the Common Law in England, 1540–1660," in *The Family in Early Modern England*, ed. Helen Berry and Elizabeth Foyster (Cambridge: Cambridge University Press, 2007), argues that Stone overplays how difficult it was to break up a marriage.

119. For instance *A Full Account of the Case of John Sayer, Esq; from the Time of His Unhappy Marriage with His Wife, to His Death*, 2nd ed. with additions (London, 1713), 8.

120. *The Remembrances of Elizabeth Freke, 1671–1714*, ed. Raymond A. Anselment, Camden 5th ser. 18 (London: Cambridge University Press for the Royal Historical Society, 2001), 50 (1 January 1684).

121. Laura Gowing, *Domestic Dangers: Women, Words, and Sex in Early Modern London* (Oxford: Clarendon, 1996), 215.

122. *The Autobiography of William Stout of Lancaster, 1665–1752*, ed. J. D. Marshall (Manchester: Chetham Society, 1967), 214–15 [1731].

123. *Narrative of the Life of Mrs Charlotte Charke*, 2nd ed. (London, 1755), 75–76.

124. *An Itinerary Written by Fynes Moryson Gent.* (London, 1617), pt. 3, bk. 4, chap. 3, p. 221. I owe the reference to Anthony Fletcher, *Gender, Sex and Subordination in England, 1500–1800* (New Haven, CT: Yale University Press, 1995), 1.

permission to bequeath even your clothing. A common joke seized on an obvious pun. "Wives must have their Wills, while they live; because they make none, when they die."[125] Here's a more intricate version:

> One, who had been a very termagant Wife, lying on her Death-bed, desir'd her Husband, that, as she had brought him a Fortune, she might have Liberty to make her Will, for bestowing a few Legacies to her Relations. No, B——d, Madam, *say he,* You *had your* WILL *all your Life-time, and now I'll have mine.*[126]

That she's a termagant (the *OED* piles on: "A violent, overbearing, turbulent, brawling, quarrelsome woman; a virago, shrew, vixen") underlines that she gets what she deserves. Not just his firing the expletive *Blood* (for *His blood,* as in Jesus's) at her while she's dying, but also his resolutely asserting control over what the law says is his property. It took him too many years, but this long-suffering husband finally has gained the upper hand.

I've examined proverbs and jokes sanguine about wife beating and coverture. They supply no evidence of popular resistance or complaint. Then again, here's a joke that returns to our motif of popular culture marveling at what an ass a man must be to assert his patriarchal authority. "A Man chiding his Wife told her, *that she could call nothing hers but her Ring, Fillet and Hairlace, nay, her very Breech was none of hers.*" In contemporary English, *breeches* in the plural is the article of clothing, a man's pants.[127] (So the proverbial struggle for the breeches.) *Breech* in the singular is someone's rear end.[128] (Recall the careful husband, "Breeches bepist" and "scarce out of his Bed to ease his Breech.") So this man has asserted not just the law of coverture, with

---

125. Fuller, *Gnomologia*, 255, no. 5800. Contrast the devout language in T. W. T., *A Mery Balade, How a Wife Entreated Her Husband, to Haue Her Owne Wyll* (London, [1568]).

126. [William Pinkethman], *Pinkethman's Jests: or, Wit Refin'd*, 2nd ed. corr. (London, 1721), 38; with trifling variations in *Joe Miller's Jests: or, The Wits Vade-Mecum* (London, [1739?]), 46. See too W[illiam] W[instanley], *The New Help to Discourse: or, Wit and Mirth, Intermix'd with More Serious Matters*, 8th ed. (London, 1721), 124; Hicks, *Oxford Jests*, 130; *Merry Medley*, 2:305.

127. *The Agreeable Companion: or, An Universal Medley of Wit and Good Humour* (London, 1745), 381: "The Bishop of *D——m* had a slovenly Custom of keeping one Hand always in his Breeches, and being one Day to bring a Bill into the House of Peers, relating to a Provision for Officers Widows, he came with some Papers in one Hand, and had the other, as usual, in his Breeches; and beginning to speak, I have something in my Hand, my Lord, said he, for the Benefit of the Officers Widows — Upon which the Duke of *Wh——n* immediately interrupting him, ask'd, *In which Hand, my Lord?*" See too [Richard Flecknoe], *The Diarium, or Journall* (London, 1656), 60.

128. Samuel Butler, *Hudibras* [1663–78], ed. John Wilders (Oxford: Clarendon, 1967), 84: "I scorn (quoth she) thou Coxcomb silly, / (clapping her hand upon her breech, / To shew how much she priz'd his speech)." See too [Flecknoe], *Diarium*, 24.

painstaking regard for her rights in paraphernalia, but also property in his wife's body.

> Which the good and harmless Woman understanding one Night, let something drop into the Bed, which he having found out by the smell, ask'd her what was the Cause of her so doing: She told him, *that whilst she thought her Breech hers, she had command over it; but being his, she could not rule another Body's Ar——.*[129]

Shades of coal from the warming pan. Treat women like shit, even verbally, and shit is what you get.[130] And shit is what you should get: the joke's *good and harmless Woman* dictates that reading. How ludicrous to assert ownership of another's body! This joke too sends out ripples of criticism. When he instructs his wife that her breech is his, does this husband cross the line into illegitimacy? Or is that last blow exemplary of what's illegitimate about coverture across the board? What, finally, is appropriate for a husband to assert and for a good and harmless woman to endure?

I started by reviewing high-flown sources, what I dubbed conduct manuals dispensing blather, urging that patriarchal authority is natural. I argued that this language doesn't "naturalize" or "essentialize," but makes a move in a legitimation game. That forcibly suggests that others denied patriarchal authority, partially or sweepingly. I then turned to comedies, songs, jokes, and proverbs, hoping to catch glimpses of social life closer to the ground, not taking these fragments of text as faithful mirrors of reality, but reflecting instead on what was likely involved in performing or reciting or reading or listening to them. One motif surfaced repeatedly: that of the overweening husband who's a buffoon in sedulously quoting or simply acting on the puta-

---

129. *Ornatissimus Joculator*, 45; the same joke with minor variants is in [Hicks], *Coffee-House Jests*, 41.

130. Then again, see *Youth's Treasury: or, A Store-Huse of Wit and Mirth* ([London], 1688), 11–12: "An Old Man and his Wife sitting one Winters Night by the Fire without Company, the time seemed tedious unto them; Come, quoth the Old Woman, let's go to Bed Husband, what should we sit up to burn Fire and Candle for? Content, quoth the Old Man; but I fear I shall not sleep if we go to Bed so soon: 'Tis no matter for that, says the Old Woman, we'l play at *One-and-Thirty* with Farts: Alas! says the Old Man, I can't play: Well, I'le learn you. Being both agreed, to Bed they went. Now says the Old Woman, you must lay your Breech in my Lap, and the first must stand for Twenty, and so on. The Game being began, the Old Man Farts, that is Twenty, quoth she, so the Old Man proceeded to Twenty-eight, and being the first hand, resolved to stand it: Well now, quoth the Old Woman, I must lay my Breech in your Lap, to which he yielded: There's Twenty: that's right, says he; there's another, that's Twenty-one; upon the third Card, the Old man cryed out, Uds-nigs, what dost do, I think thou hast Beshit me. No, Husband, quoth she, it is a Court-Card, I am One-and-Thirty, the Game is mine. The Old man being thus baffled at One-and-Thirty, never loved Card-play afterwards."

tive wisdom of the conduct manuals. As a buffoon he can be mocked or even punished. The prevalence of that motif refutes the claim that patriarchal authority was taken to be a natural or necessary bit of woodwork of the world.

That's not the only motif. So I deliberately produced texts that resound sympathetically to the conduct manuals. But it's not my position that patriarchal authority was universally condemned, that people might have had to endure flatulent tributes to it in church or read about it if they had an eccentric taste for political theory, but that otherwise it played no role in the world. On the contrary. The law of coverture was real. Wife beating was real. Defenses of both, from the conduct manuals on down to everyday life, were real. I'll say it again: women did not enjoy equality.

But neither did they suffer in a society weirdly oblivious to what was going on or uniformly impassive about it. Early modern England produced plenty of fulsome tributes to patriarchy—and plenty of acidulous critiques of it. I'll quote a bit of canonical poetry lest you think that somehow "high culture" never voiced any criticisms of patriarchal authority. This defiant missive, "The Lady's Answer to the Knight," is from Samuel Butler's biting *Hudibras*. Hudibras, that amiably blundering knight, has written again to the lady he longs for. He's convinced that he's been persuasive, but still she scorns him:

> And if we had not weighty Cause
> To not Appear, in making Laws,
> We could, in spight of all your *Tricks*,
> And *shallow, Formal Politicks;*
> Force you our *Managements* t'obey,
> As we to yours (in shew) give way.
> Hence 'tis, that while you vainly strive,
> T'advance your *high Prerogative,*
> You basely, after all your Braves,
> Submit, and own your selves, our Slaves.
> And cause we do not make it known
> Nor Publickly our Intrests own
> Like Sots, suppose we have no shares
> In *Ordring you,* and *your Affairs:*
> When all your Empire, and Command
> You have from us, at *Second Hand.*[131]

131. Butler, *Hudibras*, 317–18. I've deleted a stray comma to follow *Hudibras* (London, 1684), p. 248. Compare *Sir Patient Fancy* [1678], in *The Works of Aphra Behn*, ed. Janet Todd, 7 vols. (Columbus: Ohio State University Press, 1992–96), 6:79–80.

She goes on to proclaim that women rule the world.[132] That suggestion too raises notorious difficulties. But notice that she credits the knight with a politics—a "shallow, Formal Politicks" at that. His beatific vision of male authority is not, she sneers, the natural order of things. It's a bad joke.

"An Old Batchelor" of seventy-two ventriloquized the same sort of response in recycling the joke about wills, which he put into the mouth of "A Lady fair of nineteen":

> We claim our *Wills* while we live, because we make none when we die—Husbands, 'tis true, won't allow this to be any Argument; they are for ever informing us what we should, and should not do, and reading Lectures on the Duty of a Wife; but they are quite out in their Politicks, if they believe we are such poor, half-sighted Ninny-hammers, to stand staring with a blushing Ignorance, amaz'd, and quite confounded with their monitory Lessons. They'll generally find a Orange, thus hard squeez'd, yields bitter Juice.[133]

English husbands, she warned, shouldn't be so "out in their Politicks" to imagine that women were stunned into submission by recitations of blather. Neither should we.

Sex and Gender

I want to map one last route to naturalizing male authority. Consider a plain-vanilla distinction between sex and gender. (I think this plain-vanilla version is the best one on offer, but that's an argument for another occasion.) Sex is a category of biology. It distinguishes male and female members of the species. Reproductive organs and secondary sexual characteristics are ob-

---

132. Compare Susanna Jesserson, *A Bargain for Bachelors: or, The Best Wife in the World for a Penny* ([London?], 1675), 5, on the virtuous wife who "commands by obeying"; the same in *The Ladies Dictionary; Being a General Entertainment for the Fair-Sex: A Work Never Attempted before in English* (London, 1694), 472–73; and the more jaundiced sentiment in [Francis Osborne], *Advice to a Son: or, Directions for Your Better Conduct* (Oxford, 1655), 57–58: "The best of Husbands are but Servants, but he that takes a Wife wanting Money, is a Slave to his affection, doing the basest of Drudgeries without wages."

133. An Old Batchelor [Ralph Nab], *An Address to the Right Worshipful the Batchelors of Great-Britain* (London, [1735?]), 20, 24–25. Compare *Merry Medley*, 2:303, from the creed of a "pretty miss": "And lastly, as for my Husband, that I shall hereafter condescend to bubble, I do verily believe he ought not to have the least Superiority over me; therefore am determined, that tho' Quadrille be my Religion, and Cuckoldom ev'ry Sabbath's Meditation; tho' I ruin him in Plays, Masquerades, Fashions, House-keeping, &c. tho' I should even accept of my very Butler as a Coadjutor to him,—he shall be—mum."

vious sex distinctions. There might be others: apparently hormones affect brain development. Then too, sex might be a continuum with a bimodal distribution, not a binary distinction. Gender is a category of culture and politics. It distinguishes what's masculine and feminine, how men and women should act so far as they are men and women. So for instance if or insofar as morality binds human beings as such, it's not gendered. The two categories are then linked in one important way. The usual grammar assumes men should be masculine, women feminine. Any girl mocked as a tomboy, any boy jeered at as a wimp, knows what it's like to be on the wrong side of the mapping.

The distinction invites two questions. The first is explanatory: do the biological facts of sex offer a satisfactory causal account of the norms of gender? If men on average have larger bodies or more muscle mass, does that explain the emergence of the view that it's manly to be powerful, strong, in control? The second is justificatory: do the biological facts of sex give us good reason to embrace the norms of gender? Suppose the muscle-mass hypothesis turns out to be true. It wouldn't yet follow that there's good reason to embrace its causal outcome; we might instead work against it. That something is the consequence of biology is normatively mute. Suppose women were mostly more nearsighted than men. Imagine inferring that they shouldn't wear glasses.

A "left" critique of this distinction between sex and gender is that our grasp of sex is always going to be saturated with our gender commitments.[134] So we're never going to be in an epistemic position where we can have any confidence in our grasp of the explanatory or the justificatory questions. Here, though, I'm interested in the "right" critique of the distinction. Some will be tempted—some have been tempted—to flatten gender back into sex, to try to make it impossible even to ask the explanatory and justificatory questions. Here again the concept of nature has done political work, because that's what happens if you think it's natural for men to be masculine, women

---

134. Donna Haraway, *Primate Visions: Gender, Race, and Nature in the World of Modern Science* (New York: Routledge, 1989), and Londa Schiebinger, "Why Mammals Are Called Mammals: Gender Politics in Eighteenth-Century Natural History," *American Historical Review* 98, no. 2 (1993): 382–411, remain indispensable. Thomas Laqueur, *Making Sex: Body and Gender from the Greeks to Freud* (Cambridge, MA: Harvard University Press, 1990), mounts a remarkable and (over)ambitious argument that for centuries people thought there was only one sex and gender was the primary notion. For apt cautions on the uptake of Laqueur's view, see Valerie Traub, *The Renaissance of Lesbianism in Early Modern England* (Cambridge: Cambridge University Press, 2002), 192–93.

to be feminine, and nothing more needs to be said. But there are many possibilities for criticism. People can dispute the content of masculinity and femininity. They can dispute the desirability of their very existence as categories. They can dispute the tight link between sex and gender. And so on. For all such criticisms, it will help if they first notice the distinction. Did contemporaries notice it?

Famously, the *Tatler* gingerly warned women that he meant no offense, but insisted "there is a Sort of Sex in Souls. . . . I must go on to say, That the Soul of a Man and that of a Woman are made very unlike, according to the Employments for which they are designed. . . . The Virtues have respectively a Masculine and a Feminine Cast."[135] The language is elusive, but it certainly looks as if it collapses gender into sex. The *Tatler* was hugely popular. But this claim too was controverted. Indeed, it came decades after a woman in one of Dryden's plays briskly rebuffed the suggestion that she was "of a softer Sex" and declared, "there is no Sex in Souls."[136] That same year, a religious writer cited Galatians 3:28 ("There is neither Jew nor Greek, there is neither bond nor free, there is neither male nor female: for ye are all one in Christ Jesus") in arguing that there was "one transcendent Excellency of Human Nature," "no distinction of Sexes" in souls. In a routine move,[137] he urged further that "what ever vicious impotence Women are under, it is acquired, not natural; nor derived from any illiberality of Gods, but from the ill managery of his bounty."[138] Our affection for the *Tatler*'s urbanity shouldn't conceal the blasphemy he was flirting with. And the *Tatler*'s famous claim came years after John Dunton declared that "*There is no difference of Sex among Souls; and a Masculine Spirit may inhabit a Woman's Body.*"[139] That claim not only affirms a distinction between sex and gender. It also relaxes the usual tight link

---

135. *Tatler*, no. 172 (16 May 1710), in *The Tatler*, ed. Donald F. Bond, 3 vols. (Oxford: Clarendon, 1987), 2:444.

136. *Amboyna: A Tragedy* [1673], in *The Works of John Dryden*, ed. Edward Niles Hooker et al., 20 vols. (Berkeley: University of California Press, 1956–94), 12:68.

137. See for instance Daniel Defoe, *An Essay upon Projects* (London, 1697), 302–3; [Mary Astell], *The Christian Religion, as Profess'd by a Daughter of the Church of England* (London, 1705), 103–4; Wetenhall Wilkes, *An Essay on the Pleasure and Advantages of Female Literature* (London, 1741), 19–20.

138. [Richard Allestree], *The Ladies Calling in Two Parts* (Oxford, 1673), preface, n.p., italics reversed. See too A Lady, Who Onely Desires to Advance the Glory of God, and Not Her Own, *Eliza's Babes: or, The Virgins-Offering* (London, 1652), 100; I owe this reference to Erica Longfellow, *Women and Religious Writing in Early Modern England* (Cambridge: Cambridge University Press, 2004), 140. And see *The Female Spectator*, 3rd ed., 4 vols. (Dublin, 1747), 3:117.

139. [John Dunton], *Petticoat-Government: in A Letter to the Court Ladies* (London, 1702), 13.

between sex and gender: or, if you like, it's blasé about psychological cross-dressing. In *The Roaring Girl*, Moll challenges Trapdoor: "What should move you to offer your service to me, sir?" "The love I bear to your heroic spirit and masculine womanhood," he says readily.[140] "Thou more then woman," gushes Maximinian to Aurelia in *The Prophetess*, "Thou masculine Greatnesse, to whose soaring spirit / To touch the stars seems but an easie flight; / O how I glory in thee!"[141] If the *Tatler* was naturalizing gender, plenty of other contemporaries weren't.

A thunderous chorus fretted about effeminacy. Sometimes they meant weakness, whether male or female.[142] Locke devoted his *Thoughts concerning Education* to helping a friend raise his son. But he wrote, "The Accusations of Children one against another, which usually are but the Clamors of Anger and Revenge desiring Aid, should not be favourably received, nor hearken'd to. It weakens and effeminates their Minds to suffer them to *Complain*."[143] I don't think *Children* here means only *sons*. Sometimes they addressed women. Abuses of apparel would lead to "*delicacy*, which weakens and effeminates the *spirit*," Richard Brathwait warned English gentlewomen.[144] Here we have the instructive possibility that women, or at least gentlewomen, shouldn't be effeminate either. But some clearly worried about effeminate men and definitely had gender, not just weakness, in mind. That worry tightens the link between sex and gender by insisting that men should be masculine. But it also depends on noticing the distinction itself. William Prynne's tantrum against the dramatic stage included this gem: "That which effeminates mens mindes, mens manners, and makes them womannish both in their mindes, their bodies, speeches, habites, and their whole deportement: must needs bee abominable unto Christians, intolerable in a Common-weale. . . . But this doe Stage-

140. Thomas Middleton and Thomas Dekker, *The Roaring Girl* [1611], in Thomas Middleton, *The Collected Works*, ed. Gary Taylor and John Lavagnino (Oxford: Clarendon, 2007), 740.

141. *The Prophetess* [1652], in *The Dramatic Works in the Beaumont and Fletcher Canon*, ed. Fredson Bowers et al., 10 vols. (Cambridge: Cambridge University Press, 1966–96), 9:295. See too *The Feign'd Curtizans: or, A Nights Intrigue* [1679], in *Works of Behn*, 6:93.

142. For Machiavellian worries, see Fra[ncis] Quarles, *Enchiridion* (London, 1644), chap. XXII; [Francis Osborne], *Politicall Reflections upon the Government of the Tvrks* (London, 1656), 25; Leonard Willan, *The Exact Politician: or, Compleat Statesman* (London, 1670), 100. Compare William Warner, *Pan His Syrinx, or Pipe, Compact of Seuen Reedes* (London, [1584]), cap. 10, on lust, with "Adulteries of Men," in [Cavendish], *The Worlds Olio*, 77, on how adultery is bad for men.

143. John Locke, *Some Thoughts concerning Education* [1693], ed. John W. and Jean S. Yolton (Oxford: Clarendon, 1989), 169.

144. Richard Brathwait, *The English Gentlewoman, Drawne out to the Full Body* (London, 1631), 13.

playes."[145] Over a century later, we find this warning: "For if in Valour real Manhood lies, / All Cowards are but—Women in Disguise."[146]

Defoe's Roxana rebuffs a proposal of marriage. The marriage contract, she charges, is "nothing but giving up Liberty, Estate, Authority, and every-thing, to the Man, and the Woman was indeed, a meer Woman ever after, that is to say, a Slave." Her suitor persists, insisting on how much responsibility the husband has, while "the Woman's Life was all Ease and Tranquility." Roxana doesn't budge.

> I return'd, that while a Woman was single, she was a Masculine in her politick Capacity; that she had then the full Command of what she had, and the full Direction of what she did; that she was a Man in her separated Capacity, to all Intents and Purposes that a Man cou'd be so to himself; that she was controul'd by none, because accountable to none, and was in Subjection to none. . . .
>
> I added, that whoever the Woman was, that had an Estate, and would give it up to be the Slave of *a Great Man,* that Woman was a Fool, and must be fit for nothing but a Beggar; that it was my Opinion, a Woman was as fit to govern and enjoy her own Estate, without a Man, as a Man was, without a Woman; and that, if she had a-mind to gratifie herself as to Sexes, she might entertain a Man, as a Man does a Mistress; that while she was thus single, she was her own; and if she gave away that Power, she merited to be as miserable as it was possible that any Creature cou'd be.[147]

Roxana once uses *Masculine* and *Man* interchangeably. But she seizes on the distinction between sex and gender. Though a woman, she would enjoy the freedom supposed to belong to men, to be masculine. She would be "her own," not subjected to another. She's not even tempted to think that she should be dutifully feminine, that gender is destiny. A woman, she scoffs, would have to be a fool to fall for that gambit. Recall Mrs. Brittle's defiant riposte to her husband: "were I fool enough," he'd use her as a slave.

"By God come out and see which is the best man." So John Head testified

145. William Prynne, *Histrio-mastix: The Players Scovrge, or, Actors Tragaedie, Divided into Two Parts* (London, 1633), pt. 1, pp. 546–47. On effeminate fops, see Philip Carter, *Men and the Emergence of Polite Society: Britain, 1660–1800* (Harlow: Longman, 2001).

146. "An Epilogue" [1746], in Henry Fielding, *"The True Patriot" and Other Writings,* ed. W. B. Coley (Middletown, CT: Wesleyan University Press, 1987), 426.

147. [Daniel Defoe], *The Fortunate Mistress* (London, 1724), 180–81. On these matters, Amy M. Froide, *Never Married: Singlewomen in Early Modern England* (Oxford: Oxford University Press, 2005), is first-rate.

that his wife called out before almost strangling him.[148] To be a man socially, not biologically—that is, to be masculine—was to be ready to fight and eager to prevail. Or prone to violence: consider the newspaper report that "a noted masculine Woman" had been committed for "violently assaulting" and robbing a man.[149] These women may have raised shudders with their manly ways—even valiant Long Meg prostrates herself to her husband[150]—just as some men raised snickers by being effeminate. (Or both at once: when a woman leapt to her husband's defense in a 1594 fight, his opponent taunted him: "lett thy wife weare thye breeches, for she is worthie of them, she is the better man.")[151] The *Spectator*, successor to the *Tatler*, offers a memorable "Cott-Quean" sketched by his unhappy wife:

> I have the Misfortune to be joined for Life with one of this Character, who in reality is more a Woman than I am. He was bred up under the Tuition of a Tender Mother, till she had made him as good an Housewife as her self. He could preserve Apricots, and make Gellies, before he had been two Years out of the Nursery. He was never suffered to go abroad, for fear of catching Cold; when he should have been hunting down a Buck, he was by his Mother's Side learning how to Season it, or put it in Crust; and was making Paper Boats with his Sisters, at an Age when other young Gentlemen are crossing the Seas, or travelling into Foreign Countries. He has the whitest Hand that you ever saw in your Life; and raises Paste better than any Woman in *England*. These Qualifications make him a sad Husband. He is perpetually in the Kitchin, and has a thousand Squabbles with the Cookmaid. He is better acquainted with the Milk Score, than his Steward's Accounts. I fret to Death when I hear him find fault with a Dish that is not dressed to his liking, and instructing his Friends that dine with him in the best Pickle for a Wallnut, or Sawce for an Haunch of Venison. With all this, he is a very good-natured Husband, and never fell out with me in his Life but once, upon the over-roasting of a Dish of Wild Fowl. At the same time I must own I would rather he was a Man of a rough Temper, that would treat me harshly sometimes, than of such an effeminate busie Nature in a Province that does not belong to him. Since you have given us the Character of a

---

148. Foyster, *Marital Violence*, 104.

149. *General Evening Post*, 29 March 1735. I owe the reference to Robert Shoemaker, "Male Honour and the Decline of Public Violence in Eighteenth-Century London," *Social History* 26, no. 2 (2001): 202.

150. *The Life of Long Meg of VVestminster* (London, 1635), 23.

151. Alexandra Shepard, *Meanings of Manhood in Early Modern England* (Oxford: Oxford University Press, 2003), 127.

Wife who wears the Breeches, pray say something of a Husband that wears the Petticoat. Why should not a Female Character be as ridiculous in a Man, as a Male Character in one of our Sex?[152]

Better to be beaten, if that's what harsh treatment refers to, than have a husband who preserves apricots? Such sanctimonious horror might tempt you to summon up the specter of monolithic gender norms. Resist the temptation. A society that turns *Roxana* into a best-seller, that makes a broadly winking joke out of "A Song Call'd My Mistress Is All the Genders"[153] (masculine, feminine, "Neuter," and "doubtful"), can't be pigeonholed so readily. Here too controversy and ironic play were the order of the day.

Consider three last bits of evidence to bring to bear on my thesis that people did not passively slurp up the blather of the conduct manuals: two from Henry Fielding, one from a disgruntled preacher. Puzzletext delivers the opening song of Fielding's *Grub-Street Opera:*

> What a wretched life
> Leads a man a tyrant wife,
> While for each small fault he's corrected:
> One bottle makes a sot,
> One girl is ne'er forgot,
> And duty is always neglected.

So far, so patriarchal: but Puzzletext next reports that men don't seem to be in charge of their households—and that they are willing publicly to acknowledge it.

> But tho' nothing can be worse
> Than this fell domestic curse,
> Some comfort this may do you,
> So vast are the hen-peck'd bands,
> That each neighbor may shake hands,
> With my humble service to you.[154]

152. *Spectator*, no. 482 (12 September 1712), in *The Spectator*, ed. Donald F. Bond, 5 vols. (Oxford: Clarendon, 1965), 4:210. Compare D[aniel] R[ogers], *Matrimoniall Honovr: or, The Mutuall Crowne and Comfort of Godly, Loyall, and Chaste Marriage* (London, 1642), 215.

153. W[illiam] H[icks], *Oxford Drollery; Being New Poems and Songs* (Oxford, 1671), pt. 1, pp. 26–28.

154. *The Grub-Street Opera* [1731], in Henry Fielding, *Plays*, ed. Thomas Lockwood, 2 vols. to date (Oxford: Clarendon, 2004–), 2:73, italics removed; with variants in *The Welsh Opera* [1731], in Fielding, *Plays*, 2:37–38, and *The Genuine Grub-Street Opera* [1731], in Fielding, *Plays*, 2:627.

They must be acknowledging each other as henpecked.[155] Here's more evidence of the gap between blather and daily life. Still, the audience's laughter might well be tinged with the sense that everything would be better if the men weren't henpecked, let alone so meek about it. Put differently, this passage suggests some slippage between patriarchal sentiments and behavior on the ground. But it needn't suggest any lack of allegiance to those sentiments. For that matter, both patriarchal script and Puzzletext's song could readily be described as misogynist.

The next bit is harder to reconcile with the view that patriarchal authority was naturalized. In Fielding's *Joseph Andrews*, a careening farce smashing one pious fantasy after another, Parson Adams "bid his Wife prepare some Food for their Dinner; she said, 'truly she could not, she had something else to do.'" He knows how to deal with her insubordination: "*Adams rebuked her for disputing his Commands, and quoted many Texts of Scripture to prove, that the Husband is the Head of the Wife, and she is to submit and obey.*" But she's unmoved. "The Wife answered, 'it was Blasphemy to talk Scripture out of Church; that such things were very proper to be said in the Pulpit: but that it was prophane to talk them in common Discourse.'" Hoping to smooth troubled waters, Joseph suggests they go to an alehouse to eat. Tellingly, Mrs. Adams accepts first and her husband dutifully follows.[156] We've seen this motif before: such recitations of scriptural wisdom may be fine in church, but they're ridiculous in daily life. Maybe people thought they shouldn't talk this way, but they still unthinkingly assented to the wisdom on offer. But that won't begin to make sense of her promptly undoing his command and his acquiescing. Nor does the novel invite the reader to reject her assertiveness.

No more here than Fielding's literary romps? My last bit of evidence suggests that Fielding understated people's impatience with blather. One preacher took as his copy text the proverb "Whoso findeth a Wife, findeth a good Thing, and obtaineth Favour of the Lord." He would denounce an "*evil Woman*" as a "*Monster*" and salute man's "*Help-meet,*" who would be "a

---

155. For cuckolds cheerfully recognizing each other as cuckolds, see *The Catalogue of Contented Cuckolds* (London, n.d.), in Chappell et al., *Roxburghe Ballads*, 3:481–83.

156. Henry Fielding, *Joseph Andrews* [1742], ed. Martin C. Battestin (Oxford: Clarendon, 1967), 323. Compare the facetious account of the submissive wife at 164–65. For an equally facetious "Description of a domestic Government founded upon Rules directly contrary to those of Aristotle," with Mrs. Partridge ruling the roost, see Henry Fielding, *The History of Tom Jones: A Foundling* [1749], ed. Fredson Bowers, 2 vols. (Middletown, CT: Wesleyan University Press, 1975), 1:81.

constant Comfort and Support to her Husband." Husbands ought to love their wives, he repeated, and then he declared, "tho' there is an Equality between Man and Wife, there are, however a great many Things in which the Husband ought to have the Preheminence." But he balked at the likely reaction of the faithful.

> The Subject my Text naturally leads me to discourse of, I know not why it should so seldom be inquir'd into from the Pulpit, unless that we are generally discourag'd and driven from it by the ludicrous Temper of the Age. But is it therefore the less necessary, because People make it a Matter of Merriment and Ridicule, and will hardly attend to it with a Spirit of Seriousness and Concern?[157]

People in the pews chafed at staunch tributes to docile wives, tributes apparently profane even from the pulpit. So too Jenny Distaff, appearing in the *Tatler*, denigrated *The Batchelor's Scheme for Governing His Wife:* "I have not Patience with these unreasonable Expectations."[158]

"I say, No." So Barnaby Brittle barked at his wife when she said she wanted to go to the theater. Mrs. Brittle was defiant: "But, I say, Yes." The Brittles were the creation of a male playwright and I'll bet long odds Jenny Distaff, with her eponymous name, was the mouthpiece of Joseph Addison or Richard Steele. But we're not searching for authentic female voices raised against patriarchy, though we've heard some of those, too. We're thinking about audience responses. You can doubt my reading of any comedy, song, joke, proverb. But consider living amid the texts I've quoted and many more like them circulating freely. It's not plausible that more or less everyone unthinkingly took the likes of Mrs. Brittle and the women fouling their beds as unnatural miscreants needing another dollop or wallop of male authority. Too many of these texts explicitly sympathize with the women. Too many question how particular husbands exercise their authority. Too many question patriarchal authority itself. Men and women alike heard these challenges. They watched them onstage, laughed at the jokes, sang the songs, and recited the proverbs. That "discourse" ran one way, "material life" another is a confused and bizarre fantasy. Surely many married couples grappled with the same

---

157. [Edward Creffield], *A Good Wife a Great Blessing: or, The Honour and Happiness of the Marriage State, in Two Sermons* (London, [1717?]), 21, 22, 25, 45, 3–4; see Proverbs 18:22.

158. *Tatler*, no. 10 (3 May 1709), in Bond, *Tatler*, 1:87.

challenges. Surely it beggars belief to suggest that parties to the fray were unconscious that they were having a political struggle about male authority. Neither men nor women were such poor, half-sighted ninny-hammers as that. Patriarchal authority in early modern England was not "naturalized" or "essentialized."

CHAPTER 3

Public Man, Private Woman?

Nor did a disreputable public/private distinction simultaneously doom women to subordination and drape that subordination in a cloak of invisibility. This view, too, deeply misunderstands the terms of sexual inequality. And inequality is indeed what we're up against.

The point is familiar enough, for some tired or tiresome enough, that it's hard to remember how startling—and how hard to explain—it is: "Women never have had equal rights with men."[1] That's Harriet Taylor Mill's way of putting it in urging that women get the vote. After all, the legal exclusion of women from voting and serving in office is dramatic. Its relentless recurrence across centuries, continents, and cultures remains baffling. True, there are occasional exceptions: Lady Anne Clifford recorded the "very remarkable" case of Isabella de Veteripont, sitting as sheriff of Westmoreland and hearing capital cases in her own name—in the thirteenth century.[2] There's the glacial

---

1. Harriet Taylor Mill, "Enfranchisement of Women," *Westminster and Foreign Quarterly Review,* July 1851, in John Stuart Mill, *Essays on Equality, Law, and Education* (Toronto: University of Toronto Press, 1984), 398.

2. Anne Clifford, "The Great Book," in *Women's Political Writings, 1610–1725,* ed. Hilda L. Smith, Mihoko Suzuki, and Susan Wiseman, 4 vols. (London: Pickering & Chatto, 2007), 1:14. On *Olive v. Ingram,* 7 Mod. 263, the 1739 King's Bench opinion that came to stand for more than one might have thought, see Hilda L. Smith, "Women as Sextons and Electors: King's Bench and Precedents for Women's Citizenship," in *Women Writers and the Early Modern British Political Tradition,* ed. Hilda L. Smith (Cambridge: Cambridge University Press, 1998). For the opinion itself, see Thomas Leach, *Modern Reports: or, Select Cases Adjudged in the Courts of King's Bench, Chancery, Common Pleas, and Exchequer,* 5th ed. corr., 12 vols. (London and Dublin, 1793–96), 7:263–74. See too Amy M. Froide, *Never Married: Singlewomen in Early Modern England* (Oxford: Oxford University Press, 2005), 145–47.

breakdown of this regime, such as the halting steps from 1869 to 1894 that enfranchised some women to serve in local governments in the United Kingdom.[3] However humdrum rote familiarity has made it, the huge stretch of time and space featuring the categorical exclusion of women is remarkable.

No surprise that John Stuart Mill's quixotic attempt to amend the second Reform Bill to extend the vote to women was met with laughter, ironic applause, and a caricature in *Vanity Fair* captioned, "A Feminine Philosopher."[4] Watch Mill deliberately equivocate between normative and descriptive:

> Politics, it is said, are not a woman's business. Well, Sir, I rather think that politics are not a man's business either; unless he is one of the few who are selected and paid to devote their time to the public service, or is a member of this or of the other House. The vast majority of male electors have each his own business, which absorbs nearly the whole of his time; but I have not heard that the few hours occupied, once in a few years, in attending at a polling booth, even if we throw in the time spent in reading newspapers and political treatises, ever causes them to neglect their shops or their counting-houses. I have never understood that those who have votes are worse merchants, or worse lawyers, or worse physicians, or even worse clergymen than other people.[5]

Admire this jewel, too: "Then it is said, that women do not need direct power, having so much indirect, through their influence over their male relatives and connections. . . . Rich people have a great deal of indirect influence. Is this a reason for refusing them votes?"[6]

Why the common exclusion of women from the franchise and office? Is this exclusion relatively superficial and cultural or is it deep and social-structural? Should we accept the mappings in that query? Why the sense that there is something laughable about changing that? Why our own sense—I mean "our" to include even today's conservatives, who are not, at least publicly, or at least not that I've noticed, or anyway not more than a handful of them, demanding that we strip women of the franchise, nor even, I conjecture, plaintively sighing behind closed doors for the good old days of a male

---

3. 32 & 33 Vict. c. 55 (1869); *R. v. Harrald*, 7 L.R.Q.B. 361–64 (22 January 1872); 56 & 57 Vict. c. 73 (1894).

4. *Vanity Fair*, 29 March 1873, available at http://www.antiquemapsandprints.com/p-10990.jpg and on my office wall.

5. "Speech of John Stuart Mill, M.P. on the Admission of Women to the Electoral Franchise: Spoken in the House of Commons, May 20th, 1867," in John Stuart Mill, *Public and Parliamentary Speeches*, ed. John M. Robson and Bruce L. Kinzer, 2 vols. (Toronto: University of Toronto Press, 1988), 1:153–54.

6. Mill, *Speeches*, 1:157.

monopoly on voting and government—that the old practices are irreversibly behind us, faintly or vividly embarrassing, but part of a vanished social world? Why the accompanying alacrity in casting some of today's Arab regimes as in this way "backward," with a burst of retro-Whiggish teleology we abjure in other settings? What about the sense some of us have that the formal exclusions might have melted away, but they were just the tip of an iceberg that we still crash into regularly?

I won't attempt to answer those questions. I'm going to restrict my attention to early modern England—and alas, I'm not going to furnish an explanation even for that case. Instead I'm going to dismantle one. My account might turn out to be, in the category so adored by a certain kind of social scientist, generalizable. But it might not. I'd have thought we want to explore historical and comparative materials to surface stuff that's genuinely different and think about how and why it's different, not to assure ourselves that everything everywhere is somehow the same. The world is boring enough without academics trying to show it's even more boring. More polemically yet, there's something infantile, something redolent of thumb sucking and treasured ragged blankies, in the insistence that worthwhile insights must be transportable.

But back to sobriety or anyway closer to it. The first step in describing the exclusion of women is straightforward: we have a social division of labor on sex (not gender) lines, so that the state / society line has only males on the state side. (But not only females on the society side, so it would be a mistake to map the state / society distinction onto the male / female distinction.) That could in turn both give rise to and be underwritten by a highly stylized gender norm, so that state affairs are masculine and other social activities feminine. Ordinarily, though, the gender norms are far more complicated and conflictual than that.

So what's the next step? Some have been tempted by the doctrine of separate spheres. The doctrine is open to competing interpretations. Generally, though, the thought that women's special preserve is (supposed to be) the family or domestic life and the further thought that that claim becomes central to modern society have been assaulted and undercut.[7] We are hazy

---

7. See Robert B. Shoemaker, *Gender in English Society, 1650–1850: The Emergence of Separate Spheres?* (Harlow: Longman, 1998), for a measured review of the literature to date, and especially Amanda Vickery, "Golden Age to Separate Spheres? A Review of the Categories and Chronology of English Women's History," *Historical Journal* 36, no. 2 (1993): 383–414. For what may prove the highwater mark of separate-spheres writing, see Leonore Davidoff and Catherine Hall, *Family Fortunes: Men and Women of the English Middle Class, 1780–1850*, rev. ed. (New York: Routledge, 2002).

about just when the ideology of separate spheres arose and just what sort of prior social order it replaced. We might hesitate in recalling that the women of ancient Athens were to be concealed in interior chambers if any male visitor stopped by[8] or that through most of Roman history, women didn't have first names.[9] Ancient society aside, in 1645 one woman at court learned that other women there liked to talk about "state affaires." "I that was young, innocent, and to that day had never had in my mouth, 'What news,' begun to think there was more in inquiring into business of publick affaires than I thought off, and that it being a fashionable thing would make me more beloved of my husband (if that had been possible) than I was." But her husband didn't want to betray the prince's confidence.[10] In 1716 the *Free-Holder* moaned,

> This sharp political Humour has but lately prevailed in so great a Measure as it now does among the beautiful Part of our Species. They used to employ themselves wholly in the Scenes of a domestick Life, and provided a Woman could keep her House in Order, she never troubled herself about regulating the Commonwealth. The Eye of the Mistress was wont to make her Pewter shine, and to inspect every Part of her Houshold Furniture as much as her Looking-Glass. But at present our discontented Matrons are so conversant in Matters of State that they wholly neglect their private Affaires, for we may always observe that a Gossip in Politicks, is a Slattern in her Family.[11]

The social change alleged here is the opposite of the separate-spheres thesis, even if the polished pewter tells us the implicit middle-class frame is identical: the *Free-Holder* is in agony over the erosion of separate spheres, not celebrating or anticipating their rise. Two years later, writing from Dublin, Jonathan Swift reported, "Jo Beaumont is my Oracle for publick Affairs in the Country and an old Presbyterian Woman in Town."[12] I bet that separate spheres are always already in disarray and the more disarray they're in, or perceived to be in, the more ardently writers pay tribute to them. I might be wrong about

8. *The Oxford History of the Classical World*, ed. John Boardman, Jasper Griffin, and Oswyn Murray (Oxford: Oxford University Press, 1986), 216.

9. M. I. Finley, *Aspects of Antiquity* (London: Chatto & Windus, 1968), 31.

10. *The Memoirs of Anne, Lady Halkett and Ann, Lady Fanshawe*, ed. John Loftis (Oxford: Clarendon, 1979), 115–16.

11. *Free-Holder*, 19 March 1716. This journal was the work of Joseph Addison.

12. Swift to Knightley Chetwode, 2 September 1718, in *The Correspondence of Jonathan Swift, D. D.*, ed. David Woolley, 4 vols. (Frankfurt: Peter Lang, 1999–2007), 2:270; see too Swift to Robert Hunter, 22 March 1709, *Correspondence*, 1:244.

that. But nothing that follows depends on your beliefs about separate spheres, a construct I now shove aside.

Instead, I want to dissect a different second step: that the public/private gap maps onto sex or gender—thus public man, private woman—and so makes the political oppression of women invisible. I'll include the hybrid thought that women's special preserve is the family precisely because the family is private. Let's pause over the elegant cadences of the *Spectator:*

> We have indeed carried Womens Characters too much into publick Life, and you shall see them now a-Days affect a sort of Fame: But I cannot help venturing to disoblige them for their service, by telling them, that the utmost of a Woman's Character is contained in Domestick Life; she is Blameable or Praise-worthy according as her carriage affects the House of her Father or her Husband. All she has to do in this World, is contained within the Duties of a Daughter, a Sister, a Wife, and a Mother: All these may be well performed tho' a Lady should not be the very finest Woman at an Opera, or an Assembly.[13]

I'll return to this passage and the *Free-Holder*'s lament after probing the public/private distinction.

That the family is wrongly taken to be private and so nonpolitical, or that sexuality is, or that women are, or that gender is: these have been stock complaints, even conventional wisdom, among feminists, critics of liberalism, and others.[14] I've used the passive voice—"is wrongly taken"—because there are multiple candidates for who's missing the point. Sometimes it's classical liberal theorists. Sometimes it's some of today's historians and theorists. Sometimes it's all of us, tripped up by a nefarious semiotics that maps

---

13. *Spectator,* no. 342 (2 April 1712), in *The Spectator,* ed. Donald F. Bond, 5 vols. (Oxford: Clarendon, 1965), 3:271–72.

14. One leading statement of the view in political theory is Jean Bethke Elshtain, *Public Man, Private Woman: Women in Social and Political Thought* (Princeton, NJ: Princeton University Press, 1981); one leading statement in history is Joan B. Landes, *Women and the Public Sphere in the Age of the French Revolution* (Ithaca, NY: Cornell University Press, 1988). For the metonymic associations of *woman* in this view, see for instance Linda M. G. Zerilli, *Signifying Woman: Culture and Chaos in Rousseau, Burke, and Mill* (Ithaca, NY: Cornell University Press, 1994). For a reading of Swift's *Lady's Dressing Room* showing the influence this view has had in literary circles, see Tita Chico, "Privacy and Speculation in Early Eighteenth-Century Britain," *Cultural Critique,* no. 52 (Autumn 2002): esp. 47–48. These mappings have long been challenged by those working on other cultural settings: see for instance Cynthia Nelson, "Public and Private Politics: Women in the Middle Eastern World," *American Ethnologist* 1, no. 3 (1974): 551–63; and Lila Abu-Lughod, *Veiled Sentiments: Honor and Poetry in a Bedouin Society* (Berkeley: University of California Press, 1986), 29–30. I'm arguing that the mappings don't work even in one classic setting where they're supposed to be at home.

public/private onto male/female, political/nonpolitical, and good/bad: that gives rise to overheated calls to scrap or transcend the public/private distinction itself. Sometimes it's the people of early modern England.

My strategy is not to find glimpses of feminist insight in the historical record, not to show that "public man, private woman" wasn't the smothering straitjacket some imagine, not to parade a few valiant women with the guts to protest that frame. That strategy would implicitly concede that "public man, private woman" is basically the right story. Instead I mean to argue that that story is fundamentally misconceived.

Repetition might help: I don't believe women enjoyed equality. Instead, I believe that understanding how women were public is crucial in understanding the terms of their domination. I say that not because I wish to invert the view I'm attacking and argue that the public/private gap is gendered, but the opposite way from what critics have claimed. I think there is no simple mapping between sex or gender, public, and private. Nor is there any simple mapping between public, private, and politics. Analytically and empirically, we have to splinter the terrain. So my strategy is to pry apart a series of independent distinctions and to probe disparate examples.

A Bit of Conceptual Analysis

There's some general sense in which *public* means a largish number—what counts as largish will vary with context—of anonymous others, outsiders, or strangers. They're not insiders: other members of your nuclear family aren't the public. But others can also be too far outside to qualify. Americans might say that the public has a right to know what's going on in the executive branch, but we wouldn't ordinarily include, say, the Nepalese of Kathmandu as part of that public. The spatial sense of *outside* here is social, not physical. Nepali tourists in Central Park, or for that matter visiting the White House, don't become part of the public with a right to know about the executive. To qualify as the public, these others have to be configured or imagined in some kinds of formations, with some kinds of status. Though not necessarily approvingly. Tobias Smollett's Matt Bramble branded the public an "incongruous monster" for its debased aesthetic tastes.[15] Edmund Burke

15. *The Expedition of Humphry Clinker* [1771], ed. O. M. Brack Jr. (Athens: University of Georgia Press, 1990), 88. Contrast the manuscript "Public Address," in *William Blake's Writings*, ed. G. E.

repeated that "France has no public" and he didn't mean no one lived there.[16] He thought the French mere slaves after the Revolution. So *public* for him too entailed some dignified status.

One could say more. Michael McKeon has suggested, "The public might be figured not as a flow or an agglomerated totality but as a quotient, a totality of qualitative subjects quantified by averaged typicality."[17] But I can't figure out what that means. I want to leave *public,* standing alone, in that rough sense—some collection of outsiders or strangers, configured or imagined in particular ways—and press on.

You might assume that there's one public/private distinction. But there are three and they're independent. So we need to learn to think of the public/private distinction as an unfortunate homonym and strive to keep clear about what sense of the distinction we have in mind at any moment. First is what's open to others as distinguished from what's hidden or off limits. That first distinction in turn has descriptive and normative glosses. When your six-year-old industriously picks her nose on the playground and you say, "Don't do that in public!" you mean where others can see her. (Here Nepali tourists would qualify.) But suppose the guy in the next apartment discovers a small hole in the wall through which he can see your bathroom—with you in it. The bathroom remains private, we'd say: he shouldn't snoop. The same normative point holds for settings obviously open to view. When you pull up to the red light, you can see the driver in the next car flossing his teeth, but it's plausible to say he's in private: you can look, but you shouldn't. Or ponder our discomfort over people on crowded sidewalks chattering on their cell phones. Visual and auditory examples come readily to mind, but this first distinction runs past them. A public park is open or accessible: strangers may enter the premises. To tip my hand on a later argument, to say a park is public is not to say that it's owned by the government. Consider a much-quoted bit of language from a 1939 First Amendment case: "Wherever the title of streets and parks may rest, they have immemorially been held in trust

Bentley Jr., 2 vols. (Oxford: Clarendon, 1978), 2:1051; Shelley to Charles Ollier, 11 December 1817, in *The Letters of Percy Bysshe Shelley,* ed. Frederick L. Jones, 2 vols. (Oxford: Clarendon, 1964), 1:579; Keats to J. H. Reynolds, 9 April 1818, in *The Letters of John Keats,* ed. Hyder Edward Rollins, 2 vols. (Cambridge, MA: Harvard University Press, 1958), 1:266–67.

16. *Letters on a Regicide Peace* [1795–97], in *The Works of the Right Honourable Edmund Burke,* 9th ed., 12 vols. (Boston: Little, Brown, 1889), 5:449, 6:67.

17. Michael McKeon, *The Secret History of Domesticity: Public, Private, and the Division of Knowledge* (Baltimore: Johns Hopkins University Press, 2005), 165.

for the use of the public and, time out of mind, have been used for purposes of assembly, communicating thoughts between citizens, and discussing public questions."[18]

I need to slow down to capture the second distinction. Start with the notion of having an interest.[19] I don't mean *being interested in*, as for instance a reader of the *National Enquirer* might be curious about the antics of celebrities. You have an interest in something, let's say roughly, when it advances some plan or project you have. So if you want to attend medical school, you have an interest in mastering organic chemistry. That's true even if you find the subject unutterably boring, so *being interested in* and *having an interest* are different. An initial stab at the second distinction would be that something is public when others have interests, private when they don't. But that's not exactly right. We need some notion of legitimate interests. If some latter-day Comstock plans to purify sexual morality, that won't turn the ostensibly private choices of consenting adults into public matters. Nor would it if there were plenty of Comstocks, though that brute numerical fact might shape our notion of legitimacy. There's the usual room here for detached reports of others' views of legitimacy. One might report that sodomy between consenting adults is a matter of public concern in some state without assenting to their understanding of legitimacy. Still, we need more than legitimate interests. Suppose the reserve army of unemployed PhDs in some field is applying for the sole tenure-track opening in their field and you're one of them. There's nothing remotely illegitimate about the interest the other candidates take. They will moan that their projects have been set back if they don't get the job. But you needn't consider those interests. Let's say, then, that something is public in this second sense if others have legitimate interests that you're obliged to consider. Here again, the others I have in mind are relative outsiders or strangers. It's private if you may suit yourself.

It needn't follow that others may rightly criticize you, demand justifications, and hold you accountable. But often that inference does follow. The fallout of this same distinction, then, is between matters on which others may hold you accountable and matters on which you owe them no account. If you order two scoops of cinnamon-nutmeg ice cream and the customer behind you in line taps you on the shoulder and demands, "How *could* you?" he's

18. *Hague v. Committee for Industrial Organization*, 307 U.S. 496 (1939), 515.

19. The now-canonical starting point for these discussions is Joel Feinberg, *Harm to Others* (New York: Oxford University Press, 1984), chaps. 1–2.

probably a lunatic or a boor bullying you about your weight. But maybe he thinks the international spice trade exploits third-world workers. Then what you took to be a private consumption decision is arguably public.

There is no necessary connection between whose interests you must heed and who is entitled—or obliged—to speak up or act on their behalf. The customer is representing the interests of people across the globe, in no position to speak up for themselves. So too the unborn, infants, and the comatose can't articulate their own interests. Other underlings could speak up for themselves, but they're vulnerable. So we might think it better for the union to file a grievance than for a worker to confront his supervisor, better for a parent to have a word with the principal than a student to complain to her teacher. (Here's another wrinkle in our practices of accountability: the person fielding the complaint may not be the person behaving badly.) But sometimes we think only those being callously treated are entitled to protest. To tiptoe closer to my concerns here, if the wife down the street is being abused, some will think that neighbors or the police should get involved. But if the abuse isn't severe, others might shrug if she isn't making an issue of it.

Often you owe only some others a justification. Your department is running a job search. If a colleague wonders why you're supporting one candidate, you ought to give reasons. Those reasons should refer to the common good of the department, not your personal interest in having a fourth for your bridge game. But if the provost nudges you, you can stiff-arm her in the name of faculty autonomy. Then again, if a legislative subcommittee worried about racial or political bias summons you to testify, you may well owe the broader community of citizens an account.

These two distinctions are independent: something can be public in one sense, private in the other. Take the secret ballot. What you do in the privacy of the voting booth is hidden. But you should make a judgment based on the common good or justice and not just suit yourself. So too for statesmen pursuing fraught negotiations behind closed doors. Their diplomacy is private in the sense that it's not accessible to outsiders. It's public in the sense that others, at least citizens of their own country, have interests they must consider. Indeed, they must find those interests decisive.

Contrast tossing a jar of Skippy peanut butter into your shopping cart at the supermarket. Other patrons can see what you're doing. The cashier will notice; the store will keep an electronic record of the purchase. Still, you're ordinarily entitled to suit yourself in choosing a brand of peanut butter. So your consumer choice is public in being open to others, private in being your own business. Likewise for the clothes you put on, at least on a day off from work. You're free to suit yourself, but others can see what you're wearing.

With both distinctions, who count as others shifts with context.[20] Some apparent disagreements are properly diagnosed as cases where both distinctions are in play. For instance we call all the firms in a capitalist economy private. That means they may pursue their own interests, say by maximizing profits. So those fond of stakeholders claim that even these nominally private firms have public obligations. But we also distinguish privately held firms from publicly traded firms in which outsiders can buy ownership shares on the stock market. It's unhelpful to ask, so are capitalist firms public or private? It depends not just on normative disputes, but also on what you mean. Or again, is the government public? Yes, in that ordinarily we expect government officials to promote the common welfare, not serve themselves. But the government is also private: much of what it does is concealed. You need to grasp both public/private distinctions to make sense of long-standing demands for transparency: publicity (exposing to view) enables publicity (regard to others' interests).[21]

"But sometimes we use *public* to refer to the government." Yes, we do: here's the third distinction. In this case, today the antonym *private* ordinarily refers to the market: so we ask if health care should be publicly or privately supplied. This usage can't support the public man, private woman story. At best, it turns that story into a tautology: "People have thought women don't belong in government because people have thought that women don't belong in government" doesn't illuminate matters. Saying your thesis is true by definition is not an especially impressive way to support it. It's no way at all. Worse, insofar as *private* here means market, the thesis gains substance but becomes spectacularly false. The reason people have doubted women belong in government is not that they think women should be CEOs. So I dismiss this usage for now. It's not that common in early modern England anyway. I have found scattered cases—the snippet from the *Spectator* is one and I'll furnish others—where *public* means *government*, but the contrasting category is usually *domestic*, which points to *family* but raises other issues.[22]

20. I think this is what Susan Gal, "A Semiotics of the Public/Private Distinction," in *Going Public: Feminism and the Shifting Boundaries of the Private Sphere*, ed. Joan W. Scott and Debra Keates (Urbana: University of Illinois Press, 2004), refers to as "fractal recursions."

21. For instance *Edinburgh Review*, September 1818, 468–69; *Edinburgh Review*, March 1819, 547–48.

22. For a sample of this usage, see Thomas Manton, *A Fifth Volume of Sermons* (London, 1701), 207–8.

So far I've drawn on intuitions about how we use *public* and *private* today. But it's an open question whether people in early modern England used the words the same way. So does the public/private distinction—do the public/private distinctions—have a history? Here the Fregean distinction between sense and reference is key. The referents—what turn out to be public and private, in the first two senses—have indeed changed. But it's not enough to point at how the referents change. First we have to get clear on the senses of the distinction,[23] which seem not to have changed in English for the past several hundred years. Or so I hope to show by scrutinizing how the early modern English deployed the language of public and private.

Contemporary Usage

Let's start with an instance where the public/private distinction seems to support the account I'm challenging. *The Young Ladies Conduct* warns, "don't

23. For instances of work attentive to reference and cavalier about sense, see Elshtain, *Public Man, Private Woman*, esp. 3–16; Nancy Fraser, *Unruly Practices: Power, Discourse, and Gender in Contemporary Social Theory* (Minneapolis: University of Minnesota Press, 1989), chap. 6; Carole Pateman, "Feminist Critiques of the Public/Private Dichotomy," in her *The Disorder of Women: Democracy, Feminism and Political Theory* (Stanford, CA: Stanford University Press, 1989); Leonore Davidoff, "Regarding Some 'Old Husbands' Tales': Public and Private in Feminist History," in her *Worlds Between: Historical Perspectives on Gender and Class* (Cambridge: Polity, 1995); Martha A. Ackelsberg and Mary Lyndon Shanley, "Privacy, Publicity, and Power: A Feminist Rethinking of the Public-Private Distinction," in *Revisioning the Political: Feminist Reconstructions of Traditional Concepts in Western Political Theory*, ed. Nancy J. Hirschmann and Christine Di Stefano (Boulder, CO: Westview, 1996); and ironically, given its interest in "explicitation," McKeon, *Secret History*.

Clear on sense, but misguided on the merits, are Susan Moller Okin, "Gender, the Public and the Private," in *Political Theory Today*, ed. David Held (Stanford, CA: Stanford University Press, 1991); and Sandra Fredman, *Women and the Law* (Oxford: Clarendon, 1997), 16–17. Lawrence E. Klein, "Gender and the Public/Private Distinction in the Eighteenth Century: Some Questions about Evidence and Analytic Procedure," *Eighteenth-Century Studies* 29, no. 1 (1995): 97–109, is overinvested in fluidity and multiplies distinctions needlessly. I'm not persuaded by the attempt to historicize *public* and *private*, still less by gestures toward empty signifiers, in Erica Longfellow, "Public, Private, and the Household in Early Seventeenth-Century England," *Journal of British Studies* 45, no. 2 (2006): 313–34. Better, but with transmission on the static channel, are Jeff Weintraub, "The Theory and Politics of the Public/Private Distinction," in *Public and Private in Thought and Practice: Perspectives on a Grand Dichotomy*, ed. Jeff Weintraub and Krishan Kumar (Chicago: University of Chicago Press, 1997), and Davidoff and Hall, *Family Fortunes*, xxiv–xxvii.

Here's another way to see the point. Catharine A. MacKinnon, *Toward a Feminist Theory of the State* (Cambridge, MA: Harvard University Press, 1989), 35, writes, "Engels presupposes throughout, as liberal theorists do, that the distinction between the realm inside the family and the realm outside the family is a distinction between public and private. 'Private' means 'inside the family.' 'Public' means the rest of the world." I don't think either Engels or liberals ever held such a view. Anyway, if they did, they'd have a sterile tautology on their hands. But the claim "What happens inside the family is private" surely isn't true by definition. Before we decide whether it is true, we need to know what it means.

mistake me, LADIES, for tho' I recommend Walking as an useful Exercise, yet I do not mean publick Walking in the Mall, and other Places of that kind; but in the Groves and Gardens of your several Apartments, and in the private Fields and Walks in your adjacent Neighbourhood."[24] One could quibble over whether or how this creepy sentiment is tied to exclusion from government. Instead, I suggest that we see it as local, contingent, not a clue that we're up against some monolithic structure. In one of Dryden's plays, Aurelia and Theodosia angrily confront Don Melchor, who's been pursuing both of them. He's evasive: "Still I say nothing, Madam; but I will satisfie either of you in private; for these matters are too tender for publick discourse."[25] Women indignantly demanding publicity and a squirrelly man coveting privacy: this isn't the dynamic the usual story would lead you to suspect—or notice. The locution *public woman* in my period isn't oxymoronic. It means *prostitute,* or a woman who's sexually accessible to others.[26]

The same use of *public* and *private* surfaces in cases having nothing to do with sex, gender, and political equality. When some 1690 highway robbers take their victims "out of the road to a privet place till they had finished their robbery," they're prudently avoiding detection.[27] Their private place is one that can't be seen. John Wynne congratulated John Locke on the *Essay concerning Human Understanding:* "I am very sensible how impertinent It would be for one of my Rank and condition to pretend to make any private

---

24. [John Essex], *The Young Ladies Conduct: or, Rules for Education, under Several Heads* (London, 1722), 81. See too A Lady, *The Whole Duty of a Woman: or, A Guide to the Female Sex,* 8th ed. (London, 1735), 38, urging that it's "easiest and safest" for women to play musical instruments "in private Company, amongst particular Friends." More ominously yet, see *Some Memoirs of the Life of Mr. Tho. Tryon, Late of London, Merchant* (London, 1705), 126: "All Women above the Age of Seven Years, shall be Vailed when they go abroad."

25. *An Evening's Love: or, The Mock-Astrologer* [1671], in *The Works of John Dryden,* ed. Edward Niles Hooker et al., 20 vols. (Berkeley: University of California Press, 1956–94), 10:297. Compare *The Conquest of Granada by the Spaniards* [1672], in *Works of Dryden,* 11:137; *The Spanish Fryar or The Double Discovery* [1681], in *Works of Dryden,* 14:137. "We are now in private," says the Gentleman in *A Yorkshire Tragedy* [1608]; "There's none but thou and I": Thomas Middleton, *The Collected Works,* ed. Gary Taylor and John Lavagnino (Oxford: Clarendon, 2007), 458.

26. For instance William Gamage, *Linsi-Woolsie: or, Two Centvries of Epigrammes* (Oxford, 1613), pt. 1, epig. 53, n.p.; Lewis Ellis Dupin, *A Compendious History of the Church,* 2nd ed., 4 vols. (London, 1715–16), 2:28; Humphrey Prideaux, *The Old and New Testament Connected in the History of the Jews and Neighbouring Nations,* pt. II (London, 1718), 79. Compare Thomas Fuller, *The History of the Worthies of England* (London, 1662), [pt. 3], pp. 196–97.

27. *The Autobiography of William Stout of Lancaster, 1665–1752,* ed. J. D. Marshall (Manchester: Chetham Society, 1967), 98. Compare [Thomas Heywood], *A Curtaine Lecture* (London, 1637), 150–51, 153.

acknowledgments for so publick and Universal A Benefit."[28] Lady Margaret Hoby adopted common usage in distinguishing her "priuat praers" from when she "praid publeckly" on the basis of whether others were present.[29]

Elizabeth Caton, on trial for stealing a watch in 1732, was in a jam. However reluctant or new to the trade, she was clearly a prostitute trying to get payment agreed on beforehand. The gentleman's testimony foundered:

> C— B—. She says that I had to do with her, but upon my Honour I had no Design whatever upon her.
> Court. Do you use to pick up Women, and carry them into a private Room without any Design?
> C— B—. I had no Design, upon Honour, for I have a Wife of my own, who is here in Court. And the Prisoner and I were in a publick Room.
> Court. The Drawer swears it was a private Room. Was any Body in the Room besides yourself and the Prisoner?
> C— B—. No; but upon my Honour it was a publick Room. I don't know what other People may call publick; but I think any Room must needs be publick, if it is in a Publick-House. I took the Watch from her myself, but I was very much fuddled, and cannot tell whether I took it out of her Bosom or from under her Arm.[30]

C— B— knew that he'd lose once he conceded he had this woman in a private room. Why else if not to have sex with her? The house was the View of Oxford, a London tavern. The tavern was public: open to strangers. The room in question was public too: open to anyone who rented it. Once rented, though, it was private: others weren't permitted to barge in.[31] Notice the squirming that had to accompany giving this testimony in public, with even his wife there, and confessing he was too drunk to know if he was handling Caton's breasts. He was exposing to others matters he would rather have kept private. You have to wonder why he pressed charges and why he announced

28. John Wynne to John Locke, 31 January [1695], in *The Correspondence of John Locke*, ed. E. S. de Beer, 8 vols. (Oxford: Clarendon, 1976–89), 5:261.

29. *Diary of Lady Margaret Hoby 1599–1605*, ed. Dorothy M. Meads (London: George Routledge & Sons, 1930), 113 (10 April 1600).

30. *Old Bailey Proceedings Online* (www.oldbaileyonline.org, version 6.0, 7 December 2011), January 1732, trial of Elizabeth Caton (t17320114–39).

31. So too contemporaries understood that not all coffeehouse conversation was properly made (more) public: A Coffee-Man, *The Case of the Coffee-Men of London and Westmin[s]ter* (London, [1728]), 27; *The Case between the Proprietors of News-Papers, and the Subscribing Coffee-Men, Fairly Stated* (London, 1729), 5; James Kelly, *A Complete Collection of Scotish Proverbs Explained and Made Intelligible to the English Reader* (London, 1721), 32.

that his wife was in the courtroom. Maybe he gambled to vindicate his innocence. Maybe he was clueless.

There's the first sense of public and private, the difference between what's open to others and what's not. What about the second sense, the difference between having to heed others' interests and being free to suit yourself? Cato warned officeholders not to betray their trust: "Every Step a publick Man takes, every Speech he makes, and every Vote he gives, may affect Millions."[32] Cato's *publick* may denote *officeholding*, a sign that early modern English too had the third sense of *public* that I set aside. Consider some other examples of that third sense. A character in one of Dryden's plays uses *private* to mean *not an officeholder:* "When Kings grow stubborn, slothful, or unwise, / Each private man for publick good should rise."[33] A splendidly bizarre attempt to clarify the logical structure of language glossed *public* as "*towards* defraying the *charge of Government.*"[34] "Sophia, a Person of Quality" scoffed, "what a wretched circle this poor way of reasoning among the *Men* draws them insensibly into. Why is *learning* useless to us? Because we have no share in public offices. And why have we no share in public offices? Because we have no *learning.*"[35] Swift wished "some able Lawyers would prescribe the Limits, how far a private Man may venture in delivering his Thoughts upon publick Matters," but he promptly staked out his own view: "Every Man who enjoys Property, hath some share in the Publick; and therefore, the Care of the Publick is, in some Degree, every such Man's Concern."[36] Pope smarmily hailed the Jacobite Francis Atterbury, who'd be

32. *Cato's Letters*, 4 vols. (London, 1723–24), 1:292.

33. *The Indian Emperor* [1667], in *Works of Dryden*, 9:80 (and see *Amboyna* [1673], *Works of Dryden*, 12:22). See too [W. B.], *A Serious Letter Sent by a Private Christian to the Lady Consideration* (London, 1655); *The Female Spectator*, 3rd ed., 4 vols. (Dublin, 1747), 1:120. "I am Tottally a stranger to all publick affairs," wrote Mrs. Isabella Duke to John Locke, 21 October 1686, in *Correspondence of Locke*, 3:57.

34. John Wilkins, *An Essay towards a Real Character, and a Philosophical Language* (London, 1668), 268. See too *True Patriot*, no. 12 (21 January 1746), in Henry Fielding, *"The True Patriot" and Other Writings*, ed. W. B. Coley (Middletown, CT: Wesleyan University Press, 1987), 194.

35. Sophia, a Person of Quality, *Woman Not Inferior to Man: or, A Short and Modest Vindication of the Natural Right of the Fair-Sex to a Perfect Equality of Power, Dignity, and Esteem, with the Men* (London, 1739), 27. Felicity A. Nussbaum, *The Brink of All We Hate: English Satires on Women, 1660–1750* (Lexington: University Press of Kentucky, 1974), 8, claims this text was simply translated from the French of Poulain de la Barrre; for a correction, see Mary Beth Norton, *Separated by Their Sex: Women in Public and Private in the Colonial Atlantic World* (Ithaca, NY: Cornell University Press, 2011), 130, 222–23n43.

36. Jonathan Swift, *A Letter to the Lord Chancellor Middleton* [1735], in *The Prose Works of Jonathan Swift*, ed. Herbert Davis, 14 vols. (Oxford: Basil Blackwell, 1939–68), 10:108 (and see 10:110). See too [William Penn], *Some Fruits of Solitude: In Reflections and Maxims Relating to the Conduct of Human Life* (London, 1693), 91–92.

exiled from England: "Thanks be to God, that I a Private man, concerned in no Judicature, and employed in no Publick cause, have had the honour, in this great and shining incident, (which will make the first figure in the history of this time) to enter, as it were, my Protest to your Innocence, and my Declaration of your Friendship."[37]

But Cato's sense of *public* might also be *obliged to take others' interests into account:* the early modern English vehemently denounced government officials' corruption when they pursued their own interests. There's no ambiguity in one pamphleteer's rousing defense of Sacheverell, whose High Church extremism created a scandal, against John Dolben, himself the son of a bishop —and the member of Parliament who first assailed Sacheverell's sermons as seditious libels.[38] This passage drips scorn: "it may be alledg'd, that you cou'd not possibly give a more convincing Evidence of a true Patriot, of a publick-spirited Man; than thus to forget your Father's House, to contemn all the Sacred Bonds of Nature, Blood, and Friendship, when they came in competition with a general National Good[.]"[39] Yet the scorn depends on and so doesn't undercut the invocation of *public* as *regarding others' interests.*

Contemporaries registered the same wrinkles in their practices of accountability that we do. James I and Charles I acknowledged fiduciary obligations to promote the welfare of their English subjects, but insisted they were accountable only to God for how they handled that trust.[40] Or, to peek after my official period here for an adorable example, take Bishop Horsley's explosive claim that "he did not know what the mass of the people in any country had to do with the laws but to obey them."[41] Horsley's vigorous contempt for

---

37. Pope to Atterbury, May 1723, in *The Correspondence of Alexander Pope*, ed. George Sherburn, 5 vols. (Oxford: Clarendon, 1956), 2:169.

38. On Dolben, see Josiah C. Wedgwood et al., *The House of Commons, 1690–1715* (Cambridge: Cambridge University Press, 2002), 897–98.

39. L.M.N.O., *A True Defence of Henry Sacheverell, D.D. in A Letter to Mr. D——n* (London, 1710), 2–3.

40. "Speech to Parliament," 21 March 1609, in *The Political Works of James I*, ed. C. H. McIlwain (Cambridge, MA: Harvard University Press, 1918), 307; Samuel Rawson Gardiner, *History of England from the Accession of James I to the Outbreak of the Civil War, 1603–1642*, 10 vols. (London: Longmans, Green, 1887–91), 2:235; *The Stuart Constitution, 1603–1688: Documents and Commentary*, ed. J. P. Kenyon, 2nd ed. (Cambridge: Cambridge University Press, 1986), 43, 150; *King Charls His Tryal: or, A Perfect Narrative of the Whole Proceedings of the High Court of Justice in the Tryal of the King in Westminster Hall* (London, 1649).

41. *Parliamentary History* (11 November 1795) 32:258; and see *The Speeches in Parliament of Samuel Horsley* (Dundee, 1813), 168–83, for Horsley's not particularly apologetic apology of 30 November.

democracy is wholly compatible with thinking that Parliament ought to legislate in the people's interests.

These distinctions were familiar enough to be formalized in dictionary entries, the best evidence of explicit linguistic consciousness. From 1713, "Private, *particular, secret*";[42] from 1728, "PUBLICK [*public*, F. publicus, L.] common, belonging to the People; manifest, known by every body."[43] Decades later, Samuel Johnson's magisterial *Dictionary* would generate five meanings apiece for the adjectival forms of *publick* and *private*, but they readily collapse to the same two. For *publick* as a noun, Johnson offers just two: "The general body of mankind, or of a state or nation; the people," and "Open view; general notice."[44] So the early modern English saw that there were (at least) two public/private distinctions and that they crosscut one another.

Time for more splintering. Suppose—I'll dwell on this Aristotelian insight in opening the next chapter—we take politics as the realm of conflict (narrowly) over legitimate authority, or (more broadly) over the legitimacy of social practices. So construed, politics isn't restricted to the government. We find disputes about authority and legitimacy in every social setting, emphatically including the family. It has been no surprise to anyone, ever, that male heads of households have claimed the right to rule or that the household can be cast as a "little commonwealth."[45] To emphasize the husband's "Authority and right to Govern," Mary Astell didn't deploy this republican conceit. A husband was "a Monarch for Life," she insisted.[46] (In

42. J[ohn] K[ersey], *A New English Dictionary* (London, 1713), s.v. *private*.

43. N[athan] Bailey, *An Universal Etymological English Dictionary*, 4th ed. (London, 1728), s.v. *publick*, echoed verbatim in B[enjamin] N[orton] Defoe, *A Compleat English Dictionary* (Westminster, 1735), s.v. *publick*. Note too Edward Phillips, *The New World of Words: or, Universal English Dictionary*, 6th ed. rev. and corr. by J. K. (London, 1706), s.v. *publick*.

44. Samuel Johnson, *A Dictionary of the English Language*, 2nd ed., 2 vols. (London, 1755–56), s.vv. *private, publick*.

45. *The House-keepers Guide, in the Prudent Managing of Their Affairs* (London, 1706), 1; Richard Fiddes, *Theologia Practica: or, The Second Part of a Body of Divinity under That Title* (London, 1720), 512; Henry Stebbing, *An Essay concerning Civil Government, Consider'd as It Stands Related to Religion* (London, 1724), 69; Nicholas Brady, *Several Sermons, Chiefly upon Practical Subjects*, 3 vols. (London, 1730), 2:138. For canonical texts, contrast *The Prerogative of Popular Government* [1658], in *The Political Works of James Harrington*, ed. J. G. A. Pocock (Cambridge: Cambridge University Press, 1977), 414–15, and *Patriarcha* [1680], in Sir Robert Filmer, *"Patriarcha" and Other Writings*, ed. Johann P. Sommerville (Cambridge: Cambridge University Press, 1991), 19, with Locke's *Two Treatises of Government*, bk. 2, § 86.

46. [Mary Astell], *Some Reflections upon Marriage, Occasion'd by the Duke & Dutchess of Mazarine's Case* (London, 1700), 41, 32; and see esp. 59–61.

1664 a woman poet hailed another woman as the monarch of her house.)[47] A 1609 writer casually referred to the "master of the familie . . . in whom resteth the priuate and proper gouernment of the whole household."[48] There's nothing oxymoronic about private government, about his exercising authority without having to answer to others. "You must know how to rule your house," a 1657 writer instructed "family-governors."[49] The next century, a correspondent to the *Tatler* revealed that Isaac Bickerstaff, the authorial persona, had written "a Treatise concerning *The Empire of Beauty,* and the Effects it has had in all Nations of the World upon the publick and private Actions of Men; with an Appendix, which he calls, *The Batchelor's Scheme for Governing his Wife.*"[50] This language straightforwardly describes the family as a political community. Remember too that the *Scheme* is the very publication the *Tatler* had Jenny Distaff sneering at. Again, we are explicitly in the realm of controversy, not that of "naturalized" or "essentialized" or unalterable facts.

Indeed, I suspect prior generations grasped family politics more firmly than we do. They hired governesses; we hire nannies and au pairs. We've already seen some publications adamant about household government. Contemporary readers could have encountered plenty more. In 1598 they could have learned from *A Godlie Forme of Hovsehold Governmente* that "A Householde is as it were a little common wealth, by the good gouernment wherof, Gods glorie may be aduanced, the common wealth which standeth of seuerall families, benefited, and al that liue in that familie may receiue much comfort and commoditie."[51] In 1631 they could have peered over the shoulder of an author anxiously surveying "so many evils," "calamities," and "great disor-

47. K[atherine] P[hilips], *Poems* (London, 1664), 83.

48. W[illiam] Perkins, *Christian Oeconomie: or, A Short Svrvey of the Right Manner of Erecting and Ordering a Familie, According to the Scriptures* (London, 1609), 163.

49. John Norman, *Family-Governors Perswaded to Family-Godliness* (London, 1657), 11. See too Josias Nichols, *An Order of Hovshold Instrvction* (London, 1595), sig. B3 recto; Mathew Griffith, *Bethel: or, A Forme for Families* (London, 1633), 7; Th[omas] Paget, *A Demonstration of Family-Dvties* (London, 1643), 65–75, 135–40; Robert Abbott, *A Christian Family Builded by God, Directing All Governours of Families How to Act* (London, 1653), 38; John Worthington, *Forms of Prayer for a Family* (London, 1693), "To the Reader," n.p.

50. *Tatler,* no. 10 (3 May 1709), in *The Tatler,* ed. Donald F. Bond, 3 vols. (Oxford: Clarendon, 1987), 1:87.

51. R[obert] C[leaver], *A Godlie Forme of Hovseholde Government: For the Ordering of Private Families, According to the Direction of Gods Word* (London, 1598), 13.

der," and triumphantly revealing "the occasion of all mischief to be the want of good Houshold Government."[52] Again, we are in no position to whisper the alleged secret that the family is political to people who spoke so readily of household government.

Nor is the family simply private. The family can be public, in the sense of exposed to others: remember the paper-thin walls separating London apartments or the foul smells and smoke that led plenty of people to spend time on their thresholds or in the streets.[53] The family can be public, too, in the sense of outsiders having interests. The pressing question is, when may outsiders criticize, demand justifications, and intercede? Let's stick with the time-honored patriarchal family for a moment. The master of the household has the right to rule. But there are limits to what he may do. If he exceeds the bounds of his jurisdiction, his rule is illegitimate and outsiders may step in and hold him accountable.[54] So we find controversies about when and how outsiders should intervene.

1677 murder proceedings provide a memorable example. The accused was beating his wife, or preparing to, outdoors and a passerby "concern'd himself so far as to expostulate with the husband enquiring why he so much abused his wife." Enraged, the accused rushed at the passerby with a half-pike and had the bad luck to kill him on the spot.[55] These unhappy events took place open to view, so in public. But the killer thought the passerby should have been minding his own business, that how he treated his wife was private. Similarly, Ann Collins called out in 1740 when Samuel Badham was throttling a woman who passed for his wife. Badham "called me Bitch," she testified, "and bid me mind my own pocky, itchy Child."[56] Then too, a husband can exceed his jurisdiction along multiple boundaries. Take this London nuisance ordinance: "No Man shall, after the Hour of Nine at the Night, keep any Rule

---

52. William Iones, *A Briefe Exhortation to All Men to Set Their Houses in Order* (London, 1631), 1–2.

53. For a disgusting wealth of information, see Emily Cockayne, *Hubbub: Filth, Noise & Stench in England, 1600–1770* (New Haven, CT: Yale University Press, 2007).

54. See [Richard Allestree], *The Gentleman's Calling* (London, 1662), 16.

55. *OBP,* 1 June 1677 (t16770601–8). See *A Caution to Married Couples: Being a True Relation How a Man in Nightingale-lane Having Beat and Abused His VVife, Murthered a Tub-man that Endevoured to Stop Him from Killing Her with a Half-pike* (London, 1677).

56. *OBP,* 9 July 1740, Samuel Badham (t17400709–2); see too Joanne Bailey, "'I dye [*sic*] by Inches': Locating Wife Beating in the Concept of a Privatization of Marriage and Violence in Eighteenth-Century England," *Social History* 31, no. 3 (2006): 286.

whereby any such sudden Outcry be made in the Still of the Night, as making any Affray, or beating his Wife, or Servant, or singing or revelling in his House, to the Disturbance of his Neighbours, under Pain of Three Shillings and Four Pence."[57] Here it's fine to beat your wife, just not too late and too noisily.

Daniel Defoe joined the fray, with the drearily familiar conviction that wife beating is the special hobby of the lower orders:

> they tell me, that 'tis so frequent now, especially among the meaner sort of People, that to hear a Woman cry Murther now, scarce gives any Alarm; the Neighbours scarce stir at it, and if they do, if they come out in a Fright, and ask one another what's the Matter, and where is it that they cry Murther? the common Answer to one another is only thus; 'tis nothing Neighbour, but *such a one* is beating his Wife; *O dear,* says the other, *is that all?* and in they go again, compos'd and easie, as hearing a thing of no great Consequence, that has no great Novelty in it, nor much Danger, and what, if it had, they don't much care to meddle with.[58]

The neighbors know a woman is being beaten. In that sense it's public information. Why don't they "care to meddle"? Maybe they're scared, but the verb *meddle* suggests that they think it's none of their business. Defoe returned to the battlefield four years later:

> And now I have mentioned the Villainy of some Husbands in the lower State of Life, give me leave to propose, or at least to wish, that they were restrained from abusing their Wives at that barbarous Rate, which is now practised by Butchers, Carmen, and such inferior Sort of Fellows, who are publick Nusances to civil Neighbourhoods, and yet no Body cares to interpose, because the Riot is between a Man and his Wife.
>
> I see no Reason why every profligate Fellow shall have the Liberty to disturb a whole Neighbourhood, and abuse a poor honest Creature at a most inhuman Rate, and is not to be call'd to Account because it is his Wife; this sort of Barbarity was never so notorious and so much encourag'd as at present, for every Vagabond thinks he may cripple his Wife at pleasure, and

57. Robert Seymour [John Mottley], *A Survey of the Cities of London and Westminster, Borough of Southwark, and Parts Adjacent,* 2 vols. (London, 1733–35), 2:201. Compare the 1595 rule, worded differently but to the same effect, quoted in Cockayne, *Hubbub,* 115.

58. [Daniel Defoe], *The Great Law of Subordination Consider'd: or, The Insolence and Unsufferable Behaviour of Servants in England Duly Enquir'd Into* (London, 1724), 6–7.

'tis enough to pierce a Heart of Stone to see how barbarously some poor Creatures are beaten and abused by merciless Dogs of Husbands.[59]

People believe that they ought not intrude when a husband beats his wife. In that sense, it's private, even though in another sense it's also noisily and distressingly public and so a nuisance. Defoe protests this view. He thinks such husbands ought to be called to account for their wretched behavior. So his complaint is political: he thinks the current exercise of patriarchal authority illegitimate. He goes on to discuss the problems and possibilities of government action.

> It gives an ill Example to the growing Generation, and this Evil will gain Ground on us if not prevented: It may be answer'd, the Law has already provided Redress, and a Woman abus'd may swear the Peace against her Husband, but what Woman cares to do that? It is revenging herself on herself, and not without considerable Charge and Trouble.
>
> There ought to be a shorter way, and when a Man has beaten his Wife (which by the Bye is a most unmanly Action, and great Sign of Cowardice) it behoves every Neighbour who has the least humanity or Compassion, to complain to the next Justice of the Peace, who should be impowered to set him in the Stocks for the first Offence; to have him well scourg'd at the Whipping-Post for the second; and if he persisted in his barbarous Abuse of the holy Marriage State, to send him to the House of Correction 'till he should learn to use more Mercy to his Yoke-fellow.[60]

Defoe's "swear the Peace" refers to surety of the peace, the legal measure we've already seen that put a man on notice that continued misbehavior would have him hauled back into court to face punishment. But Defoe, knowingly or not, is suggesting an amendment. Such procedures were available not whenever any husband beat his wife, but only if he beat her "outrageously."[61] Defoe thinks these procedures thankless. He prefers not just

59. [Daniel Defoe], *Augusta Triumphans: or, The Way to Make London the Most Flourishing City in the Universe* (London, 1728), 28–29. See too Henrie Smith, *A Preparatiue to Mariage* (London, 1591), 69–74; W[illiam] H[eale], *An Apologie for Women* (Oxford, 1609); William Gouge, *Of Domesticall Dvties: Eight Treatises* (London, 1622), 389–92; *The Great Advocate and Oratour for Women: or, The Arraignment, Trial, and Conviction of All Such Wicked Husbands (or Monsters) Who Held It Lawful to Beate Their Wives and to Demeane Themselves Severely and Tyrannically towards Them* (n.p., 1682).

60. [Defoe], *Augusta*, 30.

61. William Hawkins, *A Treatise of the Pleas of the Crown*, 2 vols. ([London], 1716–21), 1:127; see too Giles Jacob, *A New Law-Dictionary* ([London], 1729), s.v. *Alimony*. The enabling statute seems to be 34 Edw. 3 c. 1 (1361); for discussion and analysis, including of the claim that the law French of the statute

criminal sanctions but also public shaming. That he impeaches such husbands' manliness raises gender complications I set aside.[62]

Nor did it take physical violence for outsiders to step in. Skimmingtons loom larger in historical imagination than their frequency warrants. Still, despite increasingly firm opinions from the late 1600s that they were illegal,[63] they went on. Married couples offending against gender or sexual norms—or, as Marvell puts it, effortlessly casting women as blameworthy, "Masculine wives transgressing Nature's law"[64]—could awake in the middle of the night to find their neighbors outside their windows, banging pots and pans, singing raucous songs, and calling them to account, making it clear that they'd be ostracized or have to leave town if they wouldn't clean up their acts. So forty were accused in 1737 of

> riotously, routously, and Unlawfully Assembling themselves together with at least 100 other people in order to disturb and break the King's Peace and being so riotously Assembled before the doors of the dwelling house of Charles Jones, Gent. did make an Assault upon Mary his wife and in a sporting manner did demand where the black Bull was, meaning the said Charles Jones, and in such Riotous manner did run up and down the Church Town of Aveton Gifford with black and Disguised Faces carrying a large pair of Rams Horns tipt like Gold and adorned with Ribbons and Flowers with a mock child made of raggs, and having an Ass whereon the said John Macey and John Purcell rid, dressed in a Ludicrous manner, back to back, with beating of Drums and winding of Hunting Horns and throwing of lighted Squibbs, And Reading a Scandalous Libellous paper, making

rolls was mistranslated, see *Lansbury v. Riley*, 3 K.B. 229 (1914). For Scottish battering leading to a nominal sentence, see [Sir George Mackenzie], *Pleadings in Some Remarkable Cases, before the Supreme Courts of Scotland, since the Year 1661* (Edinburgh, 1704), 247–58.

62. But see too M[artin] P[arker], *Hold Your Hands Honest Men* (London, [1634]): "if you desire to be held men compleat, / Whatever you doe your wives do not beat."

63. Martin Ingram, "Ridings, Rough Music, and the 'Reform of Popular Culture' in Early Modern England," *Past & Present*, no. 105 (1984): 100–101. For a useful survey of the broad class of phenomena described as "rough music," see E. P. Thompson, *Customs in Common* (New York: New Press, 1991), chap. 8; for a helpful reminder of the (sometimes magical) power of linguistic and enacted satires, see Douglas Gray, "Rough Music: Some Early Invectives and Flytings," *Yearbook of English Studies* 14 (1984): 21–43.

64. "The Last Instructions to a Painter" [1667], in *The Poems of Andrew Marvell*, ed. Nigel Smith (London: Pearson, 2003), 378, musing on a Greenwich skimmington also noted in *The Diary of Samuel Pepys*, ed. Robert Latham and William Matthews, 11 vols. (Berkeley: University of California Press, 2000), 8:257 (10 June 1667), and provoked by a wife's beating her husband.

loud Huzzahs Hallows and out Cries and so continuing for the space of 5 hours.[65]

The pageantry meant that Mary was unacceptably dominant and had cuckolded Charles. The hundreds flouting the criminal law to lampoon the poor couple would have been stunned to learn that they lived in a society that imagined, uniformly and relentlessly and stupidly and ideologically, that the family was private and nonpolitical. So too for the "two thirds of the women in town" who turned out in Islington in 1748 to administer "pelting, hissings and blows" to a wife beater on his way to prison.[66]

On both public / private distinctions, then, the family is sometimes private, sometimes public: sometimes hidden, sometimes exposed to view; sometimes free to ignore others' interests, sometimes open to the rebukes and intervention of outsiders. What about sexuality? Is sexuality private? In a 1701 comedy, Lady Lovetoy says airily, "O 'tis the new manner among us to make no secrets; our Dressing, Painting, Gallantrys, are all publick, and now a Lady wou'd no more have a Lover unknown, than she wou'd a Beauty."[67] Still, ordinarily people did not have sex in plain view of strangers. This familiar practice makes sex private and privacy titillating. Witness this 1727 graffito:

> *Jenny* demure, with prudish Looks,
> Turns up her Eyes, and rails at naughty Folks;
> But in a private Room, turns up her lech'rous Tail,
> And kisses till she's in for Cakes and Ale.[68]

But for centuries poverty and architectural crowding made sex in the presence of others routine. Besides, it was so easy to peer through glass! or to find randy couples under hedges and in meadows! The straitlaced chided others for their insouciance: "Turn your Eyes up to the Chambers of Wantonness,

---

65. M. G. Dickinson, "A 'Skimmington Ride' at Aveton Gifford," *Devon & Cornwall Notes & Queries* 34, no. 7 (1981): 290. One play staged a skimmington aimed at a "man-like buxom Dame": [Essex] Hawker, *The Wedding: A Tragi-Comi-Pastoral-Farcical Opera* (London, 1729), 20. See too *Skimmington-Triumph: or, The Humours of Horn-Fair* (London, [1720?]).

66. Elizabeth Foyster, *Marital Violence: An English Family History, 1660–1857* (Cambridge: Cambridge University Press, 2005), 197.

67. [William Burnaby], *The Lady's Visiting-Day: A Comedy* (London, 1701), 27.

68. Hurlo Thrumbo, *The Merry-Thought: or, The Glass-Window and Bog-House Miscellany*, 3rd ed. with very large additions (London, [1731]; repr., Los Angeles: William Andrews Clark Memorial Library, 1982), 22.

and you behold the most shameful Scenes of Lewdness in the Windows even at Noon-day, some in the very Act of Vitiation, visible to all the opposite Neighbours."[69] Then too, one source reports spirited disagreement on the rule against having sex "in Publick" and notices a historical alternative.[70]

Dour critics glared at London's newfangled masquerades and found shameless public flirting and fondling. One correspondent to the *Spectator*, at least purporting to be a director of the Society for the Reformation of Manners, sounded the alarm: "There are several Rooms where the Parties may retire, and, if they please, show their Faces by Consent. Whispers, Squeezes, Nods, and Embraces, are the innocent Freedoms of the Place. In short, the whole Design of this libidinous Assembly seems to terminate in Assignations and Intrigues."[71] Edward Ward joined in, aghast at "nimble-footed Ladies, who seem'd equally industrious to win Hearts by the pouting of their Bubbies, the wriggle of their Bums, and the activity of their Pettitoes."[72] He was mortified, too, by the doings of a "Lewd Congregation" in Islington.[73] St. James Park was notorious for prostitutes on the roam;[74] so too Lambeth Wells.[75] "A Wife for an hour" could be had at Bartholomew Fair.[76] Prostitutes swarmed horse races at Epsom and the aptly named *Folie*, a boat on the Thames.[77] "Went to playhouse," the young Dudley Ryder confided in his

69. *Satan's Harvest Home: or, The Present State of Whorecraft, Adultery, Fornication, Procuring, Pimping, Sodomy, and the Game at Flatts* (London, 1749), 26.

70. *Jewish Letters*, 4 vols. (Newcastle, 1739–44), 4:239–40. See too M. Moxon, "The Character of a Chaste and Virtuous Woman," in *Conjugal Duty: Set Forth in a Collection of Ingenious and Delightful Wedding-Sermons* (London, 1732), 70; and the slightly sweaty treatment in Julie Peakman, *Lascivious Bodies: A Sexual History of the Eighteenth Century* (London: Atlantic Books, 2004).

71. *Spectator*, no. 8 (9 March 1711), in Bond, *The Spectator*, 1:36–37.

72. E[dward] W[ard], *The Amorous Bugbears: or, The Humours of a Masquerade* (London, 1725), 20–21. Middlesex justices prepared to discuss plans "shou'd there be another Jubilee Masquerade Ball att Ranelagh House," Middlesex Sessions Papers, 26 April 1750, in *London Lives, 1690–1800*, LMSMPS504020067 (www.londonlives.org).

73. [Edward Ward], *A Walk to Islington* (London, 1699), 4. *A Charge Delivered to the Grand Jury* [1749], in Henry Fielding, *An Enquiry into the Causes of the Late Increase of Robbers and Related Writings*, ed. Malvin R. Zirker (Oxford: Clarendon, 1988), urges attention to masquerades (25) in its spirited indictment of "profligate Lewdness" (20); *An Enquiry into the Causes of the Late Increase of Robbers* [1751], in Fielding, *Enquiry*, 84, excepting Haymarket, brands masquerades "the Temples of Drunkenness, Lewdness, and all Kind of Debauchery."

74. *London in 1710: From the Travels of Zacharias Conrad von Uffenbach*, trans. and ed. W. H. Quarrell and Margaret Mare (London: Faber & Faber, 1934), 12.

75. *The Diary of Dudley Ryder, 1715–1716*, ed. William Matthews (London: Methuen, 1939), 57 (18 July 1715).

76. *A Description of Bartholomew Fair* (n.p., [c. 1680]), in *The Pepys Ballads*, ed. Hyder Edward Rollins, 8 vols. (Cambridge, MA: Harvard University Press, 1929–32), 3:81.

77. *London in 1710*, 120, 130.

journal. "The whores are always in the passage to it and continually lay hold of me."[78]

Ryder was dismayed by prostitutes[79] but not by servant women in inns. "Pleased myself as I came along with the hope of meeting a pretty girl to kiss at the inn at Newbury. There was such a one as I could kiss but not extraordinary."[80] The next day: "I began to grow very tired and weary of riding. Came to Sandylane. Kissed the girl there."[81] Defoe denounced gentlemen who "cannot go to see a Friend, but they must kiss and slop the Maid; and all this is done with an Air of Gallantry, and must not be resented."[82] (*OED* to the rescue: *slop* here must mean *slobber*.) Servant maids were generally available —that is, often conscripted—for sexual services.[83] When Sir Ralph Verney's wife got sick, he sought a servant he could sleep with. His uncle found him one who'd earn £3 a year. A former servant, he added, "is very confident she will match your cock."[84] Samuel Richardson's Pamela shrank from her master's kissing her and his invoking "*Lucretia,* and her hard Fate."[85] That notorious lecher, Samuel Pepys, didn't grope only his servant Deb, though his wife "did find me imbracing the girl con my hand sub su coats; and endeed, I was with my main in her cunny."[86] (He lapses into this curious pidgin mix of continental languages when recording his sexual activities.) He groped other lower-class women, too, and it's not always clear whether they're consenting. "Called at my little Millener's," he wrote, "where I chatted with her, her husband out of the way, and a mad merry slut she is."[87]

78. *Diary of Ryder,* 49 (8 July 1715). See too [Richard Ames], *The Female Fire-Ships: A Satyr against Whoring* (London, 1691), 7–9; [John Dunton], *The Night-Walker: or, Evening Rambles in Search after Lewd Women, with the Conferences Held with Them, &c. to Be Published Monthly, 'till a Discovery Be Made of All the Chief Prostitutes in England, from the Pensionary Miss, Down to the Common Strumpet,* November 1696, 14–15.

79. *Diary of Ryder,* 72 (9 August 1715), 85 (24 August 1715), and especially 138 (16 November 1715).

80. *Diary of Ryder,* 238 (21 May 1716).

81. *Diary of Ryder,* 239 (22 May 1716).

82. Andrew Moreton [Daniel Defoe], *Every-Body's Business, Is No-Body's Business: or, Private Abuses, Publick Grievances,* 4th ed. corr. (London, 1725), 21–22. See too *The History of the Life of the Late Mr. Jonathan Wild the Great* [1743], in *Miscellanies by Henry Fielding, Esq.,* ed. Henry Knight Miller et al., 3 vols. (Middletown, CT and Oxford: Wesleyan University Press and Oxford University Press, 1972–97), 3:94.

83. Laura Gowing, *Common Bodies: Women, Touch and Power in Seventeenth-Century England* (New Haven, CT: Yale University Press, 2003), 59–65.

84. Miriam Slater, "The Weightiest Business: Marriage in an Upper-Gentry Family in Seventeenth-Century England," *Past & Present,* no. 72 (1976): 39. The letter is from 7 March 1650.

85. [Samuel Richardson], *Pamela: or, Virtue Rewarded,* 4th ed., 2 vols. (London, 1741), 1:35.

86. *Diary of Pepys,* 9:337 (25 October 1668).

87. *Diary of Pepys,* 5:38 (4 February 1664).

Sometimes it's clear they're not, as when Pepys reports using "some little violence" to get Betty Mitchell to rub his penis, "she making many little endeavours para ôter su mano [to remove her hand], but yielded still."[88] More could be said about contemporaries' intuitions about consent. Sex with a "woman-child" under the age of ten or perhaps twelve counted as (what we would call) statutory rape; "any woman above" that age was free to consent. But the law presumed males under fourteen "unable to commit a rape . . . impotent, as well as wanting discretion," so they couldn't be punished.[89] No awards for connecting the dots on the injustices lurking here.

Pepys dined with Lord Rutherford: "We supped together and sat up late, he being a mighty wanton man with a daughter-in-law of my landlady's, a pretty conceited woman, big with child; and he would be handling her breasts, which she coyly refused."[90] "A noted Custom-House Officer being at the Theatre in *Drury-Lane*, to see a Play acted, made several Attempts to thrust his Hands up the *Petticoats* of one of the fair Fruitresses when she was tripping over the Seats to her Customers."[91] Elizabeth Meers complained that Henry Chamberlayne, a gentleman (!), put "his Members into her hand" in the street.[92] It won't suffice to say that Chamberlayne was out of line or to remember that every social order has its deviants. Many deemed these practices acceptable.[93] The lower-class women subjected to these indignities were, like prostitutes, public, in the sense of being accessible, if by force, and if only in some social settings and only to some kinds of men. Their being public in this sense was part of their subordination: privacy would have been bliss. Sexual practices here were sometimes public, exposed to others' view. And they were political—we find disputes about their legitimacy.

So Huizinga's pregnant concept, "cruel publicity,"[94] is helpful past the Middle Ages, helpful too in thinking about sex and gender, helpful in more

---

88. *Diary of Pepys*, 7:419 (23 December 1666).

89. Matthew Hale, *Historia Placitorum Coronae: The History of the Pleas of the Crown*, 2 vols. (London, 1736), 1:628, 630, 631.

90. *Diary of Pepys*, 6:274 (23 October 1665).

91. A True-Born Englishman, *A Ramble through London* (London, 1738), 59.

92. Jennine Hurl-Eamon, *Gender and Petty Violence in London, 1680–1720* (Columbus: Ohio State University Press, 2005), 34.

93. Bernard Capp, *When Gossips Meet: Women, Family, and Neighbourhood in Early Modern England* (Oxford: Oxford University Press, 2003), 227–28.

94. Johan Huizinga, *The Waning of the Middle Ages: A Study of the Forms of Life, Thought, and Art in France and the Netherlands in the XIVth and XVth Centuries* (Garden City, NY: Doubleday Anchor, 1955), 1.

than bringing into focus men groping women. Take wife sales.[95] Divorces, recall, were generally unavailable. Instead, in one village after another, an unhappy husband would lead his wife, tied with a rope and a halter as if she were livestock, to market and auction her off. The buyer would typically be the man she was already having an affair with. The ceremony, of no legal force, served informally as divorce and remarriage. The women so transferred were in some sense better off. But being sold as an animal says something nasty about being a wife. Nor does the sensible reminder that the handoff must be public to work explain why the publicity took this demeaning form.

Sexuality wasn't only visible to others; people also regularly claimed interests in others' sexual activities. To take the most obvious case, some showered contempt on mollies and sodomites. In 1695, John Stubbs tossed printed sheets into a Fleet Street shop:

> At the Golden-Turk's-Head in Fleet Street
> Is a Suck-Prick Hoberde-Hoy, Pimp and Atheist,
> to be seen with a Barr gown on,
> Bugger'd Davis the Pimp and Sodomite.[96]

Watch the distinctions: Stubbs wanted to make Mainwaring Davis publicly visible, to shame him, and would have insisted that his sexual deviance, from oral to anal sex with other men, with cross-dressing[97] thrown in for good measure (that "Barr gown" is probably a cocktail dress), was a matter of public concern, that others had a legitimate interest in it. When Thomas Doulton stood in the pillory for attempted sodomy, "the Women express'd their Abhorrence of the Fact, by pelting the Criminal with Dirt."[98] One

95. Samuel Pyeatt Menefee, *Wives for Sale: An Ethnographic Study of English Popular Divorce* (Oxford: Basil Blackwell, 1981); E. P. Thompson, "The Sale of Wives," in his *Customs in Common*, chap. 7; Rachel Anne Vaessen, "Humour, Halters and Humiliation [*sic*]: Wife-Sale as Theatre and Self-Divorce" (MA thesis, Department of History, Simon Fraser University, 2006). A wife sale, complete with formal papers, is the central gag of *The Phoenix* [1607], in Middleton, *Collected Works*; for the wife's opposition, see 108–9.

96. Robert B. Shoemaker, *The London Mob: Violence and Disorder in Eighteenth-Century England* (London: Hambledon & London, 2004), 241; 243 reproduces the sheet. Note J[ohn] Ray, *A Collection of English Proverbs* (Cambridge, 1670), 216: "A *Hoberdehoy*, half a man and half a boy."

97. For a jolly tale of a cross-dressing servant maid who becomes a queen, see *The Famous Flower of Servingmen: or, The Lady Turn'd Serving-Man* (n.p., [1686–88]).

98. *Weekly Journal or British Gazetteer*, 1 October 1726. For the trial proceedings, *OBP*, 31 August 1726, Thomas Dalton (t17260831–49). For the description of a notorious molly house in trials leading to a death sentence for sodomy, see *OBP*, 20 April 1726, Gabriel Lawrence (t17260420–64); *OBP*, 20 April

author dwelled morbidly on the decadent practices that turned the young gentleman into "such an enervated effeminate Animal": he watched Italian opera and other abominations onstage, but no custom was "more hateful, predominant, and pernicious, than that of the Mens *Kissing* each other." No wonder they indulged in sodomy.[99] Funny that homosexual conduct is both disgusting and easy to trigger. Regardless, this author took it for granted that the public had an interest in stamping out such repulsive behavior, so they needed a causal account.

Political Controversies

Let's take stock. There are three public / private distinctions, I've argued, not one. Whether something is political is another matter entirely. So *public man, private woman* is not a helpful way to describe the ineluctable fact that women didn't serve in Parliament or vote in elections. Worse, the slogan occludes our vision of the social landscape's intriguing contours. I want next to redouble my skepticism about familiar claims that these matters were "naturalized."[100] Contemporaries were perfectly well aware of heated controversies over what was public, what private. The reference of the distinctions—what properly fell on one side, what the other—was the subject of strenuous political debate, not merely from a tiny handful of marginal onlookers who assume bloated importance from our standpoint.

We've already met a director of the Society for the Reformation of Manners: the correspondent to the *Spectator* who denounced London's masquerades. There was a real social movement behind him. The societies—doughty

---

1726, Thomas Wright (t17260420–67); see too *The Women-Hater's Lamentation* (London, 1707), a verse account of the breakup of a club of a hundred men given to "Unnat'ral Lust" and the suicide of a few exposed participants.

99. *Satan's Harvest Home*, 45–61. For more horror, see "He-Strumpets: A Satyr on Sodomite-Club," 4th ed., in *Athenianism: or, The New Projects of Mr. John Dunton, Author of the Essay Entitl'd, "The Hazard of a Death-Bed Repentance"* (London, 1710), pt. 2, pp. 93–99; *Hell upon Earth: or, The Town in an Uproar* (London, 1729), 41; *The Female Husband: or, The Surprising History of Mrs. Mary, Alias Mr. George Hamilton, Who Was Convicted of Having Married a Young Woman of Wells and Lived with Her as Her Husband* (London, 1746), in Henry Fielding, *"The Journal of a Voyage to Lisbon," "Shamela," and Occasional Writings*, ed. Martin C. Battestin (Oxford: Clarendon, 2008), 355–84. For a vivid and horrified portrayal of a cross-dressing man having two women put him in bondage, see [Edward Ward], *The Humours of a Coffee-House*, 23–30 July 1707, 23–24.

100. Contrast Kathryn Shevelow, *Women and Print Culture: The Construction of Femininity in the Early Periodical* (London: Routledge, 1989), 10.

warriors struggling to cleanse England of its moral filth and avert divine judgment, whose (first) campaign flourished in the 1690s and early 1700s— took pressing interest in others' lives. "[P]rofanation of the Lord's Day, the execrable Sin of Cursing and Swearing; Houses of Lewdness, and notorious Uncleanness, Drunkenness, Whoredom, *and the like*"[101] left them reeling in agony. They published menacing lists fingering the men and women running bawdy houses and other dissolute rogues. The titles alone speak volumes:

A

BLACK LIST

Of the NAMES, or Reputed NAMES, of *Seven Hundred Fifty Two* Lewd and Scandalous Persons, who, by the Endeavours of a SOCIETY set up for the promoting a Reformation of Manners in the City of London, and Suburbs thereof, have been Legally Prosecuted and Convicted, as Keepers of Houses of Bawdry and Disorder, or as Whores, Night-walkers, &c. And who have thereupon been Sentenced by the Magistrates as the Law directs, and have accordingly been Punished (many of them divers times) either by Carting, Whiping, Fining, Imprisonment, or Suppressing their Licenses. All which (besides the Prosecution of many Notorious Cursers, Swearers, Sabbath-breakers, and Drunkards, not here incerted) hath been effected by the Society aforesaid.

This roster of infamy came with a helpful key: "NOTE, B. signifie Bawd, W. Whore, D. H. Disorderly House, D. P. Disorderly Person, and P. P. Pick-Pocket."[102] So the societies publicly shamed miscreants.[103] They clamored for vigorous enforcement of long-standing criminal laws. Even the johns were sometimes prosecuted.[104] (Though Defoe, eager to pursue "Sir Alexander C—ing of C—ter, Advocate, for the sin of adultery," was impatient with

---

101. John Russell, *A Sermon Preach'd at St. Mary-Le-Bow, to the Societies for Reformation of Manners, June 28 1697* (London, 1697), 8–9.

102. *A Black List* (London, 1698). See too The Society for Reformation, *Proposals for a National Reformation of Manners, Humbly Offered to the Consideration of Our Magistrates & Clergy . . . Also The Black Roll, Containing the Names and Crimes of Several Hundred Persons, Who Have Been Prosecuted by the Society, for Whoring, Drunkenness, Sabbath-Breaking, &c.* (London, 1694).

103. On the beneficent impact of shame, see John Howe, *A Sermon Preach'd Febr. 14 1698 and Now Publish'd, at the Request of the Societies for Reformation of Manners in London and Westminster* (London, 1698), 30. Compare [Dunton], *The Night-Walker*, preface, sig. B recto, and p. 7.

104. Jennine Hurl-Eamon, "Policing Male Heterosexuality: The Reformation of Manners Societies' Campaign against the Brothels in Westminster, 1690–1720," *Journal of Social History* 37, no. 4 (2004): 1017–35.

the Edinburgh Society for blinking at upper-class vice.)[105] They privately expostulated with offenders, too.

They were reviled for meddling. "And indeed nothing is more common," acknowledged a rector, "than to hear wicked Men, when at any time they are troubled (or affronted as they think) with a Friendly Advice, or a Charitable Reprimand, reply, *Mind your own Business, and trouble not your self about what I do. If I do amiss, it is I must suffer for it, and not you.*"[106] Another writer bemoaned the grief informers took—"Let a Man's Ends therein be never so honest, and pious, and charitable, yet what he doth shall be censured to proceed from Pride, Self-conceitedness, busy Bodiness, or some spightful and ill-natur'd Principle or other"—and noted the risks: "many desperate Wretches threaten to knock out their Brains, if they knew them, for doing them such a charitable Office, as to stop them in their Career to Sin and Hell."[107] The societies knew they were treading on thin ice. One vicar laid out the conventional case for subjects' deference to government officials: "We private Christians must not prescribe methods . . . to *publick* Magistrates, or *censure* their *proceedings*, and *speak irreverently* of their *persons* and *administrations*, when they determine otherwise than we had thought *fitting.*"[108] Still, one preacher after another egged on the societies. So they had to argue that others' misbehavior was properly a matter of public concern, that they weren't contemptible snoops invading others' privacy.

They brandished scripture. One preacher adduced Leviticus 19:17: "Thou shalt not hate thy brother in thine heart: thou shalt in any wise rebuke thy neighbour, and not suffer sin upon him." So "far are they from Truth, who call it a medling with things which do not belong unto you; since *God* makes it your bounden Duty," he scoffed.[109] "A publick Sinner," he con-

105. Charles Eaton Burch, "Defoe and the Edinburgh Society for the Reformation of Manners," *Review of English Studies* 16, no. 63 (1940): 306–12. For Defoe's impatience with special legal treatment for the rich, see esp. *The Poor Man's Plea, in Relation to All the Proclamations, Declarations, Acts of Parliament, &c. Which Have Been, or Shall Be Made, or Publish'd, for a Reformation of Manners, and Suppressing Immorality in the Nation* (London, 1698).

106. John Ellis, *The Necessity of a National Reformation of Manners: or, The Duty of Magistrates, Ministers, and All Others, to Put the Laws in Execution against Prophaneness and Immorality*, 2nd ed. (London, 1701), 22.

107. *The Case of Witnessing against Offenders Face to Face, Examined and Discussed* (London, 1704), 11–12.

108. John Kettlewell, *The Measures of Christian Obedience*, 5th ed. corr. (London, 1709), 284–85.

109. Josiah Woodward, *The Duty of Compassion to the Souls of Others, in Endeavoring Their Reformation: Being the Subject of a Sermon Preached December the 28th 1696 at St. Mary-le-Bow, before the Societies for Reformation of Manners in the City of London* (London, 1697), vi, italics reversed. For more on the same text, see George Stanhope, D. D. Chaplain in Ordinary to Her Majesty, *The Duty of Rebuking: A*

tinued, "does not only sin against his *own Soul*, but against the *Community* of which he is a Member; yea, against the World in which he lives. The Mischiefs which attend his Sin are general, and spread widely and universally."[110] Another chimed in with Matthew 18:17 ("if he shall neglect to hear them, tell *it* unto the church") and promptly added, "Yea, not to the Church only, but to the State also; not inform the Minister only, but the Magistrate too."[111] First on the list of evils that *"may provoke the Holy Spirit to deny or withdraw his Influence and Help,"* warned yet another, clutching the ever-convenient Genesis 4:9, was *"Cold Neutrality:* Too many are ready to say, *This is a matter that doth not concern me; am I my Brothers keeper?* Yes you are, the Authority of God has made you so, and you must be responsable to him for your neglect."[112] One author cataloged countless instances of divine judgment. His title page, too, speaks volumes:

> *A Flaming Whip for Lechery:*
> OR, THE
> Whoremasters SPECULUM.
>
> CONTAINING,
>
> A fearful Historical RELATION of such Wicked unclean Persons, as have been made Publick and Private Examples of GOD's Divine Vengeance, for polluting themselves and others with such Abomination and Defilements. Taken out of Sacred and Prophane History.
>
> ALSO,
>
> Some dreadful Examples of GOD's Righteous Judgment, not Recorded in either with curious Remarks, by way of a fuller Explanation of the most eminent Sins of this kind, particularly those mentioned in Holy Writ; much Enlightening the several Texts thereto referring; drawing from thence good Councel and Advice: With timely Warning, and serious Admonitions to Amendment of Life, and speedy Reformation of Manners.
>
> IN ORDER
> To prevent GOD's heavy Judgments hanging over this sinful Land.[113]

Sermon Preach'd at Bow-Church, December the 28th 1702 before the Right Honourable the Lord-Mayor and Aldermen of London, and the Societies for Reformation of Manners (London, 1703).

110. Woodward, *Duty,* 2. Compare [Mary Astell], *The Christian Religion, as Profess'd by a Daughter of the Church of England* (London, 1705), 225–26.

111. Daniel Chadwick, *A Sermon Preached at the Church of St. Mary in Nottingham: To the Society for Reformation of Manners on July the 6th* (London, 1698), 23.

112. Nath[aniel] Weld, *A Sermon before the Societies for Reformation of Manners in Dublin: Preached in New-Row, April the 26th, 1698* (Dublin, 1698), 13.

113. *A Flaming Whip for Lechery* (London, 1700).

These preachers also assured the societies that their neighbors' sins had horrific worldly consequences. Arguing "That it is every Man's Business to enter the Lists against Sin,"[114] they urged their audiences to "stop that raging Pestilence of Sin, which is ready to overspread the Land; and to carry Infection, and Death, and Misery into every corner of it."[115] Only the members' zealous activity could save their own children and families.[116] The noxious effects of sin and vice rippled out far beyond individual families. Merchants were "undone" by the vices of their associates, customers, and debtors: "How many a worthy Citizen has been bankrupt by other Mens Crimes, and not by his own? which, if they had been suppressed and punished formerly, the Cries, and Tears, and Ruine of many a poor Orphan, and helpless Widow in this City, might have been prevented."[117] No need, then, for the crusaders of the societies to worry that sinners branded them *"Busy Bodies"*[118] or "in derision . . . Soul-Savers."[119] Just like Defoe berating wife beaters, they had a plausible account of how they were vindicating crucial public interests.

Any word from the targets of their benevolent concern? Consider the voices of two bawds, perched precariously between journalism and fiction. "Time had been," fumed one, "when she could boast of as fine a Covey of sound, plump, and juicy Sluts in her house, as any Gentlewoman in *London*, and had kept Eighteen of as good Feather-Beds going, as a Brace of Fornicators need desire to regale their Limbs upon." But critics of the trade had driven it underground. "With Tears in her Eyes," she "solemnly declar'd that she did not *foul* more than a dozen Pair of Sheets in a whole Week."[120] The

---

114. William Harrison, *A Sermon Preach'd in the Chapel at Coleford . . . before the Society for Reformation of Manners* (London, 1702), 40.

115. Lilly Butler, *A Sermon Preach'd at St. Mary-le-Bow, to the Societies for Reformation of Manners, April 5 1697* (London, 1697), 6. On the contagion of vice, see too Daniel Burgess, *The Golden Snuffers: or, Christian Reprovers, and Reformers, Characteriȝed, Cautioned, and Encouraged: A Sermon Preach'd unto the Societies for Reformation of Manners, in London, Feb. 15 1694* (London, 1697), 45.

116. John Yate, *A Sermon Preach'd in the Parish-Church of Wendover . . . before the Society for Reformation of Manners* (London, 1702), 41.

117. John Shower, *A Sermon Preach'd to the Societies for Reformation of Mannners, in the Cities of London and Westminster, Nov. 15 1697* (London, 1698), 29.

118. Jeremiah Gill, *A Sermon Preach'd before the Society for Reformation of Manners, in Kingston upon Hull; September the 25th, MDCC* (London, 1701), 53.

119. *A Friendly Discourse concerning Profane Cursing and Swearing, Wherein Is Shewed the Heinousness of Those Sins, and the Necessity of Private Persons Giving Informations for the Suppressing of Them* (London, 1697), 12.

120. [Erasmus Jones], *A Trip through London*, 7th ed. corr. (London, 1728), 14–15. For the same with minor variants, see True-Born Englishman, *Ramble through London*, 13.

other disclosed that after the intrusion of a "disguis'd Constable," she admitted new clients only if current ones vouched for them. "By which means we are very secure; and tho' the Society for the Reformation, as they call it, does utterly Ruine all such as are Publick Houses of Assignation, yet our Trade is rather made the better by it."[121] So maybe all the societies' tireless campaigns did was conceal some illicit behavior or make it private.[122] Not enough to make them—or God—happy. But still a victory of sorts, making it possible to navigate the streets of London without being so constantly and rudely assailed by sin.[123]

Again, though, it didn't take the societies to generate public interest in errant sexuality and the publicity in question could take forms harsher than print publication. Take this 1736 snippet of news from London:

> Last Sunday Morning a young Woman did publick Penance in Greenwich Church, standing in a white Sheet in the Porch from the Time of the ringing the Bell to Divine Service, and during the Service stood in the middle Isle with a Wand in her Right Hand, and a Label on her Left Arm, signifying her Crime, viz. *I stand here for the Sin of Fornication.*[124]

There's a doubly public woman for you: others took an interest in her sex life and they put her and her secret on display. Nothing enviable about her predicament: I bet she'd have preferred privacy, in both senses. Indeed, as far as the news story reveals, that's what her male partner enjoyed. If you want to

121. *The London-Bawd*, 4th ed. (London, 1711; repr., New York: Garland, 1985), 163–64. See too *The Letter-Writers* [1731], in Henry Fielding, *Plays*, ed. Thomas Lockwood, 2 vols. to date (Oxford: Clarendon, 2004–), 1:629.

122. For arguments about driving prostitution underground or making it public and legitimate, compare, with his usual acerbic irony, Phil-Porney [Bernard Mandeville], *A Modest Defence of Publick Stews: or, An Essay upon Whoring* (London, 1724); A Genius, *Memoirs of the Bedford Coffee-House* (London, 1763), 32–34.

123. *A Help to a National Reformation: Containing an Abstract of the Penal-Laws against Prophaneness and Vice*, 5th ed. with great additions (London, 1706), 27; Thomas Bray, *For God, or for Satan: Being a Sermon Preach'd at St. Mar le Bow, before the Society for Reformation of Manners, December 27 1708* (London, 1709), 27; John Leng, *A Sermon Preached to the Societies for Reformation of Manners at St. Mary-le-Bow, on Monday, December the 29th MDCCXVIII* (London, 1719), 22–23.

124. *London Evening-Post*, 24 August 1736. For the reprints: *Daily Post*, 25 August 1736; *Old Whig: or, The Consistent Protestant*, 26 August 1736; *Country Journal: or, The Craftsman*, 28 August 1736; *Read's Weekly Journal: or, British Gazetteer*, 28 August 1736; *Universal Spectator, and Weekly Journal*, 28 August 1736. Contrast the Quaker woman disturbing church services in Rev. William Wilson to Daniel Fleming, 26 December 1666, in *The Flemings in Oxford*, ed. John Richard Magrath, 3 vols. (Oxford: Oxford Historical Society, Clarendon, 1904–24), 1:164–65. Compare Ursula Shepherd's mandated 1589 apology in church in Laura Gowing, *Domestic Dangers: Women, Words, and Sex in Early Modern London* (Oxford: Clarendon, 1996), 40.

understand this nauseating incident, the slogan you need is *public woman, private man.*

The Politics of Gender

I want last to emphasize that concerns about public and private aren't mere matters of abstract theory or institutional design. They are caught up in pedestrian and intimate matters of daily life. Here I turn briefly to gender, which isn't prior to politics,[125] isn't vaguely like politics, isn't (only) a causal influence on politics. It's already fully political on its own terms. How so? If or insofar as gender norms dictate that it's masculine to rule, feminine to submit, then they are political in my narrow sense: they are norms of authority about which we should expect, and in fact always find, controversies. Even when gender norms don't focus on rule and submission, they are political in my broader sense: they speak to the legitimacy of social practices, about which also there will be controversies. That means too, to shift from gender to sex, that women not serving or lobbying the state are engaged in politics.[126]

Some of the songs and jokes I produced are relevant. But for those Puritans who prefer their historical evidence on the social-historical straight-up-no-twist-of-pop-culture side, here's Jonathan Swift, one December day when he was forty-four years old: "Farewel, dearest MD, and love Presto, who loves MD infinitely above all earthly things."[127] That to Esther Johnson, or Stella. (*MD* is perhaps an abbreviation for *my dears:* Swift was addressing Stella and her companion, Rebecca Dingley, at whom it's oddly traditional to sneer,[128] and officially addressing both of them. But he wrote to and for Stella. *Presto,* almost surely *pdfr* in the original, is Swift himself.) Here's Swift, the very next day: "Adieu till we meet over a Pott of Coffee, or an Orange and Sugar in the Sluttery, which I have so often found to be the most agreeable Chamber in the World[.]"[129] That to Esther Vanhomrigh, or Vanessa.

125. Contrast Carole Pateman, *The Sexual Contract* (Cambridge: Polity, 1988); Susan Moller Okin, *Justice, Gender, and the Family* (New York: Basic Books, 1989).

126. Contrast Carole Pateman, "Women's Writing, Women's Standing: Theory and Politics in the Early Modern Period," in Smith, *Women Writers,* 365–66.

127. Jonathan Swift, *Journal to Stella,* ed. Harold Williams, 2 vols. (Oxford: Basil Blackwell, 1974), 2:414 (17 December 1711).

128. My sympathies are with George Sherburn's review of Harold Williams's edition of the *Journal to Stella:* see *Modern Language Review* 44, no. 1 (1949): 113.

129. Swift to Vanessa, [18 December 1711], in *Correspondence of Swift,* 1:399.

It seems lurid even to quote these passages, let alone to rehearse the gossipy questions swirling around Swift and these two women. Did Swift secretly marry Stella? Did Swift sleep with Vanessa? *Drinking coffee*, a recurrent locution in Swift's correspondence with Vanessa, sounds like code; Horace Walpole was sure it meant they were having sex.[130] What kind of room is a sluttery, anyway? (Well, the *OED* has an 1841 entry: "An untidy room; a work-room.") Was Swift impotent decades before Lady Mary Wortley Montagu lampooned his poem? Who knows? Who cares? But consider this juxtaposition. Swift seems to have been scrupulous in never being alone with Stella. "It would be difficult, if not impossible," wrote the Earl of Orrery, "to prove they had ever been together without some third person."[131] Not so with Vanessa and not just in the sluttery. He guarded their secrecy. "If you are in Ire^ld while I am there," he warned her, "I shall see you very seldom. It is not a Place for any Freedom, but where ever[y] thing is known in a Week, and magnified a hundred Degrees."[132] Vanessa shot back, "you once had a maxime (which was to act what was right and not mind what the world said) I wish you would keep to it now."[133] Observers scrutinized churchmen's romantic and sexual lives.[134] I don't say their private lives. After all, others took keen interest in their conduct and believed that they had every right to do so: these men were supposed to be moral exemplars. Swift had two opposite strategies for maintaining his reputation. He paraded his doings with Stella, but tried to keep Vanessa so tightly under wraps that no one would even know of her existence.[135] One is maximally public, the other maximally pri-

130. Walpole to Montagu, 20 June 1766, in *The Yale Edition of Horace Walpole's Correspondence*, ed. W. S. Lewis, 48 vols. (New Haven, CT: Yale University Press, 1938–83), 10:218–19. Douglas Dion suggested to me that this is an anagram: "drink**ING** **COF**fee = **FOCK**ING friend." He's more bothered by the leftover *e* than I am.

131. *Remarks on the Life and Writings of Dr. Jonathan Swift . . . in a Series of Letters from John Earl of Orrery to His Son*, 4th ed. (London, 1752), 25.

132. Swift to Miss Esther Vanhomrigh, 12 August 1714, in *Correspondence of Swift*, 2:72.

133. Miss Esther Vanhomrigh to Swift, [December] 1714, in *Correspondence of Swift*, 2:101.

134. For a 1611 lawsuit filed by a Cambridge doctor of divinity against another accusing him of sexual indiscretions, including sleeping with his male servant, see Alexandra Shepard, *Meanings of Manhood in Early Modern England* (Oxford: Oxford University Press, 2003), 116–17. Compare *The True State of the Case of John Butler, B.D. a Minister of the True Church of England: In Answer to the Libel of Martha His Sometimes Wife* (London, 1697), explaining that he didn't get his servant pregnant until deciding that his endlessly patient efforts to have his wife do her marital duties, including in bed, were futile. For another churchman fornicating with his servant, see *A Representation of the Affair of Mr. George Adam, Late Minister at Cathcart* ([Glasgow, 1748]).

135. Note "Cadenus and Vanessa," in *The Poems of Jonathan Swift*, ed. Harold Williams, 2nd ed., 3 vols. (Oxford: Clarendon, 1958), 2:712.

vate. You can judge which strategy was more likely to succeed—especially since that *no one* sails mindlessly past the prating servants.[136]

Now consider one last wrinkle on gender and politics. Swift wrote to Stella, "I don't like women so much as I did. [MD you must know, are not women.]"[137] Twelve years later, he directed Vanessa, "grow less Romantick, and talk and act like a Man of this World."[138] The next year, in a stern, even brutal, *Letter to a Young Lady, on Her Marriage*, he snarled, "I never yet knew a tolerable Woman to be fond of her own Sex."[139] Nine years later yet, he instructed Laetitia Pilkington, "You must shake off the Lea[n]ings of your Sex."[140] No wonder Sir Walter Scott commented, "he praises in his female friends those attributes chiefly which are most frequently met with in the other sex."[141]

When Stella died, an agonized Swift jotted down some reflections. "She was but little versed in the common topics of female chat," he noted. He added, "she had not much company of her own sex. . . . she rather chose men for her companions, the usual topics of ladies discourse being such as she had little knowledge of, and less relish."[142] Stella's practice was anomalous enough for Swift's great-nephew to exaggerate it.[143] No wonder Virginia Woolf would describe Stella as "one of those ambiguous women who live chiefly in the society of the other sex."[144] The gender norm that's been christened homosociality[145] was central enough—in his infamous *Advice*, for instance, Halifax silently assumed that all his daughter's friends would be female[146]—

---

136. See Pope to Caryll, 20 July 1729, in *Correspondence of Pope*, 3:40. For treacherous gossipy servants, see too *A Pleasant Comedie, Called Summers Last Will and Testament* [1600], in *The Works of Thomas Nashe*, ed. Ronald B. McKerrow, ed. and corr. F. P. Wilson, 5 vols. (Oxford: Basil Blackwell, 1958), 3:272; and see *The Proceedings upon the Bill of Divorce between His Grace the Duke of Norfolke and the Lady Mary Mordant* (London, 1700), 48.

137. *Journal to Stella*, 1:90 (10 November 1710). The brackets are Swift's.

138. Swift to Vanessa, 1 June 1722, in *Correspondence of Swift*, 2:421.

139. *A Letter to a Young Lady, on Her Marriage*, in *Prose Works of Swift*, 9:88.

140. Swift to Mrs. Pilkington, [October 1732], in *Correspondence of Swift*, 3:550.

141. Walter Scott, *Memoirs of Jonathan Swift, D. D.*, 2 vols. (Paris, 1826), 1:249.

142. "On the Death of Mrs. Johnson," in *Prose Works of Swift*, 5:230, 235.

143. Deane Swift, *An Essay upon the Life, Writings, and Character, of Dr. Jonathan Swift* (London, 1755), 92.

144. "Swift's 'Journal to Stella,'" in Virginia Woolf, *The Second Common Reader* (New York: Harcourt, Brace, 1932), 69.

145. Eve Kosofsky Sedgwick, *Between Men: English Literature and Male Homosocial Desire* (New York: Columbia University Press, 1985), presses the neologism back toward erotic desire. The category is useful even for those of us agnostic about that further claim.

146. [George Savile, Marquis of Halifax], *The Lady's New-Years Gift: or, Advice to a Daughter*, 3rd ed. corr. (London, 1688), 117–25.

that Stella forfeited her femininity, and then, in the slippage so often surrounding sex and gender, her womanhood, by immersing herself in the company of men.

We're back to the question provoked by *The Lady's Dressing-Room*. Was Swift a misogynist? I'd argue that this motif in Swift's corpus is a withering assault on contemporary understandings of femininity, but not misogyny at all. One can assault a gender norm without devaluing those who rally to it—or those who live by it. But the terrain sure is slippery. You have to grasp that you can respect people in urging that they are worthier than their actions suggest.

Swift is relying on just such a distinction between sex and gender. In Ireland, he wrote to Mary Pendarves:

> a pernicious heresy prevails here among the men, that it is the duty of your sex to be fools in every article except what is merely domestic, and to do the ladies justice, there are very few of them without a good share of that heresy, except upon one article, that they have as little regard for family business as for the improvement of their minds.
>
> I have had for some time a design to write against this heresy, but have now laid those thoughts aside, for fear of making both sexes my enemies; however, if you will come over to my assistance, I will carry you about among our adversaries, and dare them to produce one instance where your want of ignorance makes you affected, pretending, conceited, disdainful, endeavouring to speak like a scholar, with twenty more faults objected by themselves, their lovers, or their husbands. But, I fear your case is desperate, for I know you never laugh at a jest before you understand it, and I much question whether you understand a fan, or have so good a fancy at silks as others, and your way of spelling would be not intelligible.[147]

Here Swift rubbishes the feminine ideal that women be simpering idiots, even though he knows that not only (some? or many? or most?) men but also (some? or many? or most?) women embrace that ideal. If you imagine that Jonathan Swift, curmudgeonly Tory and Anglican churchman with the misfortune to live centuries ago, must have naturalized or essentialized gender, you'll miss what he's up to.

A few years later, Pendarves and fifteen other women—do you suppose

---

147. Swift to Mrs. Pendarves, [7 October 1734], in *Correspondence of Swift*, 4:3–4. Contrast the tone of *Letter to a Young Lady*, 9:91–92; and "The Furniture of a Woman's Mind," in *Poems of Jonathan Swift*, 2:415–18. But see too "The Journal of a Modern Lady," in *Poems of Jonathan Swift*, 2:444–45. And compare Pope to Lady Mary Wortley Montagu, 18 August 1716, in *Correspondence of Pope*, 1:354.

they were hoping to be manly?—would try to crash a debate in the House of Lords on the Convention with Spain.[148] Apparently Parliament was such a male preserve that women couldn't even sit in the galleries. When Charles I was on trial for his life in 1649, Lady Fairfax sat in the gallery—masked. She was obstreperous, not silent: the presiding attorney charged Charles "in the behalf of . . . the good people of England," but Lady Fairfax begged to differ. "*It was a lye,*" she called out; "not half, not a quarter of the people, *Oliver C[r]omwell* is a Rogue and a *Traytor.*" The Puritans played for keeps: a guard commanded the soldiers to present arms and fire.[149] On trial for his own life years later, that guard defended himself by insisting, "If a Lady will talk impertinently, it is no Treason to bid her hold her tongue."[150] Remember too that until the late eighteenth century, it was illegal to publish parliamentary proceedings.[151] This made Parliament intensely political, intensely male— and intensely private.

After waiting six and a half hours and enduring "the insults of the door-keepers" and "the buffets of a stinking crowd," Pendarves and her friends sent a note to the Gentleman Usher of the Black Rod, who informed them crisply that "'whilst *one lady* remained in the passage to the gallery, the door *should not* be opened for the members of the House of Commons'" waiting to observe from the galleries. Pendarves & Co. dutifully backed away, the door ceremoniously opened, the MPs rushed in—and Pendarves & Co. rushed in right behind. "Am I not a furious politician?" Pendarves asked her sister— surely her tone here is arch—before musing on how selfish politicians were and how happy she was to be "free of these engagements."[152]

Because Pendarves's action involves Westminster, it's easy to infer it was public and political. That's right: plenty of strangers watched her and she was clearly challenging the legitimacy of authority. Because it was a transgression,

148. The debate begins in *Parliamentary History* (1 March 1739) 10:1091.

149. [Heneage Finch, Earl of Nottingham], *An Exact and Most Impartial Accompt of the Indictment, Arraignment, Trial, and Judgment (According to Law) of Twenty-Nine Regicides* (London, 1679), 217–18; for less dramatic testimony, see 227.

150. [Finch], *Accompt*, 240.

151. For a narrative overview sadly lacking footnotes, see A. E. Musson, "Parliament and the Press: A Historical Survey—II," *Parliamentary Affairs* 9 (1955–56): 277–88; and see my *Poisoning the Minds of the Lower Orders* (Princeton, NJ: Princeton University Press, 1998), 71–74.

152. Mrs. Pendarves to Mrs. Ann Granville, 3 March 1739, in *The Autobiography and Correspondence of Mary Granville, Mrs. Delany*, ed. Lady Llanover, 3 vols. (London, 1861), 2:44–45. The story shifted in transmission: see Lady Mary to Lady Pomfret, [March 1739], in *The Complete Letters of Lady Mary Wortley Montagu*, ed. Robert Halsband, 3 vols. (Oxford: Clarendon, 1965–67), 2:135–37, where the "Amazons" got in by replacing their deafening "thumps, kicks, and raps, against the door" with "dead silence of half an hour," tricking the chancellor into thinking they'd gone away.

it's easy to infer that ordinarily women were private and their doings non-political. That's wrong. To be blunt, *public man, private woman* is a strait-jacket, not an incisive bit of critical theory. It's time, past time, to retire it.[153]

Postscript

I promised to return to some language in the *Spectator* and the *Free-Holder*. Recall the nub of their claims. The *Spectator* complains, "We have indeed carryed Womens Characters too much into publick Life," and con-tends their proper sphere is "Domestick Life," performing "the Duties of a Daughter, a Sister, a Wife, and a Mother." Here, whatever else it means, *public* serves as the opposite of family. Similarly, the *Free-Holder* inveighs against the "sharp political Humour" women have developed and wistfully recalls their former devotion to "domestick Life" and "private Affaires." These passages aren't alone. Daniel Rogers was horrified "that a woman should dare in publique, or in a private place after a publique manner to declare truthes of Religion: usurping over men, and encroaching upon the laws of Christ."[154] "I have not been bred, being a Woman, to publick Affairs," volunteered Margaret Cavendish.[155] One of Pope's verses is categorical:

> But grant, in Public Men sometimes are shown,
> A Woman's seen in Private life alone:
> Our bolder Talents in full light display'd;
> Your Virtues open fairest in the shade.
> Bred to disguise, in Public 'tis you hide;
> There, none distinguish 'twixt your Shame or Pride,
> Weakness or Delicacy; all so nice,
> That each may seem a Virtue, or a Vice.[156]

These sources demonstrate that contemporaries could deploy *public* and *private* in defending separate spheres or the view that a woman's place is in the home.[157]

153. I'm no Arendtian, but for a similar position, see Mary G. Dietz, *Turning Operations: Feminism, Arendt, and Politics* (New York: Routledge, 2002), chap. 6.

154. D[aniel] R[ogers], *Matrimoniall Honovr: or, The Mutuall Crowne and Comfort of Godly, Loyall, and Chaste Marriage* (London, 1642), 285.

155. Lady Marchioness of Newcastle, *Orations of Divers Sorts, Accommodated to Divers Places* (London, 1662), sig. B recto, italics reversed.

156. "Epistle to a Lady" [1735], in [Alexander] Pope, *Poetical Works*, ed. Herbert Davis (London: Oxford University Press, 1966), 296–97.

157. I'm skeptical of Mary Beth Norton's thesis that there's a sharp chronological break in the early

They could, but they rarely did. Here's the crux: if we put pressure on what these two periodicals meant in deploying the terms, we'll collapse back into tautology: women shouldn't concern themselves with government because women shouldn't concern themselves with government. No wonder we find separate-spheres sentiments not even in shouting distance of the public / private distinction. Elinor James expected resistance to her daring to defend the Church of England: "I know you will say *I am a Woman, and why should I trouble my self?*"[158] Take Daniel Rogers's sentiment: "A chast wife hath her eies open, eares watching, heart attending upon the welfare of the family, husband, children and servants: she thinks that all concerne her; estate, content, posterity: this rivets her into the house: makes her husband trust to her, commit all to her, heart and all."[159] Or this 1659 proverb: "Women in State-affairs, are like Munkies in Glas-shoppes."[160] However cogent or confused the theory of separate spheres, it gains no support from any public / private distinction.

Contemporaries had a lucid grasp of the grammar of the public / private distinctions. To suggest that they were systematically confused—that they routinely imagined women were private and that the family or patriarchal authority was nonpolitical—is to trample over what they said and did. So I have to be a recidivist: "Public man, private woman" is a straitjacket, not an incisive bit of critical theory. It's time, past time, to retire it.

1700s and that John Dunton is exemplary or responsible. See her *Separated by Their Sex*, chap. 3. The thesis leads Norton to describe one response to women's parliamentary petitions in the interregnum as "forecast[ing] the future" (65). I'm skeptical too of Norton's treatment of Margaret Cavendish. Norton acknowledges that decades before Dunton, Lady Margaret offers an apparently similar view, but argues that Lady Margaret is finally concerned with social status, not sex (99–100). Contrast Lady Margaret Newcastle [Cavendish], *The Worlds Olio* (London, 1655), preface, n.p., italics reversed: "Man is made to Govern Common-wealths, and Women their privat Families"; [Margaret Cavendish], Lady Marchioness of Newcastle, *CCXI Sociable Letters* (London, 1664), 12, 13, 27–28. Note too the diffidence expressed by women petitioning Parliament in *A True Copie of the Petition of the Gentlewomen, and Tradesmens-wives, in and about the City of London* (London, 1641), 6; contrast the women who "wonder and grieve that we should appear so despicable in your eyes" in *To the Supreme Authority of England the Commons Assembled in Parliament: The Humble Petition of Divers Wel-Affected Women* ([London, 1649]), n.p.

158. [Elinor James], *Mrs. James's Vindication of the Church of England* (London, 1687), 3.
159. R[ogers], *Matrimoniall Honovr*, 169.
160. J[ames] H[owell], *Proverbs: or, Old Sayed Sawes and Proverbs* (London, 1659), 12.

CHAPTER 4

Conflict

How could there be such a thing as household politics? Politics, you might well think, is conflict about government. If you have that view—and I do—and you think of government as an institution, namely that coercive apparatus we also call the state, then you'll think the very idea of household politics is a nonstarter. But suppose we stick with the idea that politics is conflict about government, but construe government as an activity, not an institution. To govern someone is to rule or exercise authority over her. This usage is still idiomatic today, but anyway the early modern English talked this way all the time. I've already canvassed some explicit invocations of household government, but *government* was deployed more broadly. A guide to educating well-born but clueless young men in foreign travel summoned up "the help and directions which they receive from those who usually go under the name of Governors, Companions, or what other notion you please; whose office is to take care of the Gentleman's person, improvement, and affairs. . . . These Governors so called, because they have the government of their Pupils."[1] So too a traveler reported that in Amsterdam, "the Women Governe their Women Hospitals better then the men do theirs."[2]

1. J. Gailhard, *The Compleat Gentleman: or, Directions for the Education of Youth* ([London], 1678), pt. 2, p. 7. See too Roger Ascham, *The Scholemaster* (London, 1570), 12.

2. W[illiam] C[arr], *Remarks of the Government of Severall Parts of Germanie, Denmark, Sweedland, Hamburg, Lubeck, and Hansiactique Townes* (Amsterdam, 1688), 31. For the governor and governess of a prison, see Henry Fielding, *Amelia* [1751], ed. Martin C. Battestin (Middletown, CT: Wesleyan University Press, 1983), 155–57.

Finally—and more pointedly for one relation within household government—take the incendiary exchange between Dorothy Fribble and her husband in another comedy. "I have been too tame," she reports, lamenting what a drunk he is. "Know your Lord and Master," he warns. "I am my own Mistress.[3] Did I marry a foolish Haberdasher to be govern'd by him?" she demands. Fribble apparently thinks repetition is magically effective: "Nay then, 'tis time to be in earnest. Huswife, know your Lord and Master, I say know your Lord and Master." She shoots back, "know your Lady and Mistress," so he threatens to beat her: "The Law allows me to give my Wife due correction. I know the Law, Huswife, consider and tremble." Furious, she calls him "Wittal"—a wittol is a cuckold who doesn't even protest his wife's adultery—and hits him. Provoked, he beats her and she apologetically yields, though she also sputters a threat in an aside. Bisket, another cuckold, gleefully salutes Fribble's bold assertion of masculine authority: "This is incomparable. Oh that I could govern my Wife thus!"[4]

We're inclined to reserve *politics* for the institution of government, I conjecture, because that institution is such an important locus of authority. But the government or state is not alone in governing, in exercising authority. Contemporary usage too was tugged in both directions: sometimes contemporary dictionaries defined *politics* as "the art of governing a State";[5] but sometimes they said simply, "the art of Government."[6] When the *Jacobite's Journal* wants to mock women interested in Whigs, Tories, and state policy, it sneers that "The very scandal at their Tea-Tables is political" or "my Wife's Head had taken a political turn"[7]—as if none of their other pursuits were

---

3. In *The Island Princess* [1646], in *The Dramatic Works in the Beaumont and Fletcher Canon*, ed. Fredson Bowers et al., 10 vols. (Cambridge: Cambridge University Press, 1966–96), 5:605, Quisara instructs Armusia, "I am Mistris of my selfe sir."

4. Tho[mas] Shadwell, *Epsom-Wells: A Comedy* (London, 1673), 71–73.

5. J[ohn] K[ersey], *A New English Dictionary* (London, 1713), s.v. *politicks;* see too J[ohn] B[ullokar], *The English Expositor Improv'd: Being a Complete Dictionary*, 12th ed. (London, 1719), s.v. *politicks.* See too John Wing, *The Crowne Conivgall: or, The Spovse Royall* (Middleburgh, 1620), 5–6, 16–18.

6. *Glossographia Anglicana Nova* (London, 1707), s.v. *politicks;* see too N[athan] Bailey, *An Universal Etymological English Dictionary*, 4th ed. (London, 1728), s.v. *politicks;* B[enjamin] N[orton] Defoe, *A Compleat English Dictionary* (Westminster, 1735), s.v. *politicks.*

7. *Jacobite's Journal*, 12 December 1747 and *Jacobite's Journal*, 23 July 1748, in Henry Fielding, *"The Jacobite's Journal" and Related Writings*, ed W. B. Coley ([Middletown, CT]: Wesleyan University Press, 1975), 99, 350. See too *Covent-Garden Journal*, 4 January 1752, in Henry Fielding, *"The Covent-Garden Journal" and "A Plan of the Universal Register-Office,"* ed. Bertrand A. Goldgar (Middletown, CT: Wesleyan University Press, 1988), 15.

political. Then again, Richard Brathwait warns his ideal gentlewoman not to discuss "*State-politicall action,* for the height of such a subject, compar'd with your weakenesse, were vnequall."[8] The stupid injustice of the warning isn't the point: what matters is the adjective *state-political,* which forcibly implies that there are other kinds of politics, too. Recall the *Complete Christian Dictionary*'s distinguishing three kinds of political servitude: subject to magistrate, child to parents, servant to master. Recall the words the old bachelor put in the mouth of a young lady, mockingly denying that women were so "out in their Politicks" that they'd blankly submit to husbands' echoing blather "on the Duty of a Wife." And consider now this exchange between Squire Western and his sister. The squire is forever spouting Country slogans about courtly corruption and trying to force his wayward daughter Sophia to marry the man he has chosen. His sister disapproves. The squire hurls an accusation at his sister: "'you have made a Whig of the Girl,'" he fumes. "'Brother,' answered Mrs. *Western,* with an Air of great Disdain, 'I cannot express the Contempt I have for your Politics of all Kinds.'"[9] His hatred of Westminster and his thuggish parenting both qualify as political.

Again, social life is shot through with authority: boss over worker, teacher over student, priest over flock, parent over child, surgeon over nurse, conductor over orchestra, sergeant over private, manager over baseball team, you name it. Because *government* wobbles between the institution and the activity, I'm going to substitute the gloss I've already mentioned: the core notion of *politics* is conflict over legitimate authority. Once we see that social life is shot through not just with authority but also with conflicts about that authority— once we wrest free of the thought that such authority is routinely "naturalized" or "essentialized," that the big sleep thesis is true—the way is clear to thinking about the politics of all kinds of social relations, clear too to grasping why there is nothing paradoxical about the politics of private life.

That politics is conflict over legitimate authority is concise, even cryptic.

8. Richard Brathwait, *The English Gentlewoman, Drawne out to the Full Body* (London, 1631), 91. See too *Free-Holder,* 9 April 1716; Lady Sarah's 1700 diary entry in Anne Kugler, *Errant Plagiary: The Life and Writing of Lady Sarah Cowper, 1644–1720* (Stanford, CA: Stanford University Press, 2002), 24; and Lord Mar's 1726 comment that his wife "never likt or inclined to medle in politicks," in *The Earl of Mar's Legacies to Scotland and His Son,* ed. Stuart Erskine, in *Diary of Sir Archibald Johnston . . .* (Edinburgh: University Press for the Scottish Historical Society, 1896), 177. Compare Alice Lisle's interrupting to volunteer a view of Monmouth's Rebellion during her August 1685 trial: *A Complete Collection of State-Trials, and Proceedings for High Treason,* 4th ed., 11 vols. (London, 1776–81), 4:107, 122.

9. Henry Fielding, *The History of Tom Jones: A Foundling* [1749], ed. Fredson Bowers, 2 vols. (Middletown, CT: Wesleyan University Press, 1975), 1:336; see too 2:847, 860.

So let me offer a few clarifying comments. One: as I've noticed, there are shallower and deeper kinds of conflict here. One might grant that someone has authority over someone else but protest the way in which that authority is deployed. To recur to the state, the complaint that the marginal income tax rate is too high is a political complaint even if one doesn't doubt the right of Congress to levy income taxes. That's a shallower kind of conflict. But sometimes political conflict runs deeper. Sometimes we think others have no legitimate authority whatever or that they've crossed the jurisdictional boundaries of whatever authority they do have. You might agree that your doctor has authority to instruct you to cut back on salt (though you might think she can only offer advice), but balk at her telling you to vote Democratic.

Two: we might describe some situation as political even though there is no conflict about it. Take the stereotypical capitalist, screwing his workers for all he can, feasting on foie gras while they eat scanty bowls of gruel in their frigid hovels. Suppose the workers don't grumble. Perhaps they don't see themselves as exploited or perhaps they fear being fired—or fired at, by Pinkerton guards. We might say this bleak situation is politicized only when conflict emerges. But we also might say it's political without any conflict. By that we might mean that it is ripe for conflict or properly the scene of conflict: we could be making a prediction or offering a normative proposal. It is then coherent, too, to invoke politics in describing even the unwitting zombies stumbling through life in an undead state of big sleep. It happens that that's not the sense in which I'm invoking household politics to discuss the contentious scenes of early modern England.

Three: I want to contrast authority to power, where authority embeds some claim to rule by right and power is a descriptive capacity. The schoolyard bully has the power to get the nerd's lunch money, but he has no authority over him. Conversely, after the coup d'état the vanquished Parliament may still enjoy legitimate authority, but it can't go on governing. So *legitimate authority* sounds redundant. Yet *illegitimate authority* can be idiomatic. Picture a staunch Jacobite depressed that so many subjects dutifully obey Queen Anne. He might say she enjoys illegitimate authority to acknowledge that they are doing more than submitting to the brute fact of power: they think she has a right to rule, but he thinks they're wrong. He may enthusiastically join in the '45, the uprising supposed to put bonnie Prince Charlie, inheritor of the Stuart line, back on the throne. His opponents will label Charles *the pretender* to insinuate that his claims to royal authority are illegitimate. This debate too is political and it's about the legitimacy of authority, no tautology at all.

Also I prefer sometimes saying *legitimate authority* to highlight normative disputes. Some suggestions circulating among political scientists—that politics is about who gets what when and how,[10] that all politics is distributive,[11] that we focus on pressure groups exerting power on legislatures[12]—are supposed to be hardheaded. But they conceal the stakes.[13]

Yet another reason I'll repeat *legitimate* is to advert to my broader sense of politics: controversy about the legitimacy of social practices. Here we can shift the focus from authority to legitimacy. So what sense of legitimacy is in play? Sometimes *legitimate* means *acceptable* or *good enough*. Here, though, I want to distinguish technical or efficiency concerns from those of good or bad and especially right or wrong. Even in the case of state policy, we can take this route. Return to the complaint about the marginal tax rate. We might want to focus on Congress's use of authority. But we might instead want to emphasize only that the rule is unfair and silently take for granted that it's imposed by authority. Contrast the view that the marginal tax rate is 3 percent too high and won't optimize any plausible mix of tax revenues and economic productivity: we're likely to describe that as a technical dispute, not a political one. Those studying bureaucracy remind us that buried in the ostensible technical details of implementing a rule are significant political choices, so any view on which the legislature defines the end and administrative agencies merely implement the means is drastically misleading. Whether we should care about efficiency is itself often a political question. But once there's only a technical question, it's not political.

There is then nothing mysterious about the idea of household politics or government; no reason to balk when contemporaries discuss it; no reason to imagine it as metaphorical or parasitic on "real" politics; no reason to worry that when I discuss it, I'm imposing an anachronistic vocabulary born out of feminist insights unavailable centuries ago. The early modern English understood that husbands exercised authority over wives, parents over children,

10. Harold D. Lasswell, *Politics: Who Gets What, When, How* (New York: Whittesley House, 1936).

11. E. E. Schattschneider, *Politics, Pressure, and the Tariff* (New York: Prentice-Hall, 1935).

12. Arthur F. Bentley, *The Process of Government* (Chicago: University of Chicago Press, 1908).

13. For a drily amusing tour through other definitions, see John Dunn, *The Cunning of Unreason: Making Sense of Politics* (New York: Basic Books, 2000), chap. 1; and compare his own elliptical gloss at 133.

and so on. They understood that these were relations of governance. They understood that they were politically controversial and they pursued those controversies with antic energy and high seriousness.

Much has been written in recent years about authority. Even the core intuition, that authority is the right to govern with a corresponding obligation on subjects to obey, is questionable. Take epistemic authority. Suppose we say of some distinguished scholar, "She's an authority in the field." Surely we don't mean that she has a right to tell us what to believe. Nor that we are strictly obliged to believe what she says, though it's ordinarily sensible for us to. Maybe epistemic and practical authority are two different notions. But maybe some more abstract but unified concept, keeping the sense of *ought to obey* but softening *right* and *obligation,* will generate both notions. Still, the *ought* can't collapse into a prudential ought, lest the sense in which you ought to obey the mugger with brandished gun and bulging eyes turns him into an authority and so collapses the distinction between authority and power. Then there are ongoing disputes about Joseph Raz's service conception of authority and his normal justification thesis: that authority is justified (or obtains) when the subject will do a better job complying with the dictates of reason by obeying the authority than by trying to sort things out on his own.[14] Well, a father exercises authority over his eight-year-old son in telling him not to bother brushing his teeth before bedtime. If a dentist wandering by orders the child to brush his teeth, it seems odd to say the dentist suddenly has authority. He's just butting in, even though he's right on the merits.

I don't want to join that discussion. Instead I want to focus on conflict. When we say politics is conflict over legitimate authority, there's a distinctive sense of conflict worth picking out. Even better, there's a historically prominent family of positions in social and political theory worth taking on. The family clusters around the view that social order requires consensus. But it doesn't. Conflict, I'll argue, isn't the opposite of social order. It's what social order usually is. I will be turning to domestic service in early modern England. So I shall begin with vignettes that seem to support the views I'll reject.

---

14. It's not always entirely clear whether Raz's normal justification thesis tells us (as its name forcibly implies) how we ordinarily justify authority or what authority is, that is, whether it's a substantive normative view or an analytic point about the structure of the concept: consider his "Authority and Justification," *Philosophy & Public Affairs* 14, no. 1 (1985): esp. 21–22. For the latest version of Raz's view, see his "The Problem of Authority: Revisiting the Service Conception," *Minnesota Law Review* 90, no. 4 (2006): 1003–44. For recent powerful criticisms, see Stephen Darwall, "Authority and Reasons: Exclusionary and Second-Personal," *Ethics* 120, no. 2 (2010): 257–78; Scott Hershovitz, "The Role of Authority," *Philosophers' Imprint* 11, no. 7 (2011): 1–19.

Elizabeth Branch and her daughter were sentenced to death for murdering their servant Jane Buttersworth. Buttersworth was fourteen years old.[15]

> In the Course of the Evidence it appear'd, that the Deceas'd had been sent to a neighbouring Place for some Barm, (or Yeast,) but forging a Lye, so exasperated the Daughter, that she violently struck her with her Fist about the Head, and pinch'd her Ears. That then the Prisoners jointly flung her upon her Face upon the Floor, and in the Presence of *Anne Somers*, (who was the Dairy-Maid, and the principal Evidence) the Daughter kneel'd upon the Deceased's Neck, and both Mother and Daughter whipp'd her with Twigs for a considerable Time, till she ran with Blood. That then the Daughter took off one of the Deceased's Shoes, and beat her about the Breech and Hips with the Heel thereof, keeping her with her Knee on the Ground, and the Mother still whipping. That the Deceased getting up ran into the Parlour, and was presently followed by both the Prisoners, who now had got Sticks, with which they beat her about the Head and Shoulders, driving her from Place to Place, till the Deceased was quite amazed and unable to stand. That then the Daughter threw Part of a Pail of Water on the Deceased to cool her, as she call'd it. That the Daughter afterwards rubb'd her Breech with Salt, which was all bloody with whipping.

Somers came back to find Buttersworth lying in a different cap, this one bloodied too: "presently she told her old Mistress the Girl was dead; on which she call'd her *Welch* Bitch." Mistress and daughter tried burying Buttersworth on the theory that she'd died suddenly, but after "Muttering among the Neighbours," an autopsy revealed that her skull had been broken. Twice.[16] At the Branches' trial, Henry Butler, their young servant boy, recalled being terrified at their cruelty. Mother and daughter, he testified,

> very frequently would throw Plates, Knives and Forks at my Head, because (as I being a Country Boy) I could not wait at Table genteely, or to please them. But once in particular, upon my letting fall a Plate at Dinner, the Prisoners, Mother and Daughter arose from the Table and beat me in such a Manner, that what with the Fright and Blows together my Lord, craving your Lordship's Pardon, I beshit myself, and then the Prisoners took up my Turd, thrust it into my Mouth, and made me eat it.[17]

---

15. *Inhumanity and Barbarity Not to Be Equal'd: Being an Impartial Relation of the Barbarous Murder Committed by Mrs. Elizabeth Branch and Her Daughter* (London, [1740]), 7.

16. *London Magazine*, April 1740, 191; the same report is in the *London Evening-Post*, 12 April 1740.

17. *The Cruel Mistress; Being, the Genuine Trial of Elizabeth Branch, and Her Own Daughter; for the Murder of Jane Buttersworth, Their Servant Maid* (London, 1740), 24–25. This source has a parade of

Another account has Butler reporting that the mother held him down while the daughter "took his Excrement out of his Breeches, mix'd it with Ashes, and cramm'd it into his Mouth."[18] The Branches were duly convicted[19] and hustled off to jail "under a very strong Guard in the Dead of the Night, for Fear lest the People should seize the Prisoners and tear them to Pieces."[20] The authorities scheduled the hangings for between 3:00 and 4:00 in the morning, apparently to avoid a stampede. It didn't work. A delay of a few hours—the scaffold needed rebuilding—caused "the great Disappointment of several Thousand People, who came far and near to see a publick Example made of two Wretches that so much deserv'd it."[21] Similar preparations and popular vehemence surrounded the 1689 execution of Elizabeth Deacon for murdering her servant Mary Cox.[22]

Servants, too, often played the villain's role. One "took the Opportunity of his Master's Absence to murther his Mistress and her Child, after which he rifled the House and fled."[23] One servant maid, twenty-two years old, slipped out before dawn and hurled her mistress's infant into the ocean to drown: "The miserable Wretch has only to excuse so barbarous an Action, as she pretends, that when she was uneasy in her Service, her Mistress would not suffer her to go away."[24] Another servant murdered his mistress and then her daughter, who happened to return from the mill, so he could steal £10 and two gold rings. He then burned down the house to destroy the evidence. But he lurked in the neighborhood and robbed another house, so he got caught.[25]

character witnesses; *The Trial of Mrs. Branch, and Her Daughter, for the Murder of Jane Buttersworth*, 2nd ed. (London, [1740?]), 17, recounts Butler's testimony but says it wasn't admitted because there were no character witnesses.

18. *Inhumanity and Barbarity*, 31.

19. *London Evening-Post*, 14 July 1733: "Thomas Morsh, a Weaver at Braintree, and Elizabeth his Wife, were try'd for murdering William Seabrook, their Apprentice, by starving him to Death; but it appearing that the Boy had been a disorderly Servant, and had contracted some Distempers which might occasion the same, the Jury acquitted them."

20. *Cruel Mistress*, 34–35.

21. *London Magazine*, May 1740, 241.

22. *A Remarkable Account of the Penitent Carriage and Behaviour of the Whip-makers Wife, Both before and since Her Confinement in Newgate* (London, 1689), 1–2. For a maudlin verse account of the murder, see *The VVhipster of VVoodstreet, or, A True Account of the Barbarous and Horrid Murther Committed on the Body of Mary Cox, Late Servant in Woodstreet London* ([London, 1689?]).

23. *London Journal*, 1 January 1726.

24. *Old Whig: or, The Consistent Protestant*, 9 June 1737. For a more bloodcurdlingly violent servant, see *A Lamentable Ballad of the Tragical End of a Gallant Lord and Vertuous Lady* (London, [1750?]).

25. *A Strange and Horrible Relation of a Bloody and Inhumane Murther . . . : or, The Bloody Servant* (London, 1674). These are two separate cases, despite the title's *or*; I have in mind the second one.

After "a small falling-out, about the Dressing of a Dinner," a servant tried to burn down the house, with "her Master and Mistriss, with all the rest of the Family," in bed.[26] Nor is it only a matter of wicked servants attacking their employers. Sixteen-year-old Thomas Savage finally took the advice of a woman at a bawdy house: he killed a fellow maidservant so he could rob his master.[27] When one servant failed to seduce "a very pretty young maid" he worked with, his brother and sister helped him mangle her face—an eye gouged out, the nose slashed badly enough that she could produce two bones in court—perhaps so no one else would enjoy her charms.[28] "Notorious Strumpet" Judith Brown slept with her master at least twice and then joined him in poisoning her mistress. The deed took plenty of attempts: theirs was no regrettable impulse.[29]

I could go on—the early modern English devoured crime narratives as voraciously as we do[30]—but you get the idea. No wonder that contemporaries celebrated consensus in the household. "If the Husband, the wife, the children and seruants bend all one way," as one 1634 rhapsody has it, "great is the vnity and concord of that house."[31] Listen to the imploring tones of a 1660 broadside:

> Oh ye *Children* and *Servants!* be subject and obedient unto your *Parents* and *Superiours* in the Lord, and be not *froward* and *perverse, wilful,* nor *obstinate,* but *dutiful and submissive, tractable and condescending* to every of their equal and just *requirings,* that there may be no varience, strife, emulation nor contention in your families, but that love and peace may abound among

26. *The Jesuites Firing-Plot Revived: or, A Warning to House-Keepers* (London, 1680). See too *The Poysoners Rewarded: or, The Most Barbarous of Murthers, Detected and Punished* ([London], 1687).

27. R[ichard] A[lleine], *A Murderer Punished and Pardoned* (London, 1668), or, more briefly, *Gods Justice against Murther: or, The Bloody Apprentice Executed* (London, [1668]).

28. *A True Narrative of the Proceedings at the Sessions-House in the Old-Bayly, at a Sessions There Held on April 25, and 26, 1677* (London, 1677), 6–7; or in *OBP,* 25 April 1677 (t16770425–6).

29. William Smith, *A Just Account of the Horrid Contrivance of John Cupper, and Judith Brown His Servant, in Poysoning His Wife* (London, 1686 [1684]); for a ballad treatment, *The Unfaithful Servant; and the Cruel Husband* (n.p., 1684), in *The Pepys Ballads,* ed. Hyder Edward Rollins, 8 vols. (Cambridge, MA: Harvard University Press, 1929–32), 3:132–34. For a woman who kills her drunken husband, who has beaten her, and the night after he's buried sleeps with her former apprentice, see *Great and Bloody News: From Farthing-Ally, in St. Thomas's Southwark, of the True and Faithful Relatjon of a Horid and Barbarous Murther, Committed on the Body of Walter Osily, by His Own Wife* (n.p., [1680?]).

30. For a useful reminder of what can be missing in tales of criminality, see Garthine Walker, *Crime, Gender and Social Order in Early Modern England* (Cambridge: Cambridge University Press, 2003), 50–51.

31. F[rancis] M[eres], *Wits Common Wealth: The Second Part* (London, 1634), 290–91.

you all; And see that you flee and avoid all *youthful lusts,* and that you put away *childishness,* and become *grave, sober,* and *discreet,* daily provoking one another to love and to good works, and not to lightness nor wantonness, nor to folly and vanity which doth not become Saints; And withall be ye perswaded and advised to dwell together in unity, love and peace, and be ye helpful one to another in what you may; And thereby *ingage* you one another in love to serve one another, and thereby you will come to be indeared one unto another, and so will come to be refreshed together with the sweet sincere milk of the Word of life from the breasts of consolation.[32]

I'll return to the suggestion that servants should love their masters. For now, consider juxtaposing bloodcurdling tales of domestic violence to paeans to consensus. It's plausible to enlist the tales as support for the paeans.

But again, the embrace of consensus isn't unique to domestic service in early modern England. It surfaces in other settings and under other guises. Some examples will help indicate what I have in mind. An old favorite, from 1536:

A comune welth is, as I thynke, no thynge elles but a certayne nombre of cities, townes, shires, that all agre, upon one lawe, and one hed, unyted and knytte together, by thobseruation of the lawes: these kept, they must nedes florishe, these broken, they muste nedes perisshe. The heed muste rule, if the body woll do well, and not euery man make hym selfe ruler, where only one ought to be.

Or again, from the same text:

We muste agree in religion, we must serue but one mayster, one body wyll haue but one heed. It is not possible men to agree longe, that dissent in religion. No more than it is possyble, christen men to agree with turkes. Howe be it, who wyll not thynke it moch better, to dissent, then that we all agree, upon pernytious errours? Whiche haue noo defence but this onely, that they haue regned long, and that men hath long ben subiecteto them. The nobles muste be of one beleue, of one fayth, of one religion, they must all agre vpon one heed. The gentylmen wyll folowe, the comunes can not tary longe behynde.[33]

---

32. *William Catons Salutation and Advise unto Gods Elect* (London, 1660).

33. [Sir Richard Morison], *A Remedy for Sedition, Wherin Are Conteyned Many Thynges, concernyng the True and Loyal Obeysance, That Commes Owe vnto Their Prince and Soueraygne Lorde the Kynge* ([London], 1536), n.p.

You may not like that spelling, but how about the prose style of this modern social theorist?

> Finally, to crown the hierarchy, in connection with the same theory of social utility there has been found to emerge a version of the sociologistic theorem. At the rationalized pole . . . it takes the form of the conception of the "end a society should pursue by means of logico-experimental reasoning." This may be restated to the effect that the actions of the members of a society are to a significant degree oriented to a single integrated system of ultimate ends common to these members. More generally the value element in the form both of ultimate ends and of value attitudes is in a significant degree common to the members of the society. This fact is one of the essential conditions of the equilibrium of social systems.[34]

That's pretty much what Albania figured out in Enver Hoxha's glory days. From Article 38 of the 1976 constitution:

> The rights and duties of citizens are built on the basis of the reconciliation of the interests of the individual and the socialist society, giving priority to the general interest.
> The rights of the citizens are inseparable from the fulfilment of their duties and cannot be exercised in opposition to the socialist order.
> The further extension and deepening of the rights of citizens are closely linked with the socialist development of the country.[35]

Historians might wince at swooping across centuries, continents, and issues this way. But the bird's-eye view brings out a striking family resemblance among the doughty opponent of the Pilgrimage of Grace, the earnest if tongue-tied assistant professor of sociology, and the official storytellers of Albania. You might merrily chime in with plenty more examples: cozy *gemeinschaft* against aloof *gesellschaft*, the putative good old days of racial and ethnic homogeneity, the center will not hold, the times are sick and out of joint, the Roman Catholic Church's ongoing dirge for the unity of Christendom, the protest that departmentalism must be a faulty theory of American constitutionalism, and so on; and since I am being sober about this, I shan't add *ad nauseam*. Or you might impatiently wish that I would start drawing

34. Talcott Parsons, *The Structure of Social Action: A Study in Social Theory with Special Reference to a Group of Recent European Writers* (New York: McGraw-Hill, 1937), 707.

35. *Special Supplement: The People's Republic of Albania*, in *Constitutions of the Countries of the World*, ed. Albert P. Blaustein and Gisbert H. Flanz (n.p.: Oceana, 1976).

some distinctions. Surely these aren't all exactly the same view. Perhaps some are more plausible than others. Perhaps some are even right.

Sure. In fact I will endorse one version of the thesis that social order requires consensus, even while rejecting what so many of its champions maintain. So I want now to pick out a concept of conflict that will illuminate both the suggestion that politics is conflict over legitimate authority and the deficiencies of these hallowed bids for consensus.

Distinguishing Conflict and Enmity

Let's distinguish conflict and enmity. This might summon up how intense some antipathy is—say, the difference between polite disagreement and steaming hatred—but I don't mean that. I want instead a distinction between disagreements pursued in relatively structured ways and those without real ground rules. The lack of ground rules doesn't mean that hostility will break out. So enmity is a subset of a broader category—say, confusion.

I can work up this distinction with a series of examples. Bobby and Ruth sit down to play chess. Bobby opens P-K4. Ruth responds P-Q3.[36] Here we have a kind of conflict: each wants, within the world created by the rules of the game, to kill the other. Bobby and Ruth's conflict is enabled by agreement on the rules of chess. Neither will try to move a bishop as if it were a knight: at least not as a serious move, though maybe as a whimsical way of conceding or indicating battle fatigue. Indeed the very category *move* can incorporate the rules of the game. If Ruth picks up a bishop and moves it three squares directly forward, we might call it an illegal move, but we might deny it was a move at all. Despite some familiar skepticism about rules, the rules of chess exhaustively cover what moves are legal. Particular players may be confused, say about how pawns capture *en passant*. Factual disputes can be tricky: you have to move a piece once you touch it, but it might not be obvious whether a player did touch a piece.

Still, the central point holds: agreement on clear rules enables sharp conflict. So it's confused to imagine that consensus is the opposite of conflict or the cure for it. Now suppose Emma and Sam sit down at a chessboard.

---

36. Compare Georg Simmel, *"Conflict"* & *"The Web of Group-Affiliations,"* trans. Kurt H. Wolff and Reinhard Bendix (New York: Free Press, 1964), 34–35. I owe a lot to Simmel, even though his interests lie more in causation and psychology than do my own. Lewis A. Coser, *The Functions of Social Conflict* (Glencoe, IL: Free Press, 1956), remains useful on Simmel's characteristically rich and difficult essay. I owe something too to Marx's analysis of how capitalists and proletariat are locked in combat.

Emma opens P-K4. Sam smashes an overripe banana into the middle of the board and glares at her. If Emma says, "Come on, that's not a move," Sam can respond cheekily, "I know that. We agree on what the moves are." So the notion of agreeing on the rules needs sharpening. They both have to be following the rules, orienting themselves to the activity the rules constitute. Take this borderline case: all of Emma's moves are legal, but they don't follow any recognizable strategy for winning; she aimlessly moves and waits for Sam to mop up. Is she playing chess?

For it to be true that we are playing chess, we need not many-leveled mutual understanding of individual intentions (so that I know you are making chess moves across from me with the intention of continuing the game, and you know that I'm doing the same across from you, and I know that you know, and . . .), but a shared intention.[37] If you're tempted by the behaviorist thought that all that matters is whether the publicly observable evidence is that the moves are legal, try this example. Two children approach a chessboard with the pieces set up properly. Neither one knows how to play chess. They take turns pushing pieces around the board. Coincidentally, every "move" is not only legal but also sensible. By the time they quit, white has a decisive positional advantage. If you think the children were playing chess without knowing it or something like that, I think you're in the clutches of old-fashioned dogmas about science that never were defensible anyway. But I leave that aside and return to the case of the mysterious banana.

Suppose Emma thought she was sitting down to a game of chess, not a session of Ionesco improvisations. Suppose Sam glares menacingly but does not reply when Emma complains that smashing a banana isn't a move. Here we have enmity but not yet conflict. There's some sense of antagonism in the air, probably enough for a Weberian to count whatever Emma does next as social action, meaningfully oriented to what Sam has done.[38] The two almost surely share interests in bodily security and the absence of pain. But as a Wittgensteinian might put it, it is entirely unclear how Emma is to proceed or even what would qualify as a sensible response. Juggle three strawberries?

37. For the basic intuitions, see Margaret Gilbert, *Living Together: Rationality, Sociality, and Obligation* (Lanham, MD: Rowman & Littlefield, 1996), chap. 6; for more formal accounts, compare J. David Velleman, "How to Share an Intention," *Philosophy and Phenomenological Research* 57, no. 1 (1997): 29–50; Michael E. Bratman, *Faces of Intention: Selected Essays on Intention and Agency* (Cambridge: Cambridge University Press, 1999), pt. 2.

38. Max Weber, *Economy and Society: An Outline of Interpretive Sociology*, ed. Guenther Roth and Claus Wittich, trans. Ephraim Fischoff et al., 2 vols. (Berkeley: University of California Press, 1978), 1:22–24.

Say sadly, "If only I had some ice cream and hot fudge"? It's unclear because she no longer knows what game they're playing, what they're up to.

It's not enough that the next move be predictable. That requirement will be met readily amid postapocalyptic rubble—if I hurl a rock, he'll duck—but that's no social order. Nor is it enough that the next move be intelligible. At least some of the ways in which actions can be meaningful don't require social order or any conventional code, either. The next move needs to be *permissible:* it has to be legitimate for the others to do what they do. Depending on the context, we might rely on the appraisals of participants or onlookers.

That permissibility is the relevant category might seem absurd. After all, conflict often arises when people act impermissibly. Now it's easy to invoke permissibility when different rules apply to the same case. The contract requires the workers to show up for work, but they go on strike. Then we can rescue the claim that their strike is permissible by shifting our focus to labor law, which contradicts and is superior to the contract provisions. The problem is harder when there's no formal alternate and superior body of rules. Kathy instructs her pupils to work quietly at their desks, but hyperactive Bill zips around the room and she reprimands him. It's straightforwardly true that he isn't permitted to do that, but it seems wrong that this is a case of enmity, not conflict. Though it might sound paradoxical, I want to suggest that there are ordinarily permissible and impermissible ways of breaking the rules. It's idiomatic to say, "You may not disobey that way." So Kathy might instruct Bill if he hurled a raw egg at her. In effect, we have rules about how to break rules. That there can be disputes at that level, too, doesn't threaten the point. There's no disturbing infinite regress here.

Conflict, then, requires some shared background. The requisite sharing seems to be richer than interests in bodily security and the absence of pain. Those feature prominently in Hobbes's state of nature, where people have a "right of nature" to use anything and everything, even others' bodies, to their own advantage. But I'd take that as pure enmity. Again, I take ordinary chess as a paradigm case of conflict. Because Bobby and Ruth share the rules of chess, they can try to destroy one another. Emma and Sam's curious variant might turn out to be fisticuffs, with rules or something less formal forbidding, say, biting or kicking in the genitals. That, too, would turn it into conflict.[39]

---

39. Contrast Chantal Mouffe's distinction between antagonism and agonism: see *The Democratic Paradox* (London: Verso, 2000), 101–5, and *On the Political* (London: Routledge, 2005), 20–23, 52. Mouffe's distinction layers together considerations I'd rather keep separate: whether the parties share some common ground (namely, adherence to democratic structures), whether they view one another as

We can turn Sam and Emma's misbegotten encounter at the chessboard in another direction. It isn't always obvious what game is being played, let alone what the rules of any particular game are. You thought we were going on our first date and I thought we were grabbing some coffee before returning to work: how awkward! So now we have to grope our way to some more or less (in)complete meeting of the minds on what we are doing. We have a rich repertoire of quiet maneuvers to signal discomfort and try to get back on track. But they're not foolproof and there's room at that level too for conflict.

My central motif here—what we share enables conflict—isn't some freak possibility. It's an endlessly reiterated feature of ordinary life. Take being locked in disagreement. You think Obama is a great president. She thinks he's a Muslim terrorist from Kenya. You argue about it regularly. The possibility of an argument here depends on lots of stuff the two of you share. If she adds that he can't be a great president because the United States is ruled by Brussels's bureaucrats or was dissolved in 1973 by the Trilateral Commission or is a figment of your imagination, it will be very hard to see how you could argue. Not least of what you need to share is language: vocabulary, rules of grammar—I mean the informal ones of everyday use, not the arcane ones your fussy English teacher adored—and so on. Yes, sharing a language enables cooing in harmony. But it also enables defiance, contempt, and the like. Yes, heated disagreements sometimes threaten social relationships. ("I can't deal with him anymore.") But sometimes they comprise those relationships. All the two of you do is argue about Obama. Were it not for that, you'd never see or even think of one another. So it's a mistake to think that your social relationship consists in what you share. Conflict here isn't an acid bath dissolving social bonds. It's what those social bonds consist in. As a moment's introspection should confirm, conflictual bonds can be far more charged, more intimate too, than cooperative or amiable ones.

I've been relying on rules to give a sense of when we might share an understanding of what can permissibly come next. But especially with chess in mind, *rule* may seem to summon up something much crisper or more formal than we need. True, rules needn't be written down. Rules for riding the elevator: every time someone gets on or off, move around to maintain

---

legitimate, and whether violence will erupt. And—I'm off the boat here—agonism has to be deep enough to extend to "a struggle between opposing hegemonic projects which can never be reconciled rationally" (*On the Political*, 21). One wonders whether this picture, coupled with her insistence on the limits of pluralism, leaves any substantial room between her and the liberals she derides or whether she merely has another vocabulary.

equal body distance from everyone else; make no sustained eye contact with anyone else, but stare at the floor numbers or your feet; engage in no sustained conversation. Probably no one ever sat you down and spelled out these rules. If someone did, it was after you embarrassed yourself with utterly clueless behavior on an elevator, or maybe you had bizarrely pedantic parents. Nor did anyone explicitly supply you with more general rules of which these are instances: say, don't get too close to strangers. Even if left tacit, these maxims are crisp enough to qualify as rules. Not so other maxims: take "Don't be a jerk" or "Take reasonable care." So we have a choice. We can relax the notion of *rule* to include the judgments here at issue. Or we can admit that considerations less structured than rules are enough to supply the shared background making conflict possible. I think the latter the better course, lest we have to distinguish different kinds of rules and so awkwardly reproduce distinctions already on offer, if roughly, in everyday English.

We can model the distinction between conflict and enmity as dimensional or binary. For the dimensional version, there are two independent considerations: how precisely the background considerations govern what we may do, and how much we share those considerations. Then we can start with a case of pure conflict and move gradually toward pure enmity. For the binary version, stick in thresholds or cut-off points, and decree that everything on one side is conflict, on the other enmity. Precisely because the rules of chess are so clear and so obviously shared, it's hard to summon up even a trace of enmity. But I want to emphasize two relax-the-constraints possibilities: the background considerations can themselves be relatively thin and the extent of our sharing them can be relatively fragmentary and uncertain. Let me take each in turn.

On the first, it's tempting to assume that we share ends or values or, in the tortured words of the sociologistic theorem, "a single integrated system of ultimate ends." But this is just another case of the mysteriously powerful allure of instrumental rationality. Against that view, consider driving. The rules of driving enable us to hurtle around in our death machines with a relatively low mortality rate. We follow the rules from some mix of prudence (accidents are dangerous, traffic tickets costly), habit, respect for morality and law, and more. But each of us drives to her own destination for her own reasons. Sharing right-hand drive and the rest is not sharing a value or an end. Yes, our regard for life and limb shapes the practice. But that's manifestly not the end of driving: if it were, we wouldn't drive at all. Consensus on the rules of driving enables a cacophony of ends: Jane drives to church, Kasia to the Village Atheist Society, but they don't know or care about that when they pull into the same intersection, where the background rules enable them to proceed smoothly and safely.

On the second, it's useful to cultivate an allergy to communitarian gestures toward "our shared" traditions, culture, and so on. Just how many people share just what is a contingent question. Often the answer is not that many and not that much. Think about your experiences downtown, on a subway, in a small town two or three states away. Not that you don't share anything with those you encounter, but that it's wrong to suppose that you must share a whole lot. Nor do we always settle on what game we're playing. Someone can always make a disruptive move; ambiguity and confusion can linger, sometimes to spectacular lengths. Strategic actors will often find confusion and opacity useful.[40] Suppose Adrian and Daryl are rival candidates in a close race. Some campaign measures are surely in bounds: each may attack the other's policy proposals or highlight the merits of his own. Some are surely out of bounds: neither may solicit the murder or kidnapping of his opponent. But the two might well dispute the legitimacy of, say, raising questions about the other's family life. Adrian might think this is private and out of bounds. Daryl might think the voters are properly interested in character. Or he might be behind in the polls and reluctantly responding to his campaign manager's urging him to go negative. So suppose Daryl issues a press release about Adrian's berating his son at a Little League game. It's not quite that Adrian wouldn't know how to carry on or what would count as a legitimate response. He wouldn't be mystified, as he would if Daryl were to hold a press conference to smash a banana into a chessboard. So Adrian could issue a press release deploring his opponent's irrelevant and malicious charge and he'd likely intimate that it was false anyway. But Adrian would think Daryl's charge illegitimate. He might regret that the rules of the game have changed and he might wonder what the new boundaries are. But he might think, okay, there's going to be mudslinging about family life and I know how to play that game, too. I want to keep disputes about legitimacy on the *conflict*

---

40. J. David Velleman, *How We Get Along* (Cambridge: Cambridge University Press, 2009), esp. chap. 3, helpfully deploys the notions of scenario and improvisational collaboration. He suggests "that departures from the going way of life must have the form of improvisational overtures, extended in the hope of gaining uptake from other improvisers" (110). That *must* seems to me excessive, whether construed as logical, empirical, or normative necessity.

side of the conflict/enmity distinction. I want to reserve *enmity* for when there's serious question about what the rules are and people don't come close to settling on even a provisional answer.

Does the outbreak of violence mean we're facing enmity? No: violence, as grisly as you like, can be part of the repertoire of extremely well-structured social interactions. Take dueling, which became as stylized as kabuki while still leading to death. Take boxing with Queensberry rules. It's impermissible to stab your opponent, permissible to deliver a right uppercut to the jaw. Take everyday references to military conflict. But should we restrict political conflict to struggles without violence? Carl Schmitt (in)famously suggested that politics bottoms out on a distinction between friends and enemies, one depending on "the real possibility of physical killing."[41] If killing is a real possibility, what happens when the shooting starts? Has politics been replaced by something else or is it even more intensively political? In urging that war is nothing but the continuation of policy by other means, Clausewitz was adamant that war remains fully political.[42] Closer to home, recall the episodes on and off the allegedly comic stage where marital bickering gave way to marital battering. Did the battering mark the end of a political conflict or ratchet up its intensity? The Branches were deviant in murdering one servant and forcing another to eat shit. Did their deviance mark the end of a political conflict or ratchet up its intensity?

I take the latter view. One can side with Schmitt here without beginning to endorse his view that liberalism is deeply antipolitical, parliamentary democracy a cheap joke. Usually we don't pursue political disputes by using violence. Sometimes we do. We may be drawn to the pacifist sentiment that violence is never justified. But most of us can also rattle off plenty of instances where we think it fully justified. I'd diagnose residual uncertainty about whether violence marks the end of political conflict as a symptom of that background ambivalence. Nor need one treat all these examples the same way. The Branches' savage violence tips over into enmity because it's hard to understand it as permissible. Happily, not much finally hangs on this aspect of how we carve the concept of political conflict. One approach means saying that the conflicts of household politics are sometimes intense enough to

41. Carl Schmitt, *The Concept of the Political*, trans. George Schwab (Chicago: University of Chicago Press, 1996), 33.

42. Carl von Clausewitz, *On War*, trans. Michael Howard and Peter Paret (Princeton, NJ: Princeton University Press, 1976), 605.

include violence; the other, that those political conflicts eventually yield to violence. The underlying facts are the same and they're ominously familiar.

A Few More Distinctions

I need a few more distinctions to hone my objections to the time-honored wisdom about consensus and social order. First, the connection between consensus and social order might be causal or constitutive. On a causal view, consensus is one state of affairs, social order another, and without the first, we won't get the second. On a constitutive view, the criteria for social order include consensus. So imagine pressing back on the 1536 claim that we must agree in religion. We might say that the United States has many religions and seems orderly enough. One response might be: ah, but the rot has set in and everything will decay. ("It is not possible men to agree longe, that dissent in religion.") That suggests a causal mechanism. But another response might be: no, sorry, you can't call a society orderly whose members aren't devoted to a single communion. Or: religious pluralism is inherently disorderly. That's the constitutive view. You can always stipulate that your criteria for social order are very rich, so that all sorts of societies that strike others as orderly really aren't so. But that approach is arbitrary.

The causal and constitutive views needn't be mutually exclusive. Suppose there are logically necessary but not sufficient conditions for social order: that would be the constitutive part of the claim. Then suppose those same conditions produce whatever else is required to secure social order: that would be the causal part of the claim. Or perhaps some conditions play a constitutive role, other conditions a causal one. Such thoughts don't license a drearily familiar equivocation: it doesn't make sense to offer a causal claim and then meet objections by retreating to a constitutive claim.

Second, we should allow that there can be good and bad instantiations of social order. Ordinarily, it's good to have order, bad not to. It doesn't yet follow that social order is itself a normative concept. It's good to drink water with no lead in it, but that doesn't make *water* or *lead* an evaluative term. Still, there might be a sense in which *social order* turns out to be normative. It's also good to drink water that is uncontaminated. Any plausible analysis of *contaminant* will refer to health—not everything besides H_2O in your glass of water counts as a contaminant—and it seems implausible that we can describe the criteria for health without saying anything about proper bodily functioning, and that will have to be normative. The concept of social order could similarly incorporate reference to normative concepts.

Yet even if *social order* turns out to be normative, it isn't going to be an all-things-considered overall commendation. You might think Singapore is orderly without approving of it. And I was once taken aback when a stranger hissed at me for jaywalking. I was in Zurich, it was after midnight, and the deathly quiet guaranteed that no cars were near us. I'm sure my ignoring the red light offended his sense of order. I'm sure too that he shouldn't have been so uptight. East Beirut and Albania have both been terrible places to live. Still it makes sense to deny that Beirut was orderly and grant that Albania was. So we should resist the temptation to smuggle all kinds of normative disputes into the rubric of social order.

I said I would endorse one version of the thesis that social order requires consensus. I might as well come clean. Recall the thought that enmity is a subset of the broader category confusion. Well, confusion is the opposite of social order. On my account, that's a constitutive claim. The fewer actors who share an understanding of what they're up to and the less they actually share, the harder it is to grasp their milieu as a social order. Not because they'll automatically come to blows: imagine magically snatching individuals at random from around the globe and depositing them in a train station—or, to avoid any putatively cross-cultural cues about the game, in an open field. Even if they didn't come to blows, they wouldn't comprise any social order at all. Often for Hobbesian reasons, confusion will tend to teeter into enmity. But you can't detect the presence or absence of social order by counting corpses. So champions of consensus are right in thinking that social order can't be confusion. They're wrong, though, in imagining that conflict is incipient disorder. Conflict is often what social order consists in.

I haven't yet said much to defend that broader thesis. So why believe it?

Can We All Get Along?

Let's distinguish the grounds of conflict from conflict. That Jenny likes jazz and Abby can't stand it is not yet even the grounds of conflict. If they're in different places or if each prefers using her iPod, no conflict will arise. But suppose the two are sitting together and want to put some music on the stereo. Jenny wants Eric Dolphy; Abby doesn't. Here we have the grounds of conflict. They can't both hear what they'd like. That might or might not give rise to conflict itself. Jenny and Abby might agree to take turns choosing what to play or flip a coin or settle on some compromise. Or they might have an increasingly heated verbal exchange ("Oh hell, more random notes and squawks," "No, come on, this is harmonically sophisticated," "The sad thing is that you actually believe that," "Philistine!") or even come to blows. Theirs is not yet a political conflict. But it would become that if Jenny claimed a right to decide and Abby denied it or if Abby granted Jenny's right but thought she was exercising it badly. Again, even if they weren't pursuing such disagreements, an observer who thought they could well pursue such a conflict could sensibly describe their conflict as political.

We often describe the grounds of conflict as conflict pure and simple. Suppose Michael and Eileen want the same job. We might say they have a conflict of interest without intimating that they're struggling over it. Indeed the two might not even know of one another's interest in the job. I have nothing invested in the language I've used for this distinction, but we need to keep its substance in focus. There's no logical necessity that there be any grounds of conflict at all. But they're utterly ordinary. It's routine for people to have different preferences. It's routine for people to have conflicts of interest. It's routine for people to hold rival principles.[43] Nor is there any logical necessity that predicaments will arise where not everyone's preferences and interests and principles can be realized. But such predicaments too are utterly ordinary. I have never even glanced at a society, in historical or anthropological work, that isn't chock-full of the grounds of conflict.

So should we expect the grounds of conflict never or only rarely to blossom into conflict itself? Norms, we sometimes think, resolve conflict. So, for instance, a norm of cooperation can lead parties stuck in an iterated prisoners' dilemma to cooperate. People can flip coins or split the difference or converge on other decision procedures for resolving the grounds of conflict. Yet we should beware inferring that generally norms save us from conflict or that they would if only we set aside selfish considerations. Suppose we take *norms* very broadly as including all sorts of considerations of practical reason besides those of individual prudence. Ordinarily, we face a jumble of competing norms. We dispute what norms properly apply to the case at

43. Here I adopt an eighteenth-century scheme that is still illuminating, though they said "affection" where we say "preference," and those categories aren't quite the same. For a canonical statement, see "Of Parties in General," in David Hume, *Essays: Moral, Political, and Literary*, ed. Eugene F. Miller (Indianapolis, IN: *Liberty*Classics, 1987).

hand. We dispute how they apply. We dispute how to handle conflicts among norms. Even people acting in good faith will reasonably disagree on how best to sort out the thicket of norms. You don't have to embrace relativism or incommensurability to agree. You have to remember how difficult these issues can be, how uncertain our judgment.[44] Here norms *create* conflict. Our shared norms help comprise our social order. They help explain why we're not a random assembly of people standing in a field. But their saving us from confusion does not entail their saving us from conflict. Conflicts of principle are every bit as real as conflicts of interest and incompatible preferences.

Worse, if only from the point of view of those devoted to consensus, compromise often seems intolerable when we're facing conflicts of principle. Suppose Danielle thinks the current system of financing public schools an affront to equality of opportunity, but Craig thinks Danielle's reform proposals violate property rights. Mutually agreeable compromises might not be available. Sometimes compromise is only the art of making everyone miserable, and miserable for lofty principled reasons, not just disappointment over loss.

No analyst worth her salt will shrug off that fact. Nor this one: there's a familiar slippage in norms and social life. At the edge of campus, one intersection is mobbed with cars and pedestrians. A policeman with a whistle stands in the middle of the intersection. Pedestrians often ignore the traffic light and seem merely amused by his whistling so fiercely that he turns beet red. Drivers honk, some of them to indicate or threaten, "Yes, I really am continuing to drive now," others to register frustrated indignation. Sometimes the policeman tickets aggressive jaywalkers. Sometimes one pedestrian will start to cross and a friend will hold her back. Sometimes the intersection is full of cars, sometimes of pedestrians, but this seems only loosely correlated with the dictates of the traffic light.

Everyone agrees, let's say, that you're not supposed to jaywalk. But that norm isn't inspiring universal compliance. That doesn't mean it's mere toothless pretext. Its effects outstrip whatever level of compliance it inspires. A jaywalker might agree that he's in the wrong or that a driver is well within his rights in leaning on his horn. Similarly, absent worries about invidiously selective prosecution, a jaywalker could be only rueful, not indignant, on getting a ticket.

---

44. See "The Domain of the Political and Overlapping Consensus" in John Rawls, *Collected Papers*, ed. Samuel Freeman (Cambridge, MA: Harvard University Press, 1999), 475–78.

But consider too our reaction to the fellow who refuses to jaywalk even when crowds are already spilling into the intersection and the cars have stopped. "The light says DON'T WALK," he explains primly. Many of us think this is rule worshipping: the sole justification for these rules is to enable the safe and efficient flow of cars and people through the intersection. The first few people to jaywalk may then be culpable. But once pedestrians swarm the intersection and cars stop, his marginal contribution to the problem—if there is a problem!—is zero. He can't plausibly claim that it's hard to know if he'd be jaywalking too soon to be part of the problem, not at least if his policy is to wait for the WALK light no matter what. More implausible yet is a slippery-slope argument: "If I permit myself to brush aside this rule, I'll start breaking lots of other rules I should follow. Or others watching me will." And if he claims that his jaywalking would express contempt for the rule of law, we can ask why it should be read that way.

Now consider our reaction to the pedestrian who intercepts a stranger about to jaywalk: hand politely but forcefully on his forearm, she nods toward the light and declares, "It says DON'T WALK." Then she beams affectionately, or is it officiously? at the poor policeman, who's gesticulating madly but in vain. Overwhelmingly, I suggest, we think this woman is priggish. She should mind her own business. That means that models relying on "metanorms," or the willingness of third parties to sanction offenders, run headlong into the inconvenient fact that in many settings we have robust norms that you shouldn't do that.[45] Students are notoriously reluctant to turn in other students for cheating, even when honor codes formally impose that obligation. These instances of disobedience qualify as permissible when appraised from other points of view.

So there's slippage between the "no jaywalking" norm and actual behavior at the intersection. But the norm might still be in good working order at other intersections in town, even with the same cast of pedestrians and drivers. I want to insist that it's a mistake to dismiss the norm as illusory or incompletely stated, to embrace the observed pattern of conduct as the real norm. It's also a mistake to ignore how much jaywalking there is or dismiss that as a trivial question about compliance. Both norm and conduct matter. It's not just that the explanatory story about the conduct of drivers and

45. Compare Robert Axelrod, "An Evolutionary Approach to Norms," *American Political Science Review* 80, no. 4 (1986): 1095–1111; Robert C. Ellickson, *Order without Law: How Neighbors Settle Disputes* (Cambridge, MA: Harvard University Press, 1991), 236–38.

pedestrians would appeal to partial compliance with the norm. It's also that jaywalkers may properly be sanctioned. Were there no law, a policeman who tried to write a ticket for jaywalking would be a rogue, his action not much more intelligible than smashing a banana into a chessboard. Similarly, were there neither law nor convention, a fellow pedestrian who touched your forearm and scolded you would be not priggish but mysterious. The very claim that you were jaywalking would be a nonstarter. The existence of the norm makes possible transgression. I don't mean the thought that followers of Durkheim and Foucault like to flirt with, that some will always find deviance inherently choiceworthy. I mean instead that actions can't logically qualify as transgressions in the absence of norms. Even when transgression is predictable, even when it's arguably justifiable, the existence of a norm supplies ammunition to critics: "Don't you know you're not supposed to . . . ?" "How could you . . . ?"

We often have a rough-and-ready sense—though here too how inclusive the "we" and how shared the sense are both easy to overestimate—of what sort of compliance with a norm is sensible, what punctilious overkill. But "No jaywalking" really does mean no jaywalking, not "Jaywalk only if you're pretty sure there are no drivers around or if enough others are already doing it," plus whatever other considerations might properly supply an exception or, as philosophers say, make the norm defeasible. Nor does it mean "No jaywalking unless you have good reason to," leaving open what might count as good reason. Down that road is the imp who says, "All your rules are for robots. I follow just one rule: do what's best in the circumstances. Sure, sometimes it's best to follow the alleged rules, in part because others are relying on them. But not always." Instead of seeing this as an enlightened stance about practical reason, we should see it as daffy and pernicious.

When we consider conduct as wretched as that of the Branches, we cringe. We yearn for harmony, unanimity, love. (Okay, I don't. But some do.) There is no hope for that vision and attempts to realize it are often repulsive: recall the Brinsden effect. It's dispiriting, if unsurprising too, that champions of harmony are so quick to blame putative inferiors. Recoil, if you will, from the assurance that marital difficulties and bad husbands alike are due to "the Indiscretion and Folly, if not to the Obstinacy and Stubbornness of disobedient Wives."[46] Recoil from the memorably cool one-liner, "Women are

---

46. John Sprint, *The Bride-Womans Counseller: Being a Sermon Preach'd at a Wedding, May the 11th, 1699, at Sherbourn, in Dorsetshire* (London, [1699?]), 4. For a swashbuckling response to Sprint's

borne to torment a man both aliue and dead."[47] Recoil from the suggestion that "Women dress purposely now-a-days to provoke Men to an Invasion of their Chastity."[48] We should embrace conflict. Not grudgingly, as something we're unhappily stuck with; but gracefully, as acknowledging the dignity of those who disagree with us. So too we shouldn't recoil from the prospect of household politics or daydream that a properly loving family wouldn't face conflicts over legitimate authority. But these sentiments are still unhappily abstract. I'll cash them out by turning to the fraught terrain of domestic service.

---

sermon, see A Lady of Quality [Mary Lee Chudleigh], *The Female Advocate: or, A Plea for the Just Liberty of the Tender Sex, and Particularly of Married Women* (London, 1700).

47. *The Terrors of the Night* [1594], in *The Works of Thomas Nashe,* ed. Ronald B. McKerrow, ed. and corr. F. P. Wilson, 5 vols. (Oxford: Basil Blackwell, 1958), 1:383.

48. *The Second Part of Whipping-Tom: or, A Rod for a Proud Lady* (London, 1722), 23.

CHAPTER 5

The Trouble with Servants

In early modern England, many households had live-in servants, most of them female. One prominent estimate is that anywhere from 4 to 25 percent of the population at any given time were servants—and in wealthy urban settings a crushing majority of households had servants.[1] The lure of the city is old: one 1577 dialog has a citizen of London warning a country lad that the servant's life is not the jolly one he imagines.[2] Most households with servants had just one, by necessity a jack-of-all-trades. But wealthier households sprouted more and more servants, with an imposingly formalized division of labor.[3] Some spent their entire adult lives as servants. Many more worked as servants while teenagers and young adults. Contemporaries noticed: "There is a great Number of young People that are Servants."[4] Service was a way of leaving home, or starting to: John Stevenson's son was off working as a servant, but he returned home with two badly swollen legs.[5] So domestic

1. Peter Laslett, *The World We Have Lost Further Explored* (New York: Charles Scribner's Sons, 1984), 69, 308n26; and see 64–65. For some later data, see W. A. Armstrong, "A Note on the Household Structure of Mid-Nineteenth-Century York in Comparative Perspective," in *Household and Family in Past Time*, ed. Peter Laslett and Richard Wall (Cambridge: Cambridge University Press, 1972), 213; and Peter Laslett, "Mean Household Size in England since the Sixteenth Century," in *Household and Family*, 154.

2. [John Fit John], *A Diamonde Most Precious, Worthy to Be Marked: Instructing All Maysters and Seruantes* (London, 1577), n.p.

3. For a statistical overview, see Tim Meldrum, *Domestic Service and Gender, 1660–1750: Life and Work in the London Household* (Harlow: Longman, 2000), chap. 2.

4. [John Graile], *Youths Grand Concern: or, Advice to Young Persons*, 2nd ed. (London, 1711), 83.

5. John Stevenson, *A Rare Soul Strengthning and Comforting Cordial, for Old and Young Christians* ([Edinburgh?], 1729), 44.

service was a stage in a familiar life cycle for many preparing to launch households of their own[6]—sometimes already pregnant and often to the sanctimonious disapproval of their masters and mistresses, sure their charges weren't financially or emotionally ready for independence. (When John Clarke got his fellow servant Elizabeth Mann pregnant, he killed her. But he was already married.)[7]

Contemporaries, though, did not reserve the concept *servant* for such live-in help. I don't mean to gesture toward the much rarer case of servants who lived outside the home but showed up during the day to work. Nor do I mean only the common case of apprentices learning a trade. The term sprawled out to cover all kinds of hierarchical relationships: "In some Sense we are all Servants, as being subject to some Powers that are over us."[8] Again we see contemporaries' firm grasp of authority.

The word *servant* appears over a thousand times in the King James Bible, from Noah's imprecation ("And he said, Cursed be Canaan; a servant of servants shall he be unto his brethren") to the angel's instruction ("These sayings are faithful and true: and the Lord God of the holy prophets sent his angel to shew unto his servants the things which must shortly be done").[9] Just this pair suggests that service can be an execrable condition, but it can also be one of joyous prostration before God[10]—or other worthy superiors, the prosaically earthly kind. Looming large over the cultural landscape was Jesus's parable of the servants, with the unprofitable one "cast . . . into outer darkness" with "weeping and gnashing of teeth."[11] There was no denying, though, that a household servant labored in inferiority. Take this morsel of indignation, routine where kinship and service blurred together: "Remember, Sir, my Wife was a First Cousin to your Aunt: under whom she received her Education, and with whom she lived as a Companion, not a Servant, as you

---

6. For doubts about how geographically common this pattern was, see Graham Mayhew, "Life-Cycle Service and the Family Unit in Early Modern Rye," *Continuity and Change* 6, no. 2 (1991): 201–26.

7. *Last Dying Speech, Birth, Parentage, and Education, of That Unfortunate Malefactor, John Clarke* ([London? 1750?]).

8. [Zinzano], *The Servants Calling; with Some Advice to the Apprentice* (London, 1725), 7.

9. Genesis 9:25; Revelation 22:6.

10. *The Devout Christian's Companion: or, A Complete Manual of Devotions* (London, 1707), 124: "I am entirely thine, I am thy Servant, and in this Title I glory more than in all the Honours of the World." See too 326.

11. Matthew 25:30. For a sermon on this parable, see John Warren, *The Unprofitable Servant: A Sermon* (London, 1655). For one of many instances of how scripture was enlisted to forge instructions for servants, see George Kenwrick, *The Surest Guide to Eternity: or, A Body of Divinity, Extracted out of the Writings of the Old and New Testament* (Oxford, 1725), 264–65.

maliciously and foolishly declare."[12] Or this crumb of consolation from a text that would run through dozens of editions: "It is true, the state of servitude is accounted the meanest and the most miserable of all others; but yet it is to be made easy: servants have more of the labours of life, but they have less of the cares; their bodies are more fatigued and exercised, but their minds are less perplexed."[13] Or this tidbit of doggerel, from Robert Dodsley, who really was a footman[14] before he became a poet:

> Purchas'd by annual Wages, Cloaths, and Meat,
> Theirs is our Time, our Hands, our Head, our Feet:
> We think, design, and act at their Command,
> And, as their Pleasure varies, walk or stand;
> Whilst we receive the covenanted Hire,
> Active Obedience justly they require:
> If we dislike, and think it too severe,
> We're free to leave, and seek a Place elsewhere.[15]

Servants eager to skip out before their contract ended could discover that the poet's closing assurance was dead wrong. Newspaper advertisements remind us what sort of contractual arrangement service was: "A Blackamoor Servant that ran away from his Master, pretty tall, strong, thick set, much impression of Pockholes in his Face, with a Green Livery Suit, Green and White Lace. Whoever gives notice of him . . . shall have forty shillings for his pains."[16] Gild this wilted lily if you will, but one time-honored stricture was undeniable: "Servants are placed in a lower room, in a place of inferiority and subjection, and so are bound to perform obedience, seeing in all places the Superiour must rule, and the inferiour be ruled, or else neither Superiour nor inferiour shall with any comfort enjoy the places allotted unto them by God."[17]

---

12. Wm. Peirs to Eustace Budgell, 21 August 1731, *Daily Courant*, 30 August 1731.

13. *The New Whole Duty of Man, Containing the Faith as Well as the Practice of a Christian* (London, [1741]), 226; and see 229.

14. James Boswell, *The Life of Samuel Johnson*, 20 March 1776. See generally Ralph Straus, *Robert Dodsley: Poet, Publisher & Playwright* (London: John Lane the Bodley Head, 1910). For a poet presenting himself as a servant defending his fellow servants, see William Bas, *Sword and Buckler: or, Serving-Mans Defence* (London, 1602).

15. R[obert] D[odsley], *The Footman's Friendly Advice to His Brethren of the Livery; and to All Servants in General* (London, [1730]), 19.

16. *London Gazette*, 1 June 1674. See too *London Gazette*, 24 February 1701; *Daily Courant*, 10 April 1707; *Daily Journal*, 19 April 1728.

17. Edward Leigh, *A Systeme or Body of Divinity* (London, 1654), 827.

Consider everyday address in print and in person. William Philips signed the dedication of his comedy, "My Lord, Your Lordship's Most Faithful and most Humble Servant, Will. Philips." The play itself features the same flourishes. "Ladies your Servant!" announces the Irish gentlemen Bellmine; the "Snarling and Ill-natur'd" Wormwood salutes that same gentleman, "Mr. *Bellmine,* Your humble Servant," which elicits the instantaneous, "Your Servant, Mr. *Wormwood."* Probably Bellmine omits *humble* to signal lesser or less gracious deference[18] — Wormwood is his inferior — but maybe these are innocent variations on a form. Piling on ever more deferential adjectives can recapture a genuine sentiment threatening to disappear in thickets of ritual verbiage. But it also can be facetious. Here's Vainly, "A Pert Conceited Fop":

> Least these Strangers shou'd mistake my humour, I'll march off; and there is a rare Opportunity, a Hackney Coach coming this way with two Masks; I'll pretend they call'd me. Heigh! you Rascal! Coach-man, don't you hear the Ladies cry hold? Dear Gentlemen, you see the Reason of my leaving you, there are some Ladies in the Coach call me; therefore I hope you will pardon the abrupt Departure of your most obedient faithful Servant.

He manages to scamper offstage with this threadbare contrivance. But he doesn't fool Wormwood, who sputters, "There's a Dog now, there's a Rogue. Why, wou'd you prevent my Drubbing him? I wou'd have kick't him into Jelly."[19] A speaker in another play celebrates "your humble servant madam" as the incantation for deceiving and seducing women.[20] Mandeville jeered at these verbal forms as impudent hypocrisy.[21]

So *servant* had a wide range of applications. I'd deny any priority thesis. I suppose the experience of household servants redounded back onto biblical passages, but so too people's sense of the Bible colored household service;

18. Compare "Part of the Seventh Epistle of the First Book of Horace Imitated," in *The Poems of Jonathan Swift,* ed. Harold Williams, 2nd ed., 3 vols. (Oxford: Clarendon, 1958), 1:172.

19. Will[iam] Philips, *St. Stephen's-Green: or, The Generous Lovers: A Comedy* (Dublin, 1700). I've deliberately chosen an unremarkable example. Compare the entirely remarkable verbal flourishes of Sir Formal Trifle in Thomas Shadwell, *The Virtuoso: A Comedy* (London, 1676), 6–7.

20. *Your Humble Servant Madam: Being The Flattering Courtier: or, The Cheating Lover* (London, 1662), n.p., the opening and closing stanzas. For reactions, see *The Ladyes Vindication: Being the Womens Answer, to "Your Humble Servant Madame"* (London, 1662), and *The Counterfeit Court Lady: or, An Answer to "Your Humble Servant Madam"* ([London, 1674–79]).

21. Bernard Mandeville, *The Fable of the Bees: or, Private Vices, Publick Benefits* [1732], ed. F. B. Kaye, 2 vols. (Oxford: Clarendon, 1924), 1:290, 2:160.

and so on for all the other domains the concept was invoked in. Anyway, back to household servants. Living at close quarters in a society constantly wrestling with the tensions between formal Christian commitments to equality and everyday social commitments to inequality made for chafing and worse, despite the conventional wisdom, put this way by Jonathan Swift: "Servants are directed to obey their Masters, Children their Parents, and Wives their Husbands; not from any Respect of Persons in God, but because otherwise there would be nothing but Confusion in private Families."[22] Daniel Defoe balefully reported that "our Servant Wenches are so puff'd up with Pride" that they wished to dress like their mistresses;[23] worse yet, to "become their own Lawgivers; nay, I think they are ours too, tho' No-body would imagine that such a Set of Slatterns should bamboozle a whole Nation," imperiously decreeing under what terms they would deign to work.[24] One gentleman promptly defended the servants against Defoe's attack: "As if Servants were not of the same Flesh and Blood, Make and Being, and had not as much Title to this World's Goods as Gentry."[25]

Lest that ringing affirmation beckon us on a thankless excursion into the conceptual stratosphere, consider this joke. (We know it's a joke, even if a lousy one, because it's published in a joke book.) "A Gentleman hir'd a Servant, and told him he must do whatever he commanded him; to which he reply'd Yes, he would most faithfully. The Gentleman presently let a Fart, Go fetch me that (says he) to his Man: Yes Sir, (says he) and lets another, There Sir (says he) 'tis."[26] The joke admits competing readings, but here's one: the gentleman wishes to demonstrate his unconditional superiority, but he is insolent in urging what's impossible and the laugh provoked by the servant's

---

22. "The Duty of Mutual Subjection," in *The Prose Works of Jonathan Swift*, ed. Herbert Davis, 14 vols. (Oxford: Basil Blackwell, 1939–68), 9:143.

23. Compare [Margaret Cavendish], Lady Marchioness of Newcastle, *CCXI Sociable Letters* (London, 1664), 125–26.

24. Andrew Moreton [Daniel Defoe], *Every-Body's Business, Is No-Body's Business: or, Private Abuses, Publick Grievances*, 4th ed. corr. (London, 1725), 6, 13.

25. John Johnson, gent., *Modern Gentility No Christianity: or, A Compleat Answer to "Every Body's Business Is No Body's Business"* (London, 1725), 36. See too W[illiam] Fleetwood, *The Relative Duties of Parents and Children, Husbands and Wives, Masters and Servants, Consider'd in Sixteen Sermons* (London, 1705), 414.

26. W. B., *Ingenii Fructus: or, The Cambridge Jests* (London, 1703), 59. Compare *"Merry Passages and Jests": A Manuscript Jestbook of Sir Nicholas Le Strange (1603–1655)*, ed. H. F. Lippincott (Salzburg: Institut für Englische Sprache und Literatur, 1974), 54.

impudence is sympathetic.[27] It means the gentleman, swaggering in his authority, gets what he deserves.

But masters shouldn't pal around with their servants, either. Take this much-reprinted advice to a young gentlewoman: "Be courteous to all the Servants belonging to your Parents, but not over-familiar with any of them, lest they grow rude and sawcy with you; and indeed too much familiarity is not good with any, for contempt is commonly the product thereof."[28] There's a tightrope to be walked here—or two tightropes, one for masters and one for servants.[29] Another guide instructed young ladies on "the Art of being duly served by the Domesticks," the importance of winning their love with neither excess familiarity nor haughty impatience.[30] The *Spectator* fretted over masters' clumsiness in their roles:

> There are . . . Masters who are offended at a cheerful Countenance, and think a Servant has broke loose from them, if he does not preserve the utmost Awe in their Presence. There is one who says, if he looks satisfied his Master asks him what makes him so pert this Morning; if a little sowre, Hark ye, Sirrah, are not you paid your Wages? The poor Creatures live in the most extreme Misery together: The Master knows not how to preserve Respect, nor the Servant how to give it.[31]

To shift the metaphor, this landscape is generously littered with landmines, only some of them conspicuous.

And it is a political landscape. We're used to thinking that talk of the monarch as the father of his people naturalizes political authority and so

27. For insolence and impudence as opposites, see my *Poisoning the Minds of the Lower Orders* (Princeton, NJ: Princeton University Press, 1998), 210–17.

28. Hannah Woolley, *The Gentlewomans Companion: or, A Guide to the Female Sex* (London, 1673), 27–28. See too [John Shirley], *The Accomplished Ladies Rich Closet of Rarities: or, The Ingenious Gentlewoman and Servant Maids Delightfull Companion*, 2nd ed. (London, 1687), 195–96.

29. For strictures on tone in letter writing, see Simon Daines, *Orthoepia Anglicana: or, The First Principall Part of the English Grammar* (London, 1640), 85–86. I owe the reference to Mark Thornton Burnett, *Masters and Servants in English Renaissance Drama and Culture: Authority and Obedience* (New York: St. Martin's, 1997), 2.

30. [John Essex], *The Young Ladies Conduct: or, Rules for Education* (London, 1722), xxxvii–xxxviii. See too *The Advice of a Father: or, Counsel to a Child* (London, 1664), 38–39; A Norfolk Gentleman [James Poole], *Advice to the Ladies: A Poem* (London, 1745), 9. Compare A Person of Quality, *The Young Lady's Companion: or, Beauty's Looking-Glass* (London, 1740), 29; F. L., *The Virgin's Nosegay: or, The Duties of Christian Virgins* (London, 1744), 136.

31. *Spectator*, no. 137 (7 August 1711), in *The Spectator*, ed. Donald F. Bond, 5 vols. (Oxford: Clarendon, 1965), 2:41.

makes it disappear. That's wrong; contemporaries regularly ran the analogy in the other direction. From 1652: "Every private Family is a little City; wherein if there should be no order, nor harmony, that distracted government would beget a private Anarchy."[32] From 1744: "All masters of families are governors and rulers in their own houses."[33] This everyday trope links high political theory and scrutiny of the household. But we don't need that trope to see politics here. All we need is controversies about the legitimacy of authority. If you think we need potential or actual violence, we find that too. We've already met Elizabeth Branch and servants as deadly as she. We'll meet more. Such infamous criminals had their counterparts in constantly renewed proposals for enforcing long-standing laws to discipline insubordinate servants,[34] for adding new laws too,[35] as well as compendia setting out laws to guide masters and servants alike[36] and helpful guides for producing such forms as a warrant for arresting a fugitive servant.[37]

Yet there are also instances of model, if not saintly, servants. Puritan divine Richard Baxter fondly recalled "the Benefit of a godly, understanding, faithful Servant (an ancient Woman near Sixty Years old) who eased me of all Care, and laid out all my Money for Housekeeping, so that I never had one Hour's trouble about it, nor ever took one Day's Account of her for Fourteen Years together, as being certain of her Fidelity, Providence and Skill."[38] MP John Hungerford left "my honest Servant *Henry Capps*, alias *Trusty*," not just horse and saddle but also an annuity of £15, to be increased to £20 tax-free upon his wife's death.[39] Samuel Wright bequeathed each of his servants

---

32. R[ichard] Brathwait, *Times Treasury: or, Academy for Gentry* (London, 1652), supplement, 31.

33. [Patrick Delany], *Fifteen Sermons upon Social Duties* (London, 1744), 220.

34. See for instance 7 Jac. c. 4, requiring Justices of the Peace to establish workhouses for "idle and disorderly persons." The rule's primary concern is vagrants.

35. Christopher Tancred, *A Scheme for an Act of Parliament for the Better Regulating Servants, and Ascertaining Their Wages, and Lessening the Future Growth of the Poor, and Vagrants of the Kingdom* (London, 1724).

36. *The Laws Relating to Masters and Servants: With Brief Notes and Explanations, to Render Them Easy and Intelligible to the Meanest Capacity* ([London], 1755).

37. Richard Kilburn, *Choice Presidents upon All Acts of Parliament, Relating to the Office and Duty of a Justice of the Peace*, 7th ed. (London, 1703); S[amuel] C[arter], *Legal Provisions for the Poor*, 4th ed. (London, 1718), 279–80; Matt[hew] Dutton, *The Office and Authority of a Justice of the Peace for Ireland* (Dublin, 1718), 386–87; G. F. Gent., *The Secretary's Guide* (London, [1741]), 91.

38. Richard Baxter, *Reliquiae Baxterianae* (London, 1696), lib. 1, pt. 1, p. 95. See too Mary Woodforde's diary in *Woodforde Papers and Diaries*, ed. Dorothy Heighes Woodforde (London: Peter Davies, 1932), 13 (14 January 1686).

39. *Universal Spectator, and Weekly Journal*, 2 August 1729.

£100.[40] A Mr. Ashton left his coachman of over twenty years £500.[41] Masters sometimes erected tombstones with glowing epitaphs to servants, too.[42]

But the contrast between dutiful servants and loathsome criminals might suggest that social order and conflict are opposites. So let's think instead about everyday snafus. One Irish lady ordered her cook to lock the cellar so another servant, too fond of alcohol, couldn't get to the beer. Vexed, "he nail'd up all the Larders & the Cook's Chamber doore."[43] Disobedient? Sure. Disobedient in a permissible way? Maybe not, so maybe this counts as enmity, not conflict. Then again, what's sauce for the goose is sauce for the gander.[44] Or let's return to flatulence: by 1699, *catch fart* had passed into the English language, at least the colorful version spoken by deviants, as slang for a footboy.[45] It was still in use at the end of the eighteenth century and one dictionary spelled out the point: "CATCH FART. A footboy; so called from such servants commonly following close behind their master or mistress."[46] I doubt that only jaundiced observers knew this lingo. Masters and mistresses farted, servants trudging behind inhaled, and everyone knew it. So the pageantry went on with embarrassed and ironic awareness, surely now and again with grumbling or worse. Notice then another reading of that joke about the dueling farts: the master is making his right to extort deference ludicrously explicit and the servant is ironically complying by offering a pungent refusal. This joke too is no "hidden transcript." It's fully public: everyone—master, mistress, servant, outsider—knows what's going on. Everyone knows that everyone else knows, too. It would take far more repression or obliviousness

---

40. *Weekly Miscellany*, 14 August 1736.

41. *Weekly Journal: or, The British Gazetteer*, 8 June 1728. Compare Locke's will in *The Correspondence of John Locke*, ed. E. S. de Beer, 8 vols. (Oxford: Clarendon, 1976–89), 8:424.

42. Silvester Tissington, *A Collection of Epitaphs and Monumental Inscriptions* (London, 1857), 215, 221; *Faithful Servants: Being Epitaphs and Obituaries Recording Their Names and Services*, ed. Arthur Munby (London, 1891), 159. I was led to these sources by Joshua Scodel, *The English Poetic Epitaph: Commemoration and Conflict from Jonson to Wordsworth* (Ithaca, NY: Cornell University Press, 1991), 368–74.

43. Lady Fermanagh to [Lord Fermanagh?], 1 December 1710, in *Verney Letters of the Eighteenth Century from the Mss. at Claydon House*, ed. Margaret Maria Lady Verney, 2 vols. (London: Ernest Benn, 1930), 1:284.

44. The proverb is in Daniel Leeds, *A Trumpet Sounded out of the Wilderness of America* (London, 1699), 119.

45. B. E. Gent., *A New Dictionary of the Terms Ancient and Modern of the Canting Crew, in Its Several Tribes of Gypsies, Beggers, Thieves, Cheats, &c.* (London, [1699]), 18.

46. [Francis Grose], *A Classical Dictionary of the Vulgar Tongue*, 3rd ed. (London, 1796), s.v. *catch fart*.

than I imagine the locals capable of to overturn that inference. Still, the pageantries had to be maintained, even in the face of such jaundiced sentiments as those of Mandeville's salvo against footmen:

> The greatest part of them are Rogues and not to be trusted; and if they are Honest half of them are Sots, and will get Drunk three or four times a Weak. The surly ones are generally Quarrelsome, and valuing their Manhood beyond all other Considerations, care not what Clothes they spoil, or what Disappointments they may occasion, when their Prowess is in Question. Those who are good-natur'd, are generally sad Whore-masters that are ever running after the Wenches, and spoil all the Maid-Servants they come near. Many of them are Guilty of all these Vices, Whoring, Drinking, Quarreling, and yet shall have all their Faults overlook'd and bore with, because they are Men of good Mien and humble Address that know how to wait on Gentlemen; which is an unpardonable Folly in Masters and generally ends in the Ruin of Servants.[47]

Footmen seem to have been an especial affliction. "I think I am uncomonly plagu'd with Footmen," Gertrude Savile moaned in her diary. She went through "5 Footmen in one Year, and one 3 times over!" and her struggles went on for years.[48] But it was all too easy for polite society to shower disdain on servants. In the fracas surrounding the publication of Pope's correspondence, the Earl of Orrery sniffed, "Certainly, Madam, this printed Collection has been stolen by some low, mean, injudicious Person, probably some Servant, who has snatched them at various opportunities."[49]

Some social critics waxed nostalgic, as if once upon a time servants minded their manners. We needn't decide whether servants in the good old days were acting obedient as against obeying for real, whatever that distinction amounts to, because they never were all that obedient. "There is not a Grievance more universally complain'd off, than that of *bad* Servants," as one 1731 report had it. "It is the common Topick of every Conversation; and all Orders of Men, however they may differ in other points, agree in this, that it is almost impossible to get a *trusty, faithful,* and *diligent* Servant."[50] In 1711,

---

47. Mandeville, *Fable,* 1:302–3.

48. *Secret Comment: The Diaries of Gertrude Savile 1721–1757,* ed. Alan Saville (Devon: Kingsbridge History Society, 1997), 56 (29 August 1727), 88 (19 December 1727), 154 (heads of the year 1728), 195–96 (heads of the year 1729), 214 (29 September 1730).

49. Earl of Orrery to Mrs. Whiteway, 2 January [1741], in *The Correspondence of Alexander Pope,* ed. George Sherburn, 5 vols. (Oxford: Clarendon, 1956), 4:235.

50. *Universal Spectator, and Weekly Journal,* 26 June 1731. For a response, see *Gentleman's Magazine,* June 1731, 249–50.

Philo-Britannicus bemoaned "the general Corruption of Manners in the Servants of *Great-Britain*."[51] Or take this 1701 lament: "this is certain, that disorderly Servants are become one great Complaint in the Country in general, and of almost every Family in particular."[52] Shall we wind back the clock to 1650? "In former times, when they had not the tythe of the means they now enjoy, servants were plain, diligent, trusty, careful to please, painful [they took pains], &c."[53] To 1600? "I counsel masters not to keepe any seruants in their houses, that are giuen to swearing, gaming, whoring, drinking, or to any such notorious crimes."[54] 1550 yields the sigh of a Christian moralist, who knew what familiar social type to invoke to lacerating effect: "we all for the most part, of us haue the nature of suche slouthful and sluggyshe seruauntes which will do nothynge well excepte, we be dryuen by cõpulsyon and euen wypped and beaten vnto it."[55] 1499 yields the same trope.[56]

Corporal punishment remained a staple of domestic discipline. The *"heedless servant . . .* will deserveth *some stripes,"* intoned one preacher. "A *stubborn servant . . .* deserveth *more stripes."* The most were deserved by the *"ungracious servant"* who deliberately hid so he could claim he had no idea what his master wanted.[57] These severe sentiments too echo scripture: "And that servant, which knew his lord's will, and prepared not himself, neither did according to his will, shall be beaten with many stripes."[58] Controversies arose over how hard beatings should be and what sort of disobedience justified them.[59] I don't know of anyone who thought they were simply out of

51. *Spectator*, no. 88 (11 June 1711), in Bond, *The Spectator*, 1:372.

52. William P[udse]y, *The Constitution and Laws of England Consider'd* (London, 1701), 161. See too *An Enquiry into the Causes of the Late Increase of Robbers* [1751], in Henry Fielding, *"An Enquiry into the Causes of the Late Increase of Robbers" and Related Writings*, ed. Malvin R. Zirker (Oxford: Clarendon, 1988), 173.

53. John Rogers, *A Godly & Fruitful Exposition upon All the First Epistle of Peter* (London, 1650), 646; and see 348.

54. W[illiam] Vaughan, *The Golden-Groue, Moralized in Three Bookes* (London, 1600), bk. 2, chap. 15, sig. O4 verso.

55. [Otto Werdmüller], *A Spyrytuall and Moost Precouse Pearle Teaching All Men to Loue and Imbrace the Crosse* (n.p., [1550]), fol. xlvii verso.

56. *The Rote or Myrour of Consolacyon & Conforte* (Westmyster, 1499), n.p.

57. Robert Sanderson, *XXXVI Sermons* (London, 1686), 279. Sanderson lived from 1587 to 1663 and his work was much reprinted. This passage is already in his *Two Sermons Preached at Paules-Crosse London* (London, 1628), 91. See too Lancelot Andrews, *The Pattern of Catechistical Doctrine at Large* (London, 1650), 354; William Sharpe, *Unity and Peace: A Seasonable Legacy* (Bristol, 1728), 6–7.

58. Luke 12:47.

59. For social discomfort over striking a servant, see Henry Fielding, *The History of Tom Jones: A Foundling* [1749], ed. Fredson Bowers, 2 vols. (Middletown, CT: Wesleyan University Press, 1975), 2:704.

bounds. Surely the law didn't.[60] Indeed, one source after another declares — shades of passive obedience — that servants must quietly submit to these beatings even when they don't deserve them.[61] The gospels laid down the rule: "Servants, be subject to your masters with all fear; not only to the good and gentle, but also to the froward. For this is thankworthy, if a man for conscience toward God endure grief, suffering wrongfully."[62]

Servants must have owed many of these stripes to the paeans to harmony of interests and love. Masters and mistresses smitten with those paeans would surely look askance at what the disabused might think the reasonable conduct of their servants. Again, the Brinsden effect, with its gratuitous nastiness and indelicate irony, is the actual payoff of syrupy salutes to love.

I could keep backing up in time, but surely growls about misbehaving servants are as old as domestic service itself. So when we find mischievous servants taunting and defying hapless or vengeful masters intent on extracting more dutiful service from the corrupt buffoons they had the misfortune to hire, we shouldn't imagine that we're witnessing social decay. Instead we're witnessing a reasonably stable social formation which has always already been a thicket of ambiguous and often conflicting norms with room for creative misreading, extemporaneous performances, violations that might or might not be excused or justified, and so on. Nor do even gross infractions — by servants and masters alike — necessarily mean the collapse of the practice. That would depend not just on whether they're punished, let alone as decisively as the Branches were, but also on whether we should expect serious unraveling effects. If your neighbors got away with murdering their servant, would you be more inclined to murder yours?

60. See for instance Thomas Wood, *An Institute of the Laws of England*, 2 vols. ([London], 1720), 2:728, echoed almost verbatim in T. S., *A Dissertation concerning the Evil Nature and Fatal Consequence of Immoderate Anger and Revenge* (London, 1725), 76. See too *The Student's Law-Dictionary* (London, 1740), s.v. *battery;* Giles Jacob, *The New Law-Dictionary* (London, 1743), s.v. *battery.*

61. Robert Abbott, *A Christian Family Builded by God, Directing All Governours of Families How to Act* (London, 1653), 61; Richard Burton, *The Apprentices Companion, Containing Plain and Useful Directions for Servants, Especially Apprentices, How to Perform Their Particular Dutys to Their Masters, so as to Please God* (London, 1681), 49; [John Graile], *Youths Grand Concern: or, Advice to Young Persons*, 2nd ed. (London, 1711), 84; T[homas] Wheatland, *A Manual for Servants: Containing the Several Instances of Their Duty, and the Advantages of Complying with It* (London, 1731), 17.

62. 1 Peter 2:18–19. [Nathaniel Hardy], *Love and Fear the Inseparable Twins of Ablest Matrimony* (London, 1658), 20, carefully distinguishes a servant's fear of his master from a wife's fear of her husband. Contrast B. D., *The Honourable State of Matrimony Made Comfortable* (London, 1685), 97.

Servants' Manuals

The ubiquity of domestic service gave rise to a genre of servants' manuals. The manuals' advice testifies to the extent of everyday insubordination. A recurrent tic is to applaud consensus and harmony of interests, though it sometimes sounds like slavish self-abnegation for the servants. (But isn't that a sadly regular way to arrive at a harmony of interests?) I don't want to caricature this literature or cherry-pick its worst excesses. But I do want to suggest it's chock-full of blather. I argued before that when we read celebrations of patriarchal authority over women, we shouldn't assume that people unthinkingly assented. I have the same view about celebrations of patriarchal authority over servants. Readers and listeners needn't be slack-jawed.

Let's start with Richard Baxter's imposing 1681 roster of "The Duty of Servants to Their Masters":

> First, to honour and reverence them, and obey them in all lawful things belonging to their places to command, and to avoid all words and carriage, which savour of dishonour, contempt, or disobedience. *2ly*. To perform all labour willingly which they undertake, and is required of them, and that without grudging: and to be as faithful behind their Masters backs as before their faces. *3ly*. To be trusty in word and deed, and abhor lying and deceit, not to wrong their Masters in buying or selling, or by stealing any thing that is theirs, no not meat nor drink against their Will: but being as thrifty and carefull for their Masters profit, as if it were their own, not to murmer at the means of food that is wholesome, nor to desire a life of fulness, ease, and idleness. *5ly*. To be more careful to do their duty to their Masters, then how their Masters shall use them, because sin is worse than suffering. *6ly*. Not to reveal the Secrets of the Family abroad, to Strangers or Neighbours. *7ly*. Thankfully to receive Instructions, and to learn God's word, and to observe the Lords day, and seriously joyn in publick and private worshipping of God. *8ly*. To bear patiently reprooff and due correction, and to confess faults and to amend. *9ly*. To pray daily for a blessing on the Family, on their labours and themselves. *10ly*. To do all this in true obedience to God, expecting their reward from him, 1 *Pet.* 2. ch. 18. *Tit.* 2 ch. 9. ver. 1. *Tim.* 6 chap. 12 ver. *Col.* 3 ch. 22. 2 *Eph.* 6 ch. 5 ver. *Matt.* 10 ch. 24 ver.[63]

---

63. [Richard Baxter], *Mr. BAXTERS Rules & Directions for Family Duties, Shewing How Every One Ought to Behave Himself in a Christian Behaviour, Suitable to That Relation in Which God Hath Placed Him* (n.p., [1681]). There is no *4ly* in the original. Compare John Reading, *A Gvide to the Holy City: or, Directions and Helps to an Holy Life* (Oxford, 1651), 275.

What do such catalogs tell us about everyday life? Recall the interpretive rule of thumb: authors promulgate norms when they object to what others are doing. We could refine this: maybe no one's actually doing it, but people worry they are or they might; or maybe the norm is aimed at a hyperbolic version of the target; or in their more considered moods, some don't like what they themselves sometimes do; and so on. And the contours of the norm will often respond to pressing problems. Why tell servants to obey their masters "in all lawful things"? Lest servants become complicit in, just for instance, murder. Baxter wrote a decade after Henry Jones got his fifteen-year-old servant to help him murder his mother. (Jones wanted to collect the £100 a year she'd inherited from her father.) The servant didn't hesitate: "this Imp of Hell, a stranger to Grace, and Rebel to Nature, scoffingly told his Master on that horrid occasion, *That his Mothers throat cut as tough as an old Ewes.*"[64] If masters are ordering their servants to help them with matricide, you have to worry about wholesale recommendations of obedience. But norms are usually defeasible: indefinitely many exceptions may arise and it's unimaginable that we could spell them all out ahead of time. Then too, some will champion more sweeping formulations: "What is the Business of a Servant, is it not to obey the Pleasure of his Lord, and yield himself up entirely in Subjection to his Commands?"[65]

Baxter's advice reveals—no, trumpets the unhappy fact—that servants dishonored their masters, did their work grudgingly, skipped it altogether when they could, exploited what today's economists call agency slack to line their pockets, groaned about their plight, longed for lives of ease, gossiped like fiends outside the house, and so on. (Baxter was especially fierce about that longing for ease. On another occasion, he insisted that a Christian "had rather if he be a servant, dwell in a family, where he may do or receive most spiritual good, than in a carnal family, where he may have more ease, and better fare, and greater wages.")[66] Not all servants. But at least some servants

64. *The Bloody Murtherer: or, The Unnatural Son His Just Condemnation* (London, 1672), 7. See too *The Deposition, and Farther Discovery, of the Late Horrid Plot, by One Mr. C——, Late Servant to Sir Tho. G——* (London, [1679]); *The Information of Eustace Comyne, Servant to Mr. Keadagh Magher Treasurer to the Papists in Ireland* (London, 1680); *A Full Account of the Case of John Sayer, Esq; from the Time of His Unhappy Marriage with His Wife, to His Death,* 2nd ed. with additions (London, 1713), 24.

65. Daniel Whitby, *A Discourse of the Love of God* (London, 1697), 60. Contrast Thomas Seaton, *The Conduct of Servants in Great Families* (London, 1720), 43–44.

66. Richard Baxter, *Directions for Weak Distempered Christians, to Grow Up to a Confirmed State of Grace* (London, 1669), pt. 2, p. 46.

at least some time: that ancient woman of sixty Baxter so fondly recalled wouldn't have been worth singling out were she typical. Nor would we find the warning, "A sleepy master makes his servant a lowt,"[67] if it weren't painfully clear what servants would do in the absence of gimlet-eyed monitoring. Nor the warning, "the Master that keeps an idle Servant is in danger of nourishing a Traytor or a Thief."[68]

Baxter's advice was published as a broadside: one large sheet suitable for being hawked on street corners. I'll quote from another broadside of several years later, more homespun but open to the same strategy of interpretation. This husband's hatreds are what weary masters and mistresses regularly confronted:

> Lastly, My Servants, if you would me please,
> You must observe, & keep such Rules as these:
> Be true and trusty; let your Hands be clear,
> And to Purloyn your Master's Goods, forbear.
> I hate a Slut, I hate a sawcy Knave,
> And in a Lyar I no pleasure have.
> I hate all those that have a vaunting Vein,
> And those that Other's Credits love to stain.
> I hate the Swearer, and the Drunken Sot,
> Who vow Obedience only to the Pot;
> By which Love, Fear, and Duty are forgot.
> I like not such, who would by fawning please,
> Nor those that love their Belly, and their Ease.
> Sly Sneaks, that would my Secrets over-look;
> Proud Fools, or Talking Ones, I cannot brook.
> I like not those, that are unapt to learn;
> Nor those, that grudgingly their VVages earn.
> Those I detest, who Cards and Dice do use,
> Quarrel with Fellow-Servants, and abuse.

---

67. G[eorge] H[erbert], *Outlandish Proverbs* (London, 1640), no. 766, sig. D4 verso. It's not anachronistic to read this proverb as another bit of principal / agent theory worrying about agency slack. We can find today's familiar usage of *principal* and *agent* as far back as 1655, with the dragon of the book of Revelations the principal, Rome his agent: John Lightfoot, *The Harmony, Chronicle and Order of the New Testament* (London, 1655), 168.

68. *The Counsels of Wisdom: or, A Collection of the Maxims of Solomon*, 2nd ed. (London, 1735), 232. See too *Walsingham's Manual: or, Prudential Maxims for Statesmen and Courtiers*, 2nd ed. (London, 1728), 33–34. See Fielding, *Tom Jones*, 1:39 for some mischievous writing about a servant taking her sweet time to respond.

The Loyterer too, who does of Errands stay,
By false Occasions making long his way.
Those too I hate, who only serve the Eye;
Nor longer labour, than whil'st I am by.
And such, by Night, who revel out of Doors,
Are only fit to serve the Galley-Oars.
The false, deceitful Soul, I hate as Hell;
Only with me the Honest Heart shall dwell,
   That's Humble, Painful, willing to Obey,
   And well deserves to Rule another Day.[69]

Jeremy Taylor rattles off a more succinct catalog: "In your Servants, suffer any offence against your self, rather than against God; endure not that they should swear, or lye, or steal, or be wanton, or curse each other, or be railers, or slanderers, or tell-tales, or sowers of dissention in the family, or amongst neighbors."[70]

Again, these writers reveal the range of everyday misbehavior: there's no point in urging servants to do things they already do—or not to do things they don't. When we read that servants "are oblig'd to see, there be no Waste of any thing under their Charge, but must manage all with as much Care and Frugality, as if it were their own,"[71] we should assume that servants weren't frugal with their masters' assets, and masters pushed back, and so it went, on and on, acrimoniously, bumblingly, comically, depressingly, enervatingly, frustratingly, glumly, homicidally, infuriatingly. . . . When we see chamber-maids instructed, "Be careful in over-looking Inferiour Servants, that they waste nothing that belongs to your Master and Mistress," we should see too that the overarching imperative of thrift created further conflict among servants.[72] Whatever the occasion, whatever the remedy, the centrality of con-

---

69. *The Husband's Instructions to His Family: Or, Houshold Observations, Fit to Be Observed by Wife, Children, and Servants* (London, 1685). For more strictures against eye-service, echoing Ephesians 6:6, see for instance *The Workes of the Reverend and Faithfvll Servant of Iesvs Christ Mr. Richard Greenham* (London, 1612), 76.

70. Jeremy Taylor, *The Golden Grove: A Choice Manual* (London, 1703), 40. For a whimsically affectionate nod to masters' cursing, see A Person of Thirty Years Experience, *Advice How to Manage in the Gout, and When Free of It*, 2nd ed. (Dublin, 1733), 11.

71. [John Gother], *Instructions for Apprentices and Servants* ([London], 1690), 14–15. This tract is largely folded into *Instructions for Masters, Traders, Labourers, &c. Also for Servants, Apprentices, and Youth* ([London?], 1718), starting at 59.

72. N. H., *The Ladies Dictionary, Being a General Entertainment of the Fair-Sex: A Work Never Attempted before in English* (London, 1694), 91–92. So too for housekeepers, 183.

flict was bleakly evident. "The Occasions of falling out amongst Servants are as numberless as the Injuries they are capable of doing one another."[73]

Other writers might as well have been sparring to see who could most enthusiastically urge devotion. When one writer announces, "it will rejoice the heart of a good Servant to see his Masters Affair prosper," he's not thinking that the servant is prudently forecasting a wage increase or better food. Deriding fear of sanctions, he coupled the divine right of kings and that old parallel between realm and family to give birth to this unctuous thought: servants ought to "have reverence for their Masters, as those that by Gods appointment are placed over them."[74] Another writer asserted, "It is enough to set a servant about his work in that it is his masters pleasure."[75] In labor history, we're not yet up to the worker as living appendage of the machinery; we're still at living appendage of another person. No wonder servants ought to cultivate "Faithfulness in keeping their Master's Secrets, promoting his Interest, vindicating his Reputation, and defending his Person, as occasion serves, and so far as it is in their Power."[76] A good servant "stoops under the authoritie of his master," offering not just reverence but also "patient bearing of rebukes though bitter and unjust."[77] Indeed, "a good servant will take a buffet patiently, and go about his Masters work."[78]

The subterranean rumblings of dehumanization sometimes surfaced loud and clear. "IT is required in a good seruant, to haue the backe of an Asse, to beare all things patiently: the tongue of a shéepe, to kéepe silence gently: and the snout of a swyne, to féede on all thinges heartily: large eares: light feet: & a trustie right hand: loth to offend: diligent to please: willing to amende, and sufferance disease."[79] Dr. Johnson captured the contempt afoot

73. Seaton, *Conduct of Servants*, 169.

74. Burton, *Apprentices Companion*, 8.

75. Thomas Manton, *One Hundred and Ninety Sermons on the Hundred and Nineteenth Psalm* (London, 1681), 25.

76. John Waugh, *The Duty of Apprentices and Other Servants: A Sermon* (London, 1713), 21.

77. Abbott, *Christian Family Builded by God*, 60–61. This echoes Mathew Griffith, *Bethel: or, A Forme for Families* (London, 1633), 383–84.

78. Manton, *One Hundred and Ninety Sermons*, 25, 299 (the latter echoed not quite verbatim at 140). Compare E. Dower, *The Salopian Esquire: or, The Joyous Miller: A Dramatick Tale* (London, 1739), 38: "I saw a Tinker the other Day beating his Wife: I asked the poor Woman how she could bear the Blows with so much Patience? — She told me Love softned every Stroke."

79. L[eonard] Wright, *A Display of Dutie, Dect with Sage Sayings, Pythie Sentences, and Proper Similies* (London, 1589), 37. See the cover illustration of *The Ages Rarity: or, The Emblem of a Good Servant Explain'd* (London, 1682). For "an excellentt footman" sprinting at a superhuman pace, see *The Memoirs of Anne, Lady Halkett and Ann, Lady Fanshawe*, ed. John Loftis (Oxford: Clarendon, 1979), 79.

in a letter from Zosima, "daughter of a country gentleman" seeking work as a servant. (Johnson must have intended her social status to invite the polite reader's sympathy.) She takes affront when the master of one house banters about her likely future of stealing "a few ribbands":

> Sir, answer'd I, why should you, by supposing me a thief, insult one from whom you had received no injury? Insult, says the lady; are you come here to be a servant, you saucy baggage, and talk of insulting? What will this world come to, if a gentleman may not jest with a servant? Well, such servants! pray be gone, and see when you will have the honour to be so insulted again. Servants insulted—a fine time.—Insulted! Get down stairs, you slut, or the footman shall insult you.[80]

Imagine being branded a slut for protesting being branded a thief.

Here talk of deference and consensus sugarcoats contempt and physical blows. Maybe this talk is strategic. After all, contemporaries understood the advantages of setting the bar high. "A Servant never yet miscarried thro' Excess of Respect," as one adage had it.[81] There might be another strategy in play, making actual masters look less peremptory than they were officially entitled to be. Already in 1639 we find the maxim, "If the master bid *goe*, the servant must *run*."[82]

Either way, chunks of that sugarcoating are a regular diet in the servants' manuals. One called for "Affection or good Will towards a Master."[83] The first duty of servants, said another, was "from their hearts, cheerefully, and willingly performe the labors and works, that their mastresses, or dames, shall command them"—indeed, "to loue them, and to be affectioned towards them, as a dutifull childe is to his father."[84] Another agreed that servants owed their masters not just fidelity, not just respect, but also love: "when Servants bear a hearty Love to their Masters, they Act in Their Concer[n]s, as they would do in their own, and they are zealously Studious both of their Profit Credit and Welfare."[85] Servants owed their masters obedience, faith-

80. *Rambler*, no. 12 (28 April 1750), in *The Yale Edition of the Works of Samuel Johnson*, ed. W. J. Bate et al., 23 vols. to date (New Haven, CT: Yale University Press, 1958–), 3:62–68.

81. Thomas Fuller, *Gnomologia: Adagies and Proverbs; Wise Sentences and Witty Sayings, Ancient and Modern, Foreign and British* (London, 1732), no. 391, p. 15.

82. [John Clarke], *Paroemiologia Anglo-Latina . . . or Proverbs English, and Latine* (London, 1639), 284, italics reversed.

83. [Zinzano], *Servants Calling*, 47.

84. R[obert] C[leaver], *A Godlie Forme of Hovseholde Government: For the Ordering of Private Families, According to the Direction of Gods Word* (London, 1598), 378, 379.

85. Will[iam] Nichols, *The Duty of Inferiours towards Their Superiours, in Five Practical Discourses* (London, 1701), discourse III, pp. 68–69, 70–71, 76–77.

fulness, and that "*Third* and last great Duty," love, chorused another writer.[86] Margaret Cavendish ratcheted up the stakes: "Good & Faithfull Servants will Dye for the Safeguard of their Masters Life, and they will indure any Torments rather than Betray their Masters; and it is the Duty of Servants so to do."[87] There's more here than a verbal form, though there is that: Sir Walter Raleigh, facing execution, was probably not bursting with affection when he wrote to James I, "whither I live or dye, your Majesties loving servant I will live and die."[88] One divine summoned up a "louing seruant [who] vpon curtesie to his old maister, though he haue left him, yet he still calleth him maister, and offereth himself and his seruice at his command."[89]

Yet again, scripture was in the background—"Owe no man any thing, but to love one another: for he that loveth another hath fulfilled the law"[90]— and sometimes explicitly.[91] Watch how scripture underwrites more incessant demands for amiable self-abnegation:

> But besides the yielding an active Obedience, you that are Servants are also obliged patiently to bear the Reproofs and Corrections of your Masters, without any Resistance, or so much as *answering again* in sausie Replies; *Tit.* 2. 9. And St. *Peter* carries your Duty yet further, requiring a Compliance with such Orders and Commands as are harsh and severe, and a patient Submission to such Reproofs and Corrections as are altogether undeserved; not occasioned by the Faults of Servants, but by the Rigour, Moroseness, and wrathful Passions of ill-tempered Masters; 1. *Pet.* 2. 16, 19, 20.[92]

But there's more than biblical citation on offer and the bonds of sentiment overflow any mere contractual arrangement. Robinson Crusoe's man Friday is fiction, but the social type he stands for is fact—at least as wistful aspiration: "never Man had a more faithful, loving, sincere Servant than *Friday* was to me; without Passions, Sullenness, or Designs, perfectly oblig'd and en-

86. [Richard Lucas], *The Duty of Servants*, 3rd ed. (London, 1710), 64, 47.

87. [Cavendish], *CCXI Sociable Letters*, 126–27.

88. *The Araignment and Conviction of Sʳ Walter Rawleigh, at the Kings Bench-Barre at Winchester on the 17 of November 1603* (London, 1648), 36, worded slightly differently in *Remains of Sir Walter Raleigh* (London, 1702), 192. Less apocalyptically, see for instance [Simon Kellwaye], *A Defensative against the Plague* (London, 1593), sig. A2 recto.

89. [Thomas Bell], *The Iesuits Antepast Conteining, A Reply against a Pretensed Aunswere to the Downe-fall of Poperie* (London, 1608), 13. Bell puts these words in his opponent's mouth, but not to distance himself from the sentiment.

90. Romans 13:8.

91. [Robert Shelford], *Lectvres, or Readings vpon the 6 Verse of the 22 Chapter of the Prouerbs* (London, 1602), 105.

92. [Graile], *Youths Grand Concern*, 84.

gag'd; his very Affections were ty'd to me, like those of a Child to a Father; and I dare say, he would have sacrific'd his Life for the saving mine, upon any Occasion whatsoever."[93] The servants of Sir Roger Coverley, that gruff and lovable character in the *Spectator*, "were not able to speak a Word for weeping" when Coverley told them he was dying.[94]

But not only as wistful aspiration or saccharine literary fantasy. There's no reason to doubt a series of contemporary reports. Archbishop William Laud confided in his diary, "Master *Adam Torles*, my Ancient loveing and faithfull servant then my Steward, after he had served me full 42. yeares, dyed, to my great losse and griefe."[95] Lord Capel's servants wept at his execution.[96] "The extraordinary Diligence of her Coachman and a Woman Servant" saved a pregnant Lady Bridgman when her Soho Square house collapsed.[97] If that strikes you as admirable but not loving, what about the servant of one Mr. Weston? When Weston was robbed at his threshold, his servant chased the robbers, earning a wounded arm for his devotion.[98] Or take the servant who plunged into a burning house to save his master's property, burning himself dreadfully in the process.[99] When a wealthy gentleman gone missing was finally found drowned, one newspaper reported a signal bit of loyalty: "His Footman, a Negro Servant, had been in search for him upwards of five Weeks."[100] (No, you may not suggest he was only trying to get paid.) The generous bequests from masters to their servants that I canvassed before suggest heartfelt gratitude. Maybe such masters were dupes taken in by two-faced servants. But honestly: all of them? Servants were family members: "I came with my whole Family (except my little Grandson, & his Nurse & some servants to looke after the house) to be in London the rest of this Winter," wrote John Evelyn in his diary.[101] Living at close quarters

93. [Daniel Defoe], *The Life and Strange Surprizing Adventures of Robinson Crusoe*, 3rd ed. (London, 1719), 247.

94. *Spectator*, no. 517 (23 October 1712), in Bond, *The Spectator*, 4:340.

95. William Prynne, *A Breviate of the Life of William Laud* (London, 1644), 25 (23 September 1641).

96. Arthur Lord Capel, *Excellent Contemplations, Divine and Moral* (London, 1683), 193.

97. *Daily Journal*, 2 August 1725.

98. *Old England*, 8 July 1749.

99. An Eye-witness, *A Sad Relation of a Dreadful Fire at Cottenham* ([London], 1676), 4.

100. *Daily Gazetteer*, 27 January 1736. For another tribute to a loving servant, see William Bagwell, *The Distressed Merchant: and The Prisoners Comfort in Distresse* (London, 1645), chap. 35.

101. *The Diary of John Evelyn*, ed. E. S. de Beer, 6 vols. (Oxford: Clarendon, 1955), 4:350 (17 November 1683); and see *Diary of Evelyn*, 5:375 (7 January 1700). See too Thomas Hobbes, *Leviathan*, chap. 20; Andrews, *Pattern of Catechistical Doctrine*, 350; Tho[mas] Gouge, *The Young Man's Guide*,

can generate warmth as well as cold hostility. It is no part of my purpose to deny that servants could love their masters, just as it is no part of my purpose to paint masters and mistresses as uniformly exploitative. On that last, Elizabeth Bury's diary speaks volumes:

> 1700. *Feb.* 29.] My Soul was humbled in me for the Wickedness and obstinate Impenitence of a Servant, which GOD had directed us to take, after we had seriously sought Divine Direction together and apart.
>
> *March* 1.] With the most melting Entreaties we could, we renewed our Exhortation, that the Criminal would make open and ingenuous Confession, and begg'd earnestly of GOD to move her Heart thereto; but the poor Wretch left our House in willful Impenitency, however we continued our earnest Prayer for her.[102]

However officious Bury's stance, there's no denying her concern. Nor that of Anne Clifford, who bought twenty-eight "bookes of Devotion" and gave twenty-two to her servants.[103] There could be strategy here—"the awe and government of your servants depends upon" "fervent, and constant" prayer, counseled one writer[104]—but there needn't be.

Still it is part of my purpose to deny that servants routinely loved their masters: a loving servant, admitted the *Female Spectator,* "is indeed a Jewel rare to be found."[105] And it is part of my purpose to argue that even love wouldn't be the opposite of conflict. If you're tempted to take these rhap-

---

through the VVilderness of This VVorld to the Heavenly Canaan (London, 1676), 152; David Jones, *A Sermon of the Absolute Necessity of Family-Duties* (London, 1692), 2–3; Lady Verney to Sir John Verney, 7 September 1702, in *Verney Letters,* 1:114; *Guardian,* 20 June 1713; William Burkitt, *The Poor-Man's Help, and Young-Man's Guide* (London, 1732), 51–52; [Samuel Richardson], *Pamela: or, Virtue Rewarded,* 4th ed., 2 vols. (London, 1741), 1:84, 1:123, 1:174, 2:3, 2:39; Henry Fielding, *Joseph Andrews* [1742], ed. Martin C. Battestin (Oxford: Clarendon, 1967), 47; *Rambler,* no. 68 (10 November 1750), in *Works of Samuel Johnson,* 3:361.

102. *An Account of the Life and Death of Mrs. Elizabeth Bury, Who Died, May the 11th 1710: Aged 76,* 3rd ed. corr. (Bristol, 1721), 138. See too Timothy Rogers, *The Character of a Good Woman, Both in a Single and Marry'd State* (London, 1697), with diary material from Elizabeth Dunton, esp. 15–17; [Edmund Hall], *A Sermon Preached at Stanton-Harcourt Church in the County of Oxford at the Funerall of the Honourable Lady Ann Harcourt* (Oxford, 1664), 54–55; Thomas Manton, *Advice to Mourners under the Loss of Dear Relations* (London, 1694), xii–xiii; [John Graile], *An Essay of Particular Advice to the Young Gentry* (London, 1711), 80.

103. *The Diaries of Lady Anne Clifford,* ed. D. J. H. Clifford (Phoenix Mill: Sutton, 2003), 243–44 (10 January 1676).

104. D[aniel] R[ogers], *Matrimoniall Honovr: or, The Mutuall Crowne and Comfort of Godly, Loyall, and Chaste Marriage* (London, 1642), 142.

105. *The Female Spectator,* 3rd ed., 4 vols. (Dublin, 1747), 2:28.

sodies as snapshots of the typical case, consider the *Spectator*'s diatribe: "A Man will have his Servant just, diligent, sober, and chaste, for no other Reasons but the Terrour of losing his Master's Favour." No wonder the *Spectator* appended a petition denouncing the use of household spies.[106]

The loving servant: we are a long way from hurling the mistress's daughter into the ocean, a long way too from the catch fart. (Happily, there are limits: I located no manual suggesting that servants should rapturously inhale their masters' flatulence.) It's bitterly amusing, perhaps, that when one servant helped his mistress murder his master, he had to listen to this yearning appeal to help find the murderer: "thou of all men diddest loue thy maister, and thy maister of all men did loue thee best."[107] Love, surely, would provide an answer to this plaintive lament: "If Servants prove idle or faithless to their Trust, is it not because a zealous Discharge of their Duty has no Savour in it; and 'tis more agreeable to comply with their own slothful or gossipping Humour?"[108] Again, I don't wish to caricature the servants' manuals. There is more in them than the thrumming refrain that servants should be dutiful, respectful, self-abnegating, devoted, loving. But that refrain is insistent. It's as if the only choices on offer were murderous servants and saintly ones. Or as if shirking, insubordination, mischief making, and the like were nothing but way stations on the slippery slope to outrageous criminality. All these framings and sentiments betray the powerful pull of a bankrupt model of social order. We can do better. At least one notable contemporary did.

Swift: Text, Genre, Context

Alas, Jonathan Swift's *Directions to Servants* enjoys a reputation as a decidedly minor work[109]—in part, I suspect, because of the misguided impulse to cast Swift's irony as saying the opposite of what he means. First published in 1745, shortly after Swift died, it is incomplete. But Swift worked on it intermittently for decades[110] and anyway its fragmentary state is part of

106. *Spectator*, no. 202 (22 October 1711), in Bond, *Spectator*, 2:292, 294.

107. *Two Most Vnnatural and Bloodie Murthers* (London, 1605), 26.

108. [John Gother], *Afternoon Instructions for the Whole Year*, 2 vols. ([London?], 1717), 2:82.

109. But see Jenny Davidson, *Hypocrisy and the Politics of Politeness: Manners and Morals from Locke to Austen* (Cambridge: Cambridge University Press, 2004), chap. 1.

110. For the textual history, see *Prose Works of Jonathan Swift*, 13:vii–xxiii. For the text, *Prose Works*, 13:17–65.

its literary charm. The apparent interruptions and the brevity of the last chapters suggest that he could go on in this vein indefinitely. Nor would it run a joke into the ground, because the text is wonderfully rich. Swift, I suggest, subverts the fatuous advice of the servants' manuals—and he offers a better way to conceive the relationship between norms and everyday life. Almost every paragraph offers a vivid vignette of household life, bracing stuff after the soporific abstractions of the servants' manuals. Swift shows in splendidly concrete detail how rich and tangled the grounds of conflict are, how easily they give rise to conflict itself.

Like other famous subversions—Machiavelli's *Prince* of the mirror-of-princes literature, Mandeville's *Fable of the Bees* of poems casting the realm as a happy beehive—Swift's text remains, but the genre it spoofs has disappeared. Similarly, our grasp of the social practice of domestic service in early modern England is shaky. I take genre and context not as causally interesting, not that is as helping to explain why Swift happened to write this little gem, but as interpretively interesting, as illuminating what it means. Then reading Swift's text can't be solely a matter of reading the text closely, though that's a great thing to do. It has to be in part summoning up the prior genre of servants' manuals and in part summoning up the actual social practice of domestic service.

The *Directions* purport to be written by a former footman: "I had once the Honour to be one of your Order, which I foolishly left by demeaning myself with accepting an Employment in the Custom-house." For persuasive authority, the narrator pleads his seven years' experience and ongoing solidarity: he hopes that footmen, "my Brethren, may come to have better fortunes." Remember that footmen elicited vehement disapproval: it's intriguing that Swift chose to make one his narrator. But who are the *Directions* written for? They're formally addressed to servants in what must be a large, prosperous house: to butler, cook, footman, coachman, groom, and so on. But that can't settle the question of their intended readership any more than the narrator's identity as a former footman can tell us something about Jonathan Swift's occupational history.[111]

---

111. Ditto for the apocryphal joke in *England's Genius: or, Wit Triumphant* (London, 1734), 17: "The famous Dean of St. *Patrick's*, being once in Company with a Gentleman of the Name of *Taylor*, said, he believed most of the Sirnames of *Taylor*, *Smith*, *Carpenter*, &c. came from Persons who had occupied those Trades, or Vocations; and then made bold to ask his Friend, if none of his Ancestors had been bred Taylors.—*No, Sir, they were all Gentlemen. Now, Mr. Dean*, adds he, *since you have been so free*

Swift, I suggest, is writing for masters and mistresses or anyway a relatively sophisticated audience, but not servants. "My treatise is chiefly calculated for the general Run of Knights, Squires, and Gentlemen," announces the footman. That doesn't prove anything either, but it does highlight the possibility. For what it's worth, the biographical evidence on Swift's attitudes about servants is mixed. Swift could be harsh. The brief "Laws" he penned for his own servants set out a scheme of monetary fines for various offenses and add an ominous assertion of absolute authority: "Whatever other laws the Dean shall think fit to make, at any time to come, for the government of his servants, and forfeitures for neglect and disobedience, all the servants shall be bound to submit to."[112] Consider an apocryphal vignette about the written recommendation Swift handed his own errant servant: "WHEREAS the bearer served me the space of one year, during which time he was an *idler* and a *drunkard;* I then discharged him as such; but how far his having been five years at sea may have mended his manners, I leave to the penetration of those who may hereafter chuse to employ him."[113] This nasty joke depends on the servant's credulity, his illiteracy, and the failure of those who read this appalling reference to tell him why they reject him. The servant was rebuffed time and again. Eventually Laetitia Pilkington advised him to try Swift's dear friend Alexander Pope, who hired him—and kept him on for life—once the man established he had worked for Swift.[114]

Then again, Swift's servants were devoted enough that they rarely left voluntarily.[115] Observe what social scientists call selection and socialization effects. When interviewing potential servants, Swift made it clear they'd be cleaning shoes—including other servants' shoes. If they balked, he'd have no more to do with them.[116] But those hired were paid "the highest rate then

with my Family, pray give me some account of your own.—Why truly, replies the Dean, my Father indeed was a Gentleman, but my Grandfather was a running Footman, which made him take the Name of sw—FT."

112. "Laws for the Dean's Servants," *Prose Works*, 13:161–62. Compare the illustration used in an argument about things indifferent in Izaak Walton, *The Life of Dr. Sanderson, Late Bishop of Lincoln* (London, 1678), 91–92.

113. *Prose Works*, 13:166. See too *"Merry Passages and Jests,"* 103–4.

114. *The Third and Last Volume of the Memoirs of Mrs. Laetitia Pilkington, Written by Herself* (London, 1754), 80–81. For Pope's generosity to a man who'd saved his life and was now seeking work as a footman, see Pope to John Brinsden, November [1740?], in *Correspondence of Pope*, 4:289.

115. Irvin Ehrenpreis, *Swift: The Man, His Works, and the Age*, 3 vols. (Cambridge, MA: Harvard University Press, 1962–83), 3:33.

116. [Patrick Delany], *Observations upon Lord Orrery's Remarks on the Life and Writings of Dr. Jonathan Swift* (London, 1754), 213–14.

known: which was four shillings a-week," and additional wages for work beyond their usual duties.[117] (Right, it's prudent to wonder how much they paid back in fines.) Even so, Swift wasn't always satisfied. "I have the best Servant in the World dying in the House," lamented Swift, "which quite disconcerts me; He was the first good one I ever had, and I am sure will be the last." That servant bequeathed Swift "a Fus[il], Quaile Pipes and Nets . . . as the last mark of Duty and Affection from a faithfull Servant." Swift presided tearfully over his funeral service and erected "an unpretentious stone slab" for him.[118] Yet Swift's servant Patrick exasperated him. "He was damnably mauled one day when he was drunk; he was at cuffs with a brother footman, who dragged him along the floor upon his face, which lookt for a week after as if he had the leprosy; and I was glad enough to see it."[119]

This biographical evidence can't bear significant weight in interpreting the *Directions*. Even other texts from Swift needn't be decisive or even relevant. One sets out his servants' duty at inns.[120] All its instructions, even an odd one about checking Swift's bed "lest a Cat or something else may be under it," are perfectly earnest: that is, he'd be happy to have his servants follow them. The difference between the *Directions* and this text is the difference between what Swift wants to say in public and what he wants to say to his own servants in private. But it will follow instantly that how Swift happened to address his own servants can't govern or even guide what he might want to say in public. Even moralists horrified by hypocrisy admit that public professions need be no guide to private conduct. The inference doesn't work any better in the opposite direction.

But what about another text Swift intended for public consumption? His "Causes of the Wretched Condition in Ireland" shows how seriously he took worries about servants:

> I THINK there is no Complaint more just than what we find in almost every Family, of the Folly and Ignorance, the Fraud and Knavery, the Idleness and Viciousness, the wasteful squandering Temper of Servants, who are,

117. [Delany], *Observations*, 185–86; and see Ehrenpreis, *Swift*, 3:833.

118. Swift to Knightley Chetwode, 13 March 1722, in *The Correspondence of Jonathan Swift, D. D.*, ed. David Woolley, 4 vols. (Frankfurt: Peter Lang, 1999–2007), 2:416–17. For the full text of the gravestone inscription and a friend's imposing on Swift not to describe himself on it as the servant's friend, see [Delany], *Observations*, 194–96.

119. Jonathan Swift, *Journal to Stella*, ed. Harold Williams, 2 vols. (Oxford: Basil Blackwell, 1974), 1:302 (30 June 1711).

120. "The Duty of Servants at Inns," in *Prose Works*, 13:163–65.

indeed, become one of the many publick Grievances of the Kingdom; whereof, I believe, there are few Masters that now hear me, who are not convinced by their own Experience. And I am very confident, that more Families, of all Degrees, have been ruined by the Corruptions of Servants, than by all other Causes put together.[121]

This diatribe, also as it happens published posthumously, poses no worries about enlisting Swift's private sentiments or life in reading the *Directions*. The jocular tone of the *Directions* might seem not to fit well with the portentous air of the "Causes." Better, I think, to realize that Swift was happy to subvert the servants' manuals without being under any illusions about the stakes.

What does social context tell us about Swift's audience? Probably most servants in Swift's day were illiterate. London is a partial exception to the rule that literacy collapsed at the bottom of the social hierarchy. But a sampling of some rural dioceses over a somewhat earlier time period shows that 76 percent of servants couldn't sign their own names, but made marks.[122] The relationship between signing and reading is murky, but that's not an encouraging figure.[123] This evidence isn't conclusive, either. Some of the prior servants' manuals are addressed to servants, some to masters. Formal address doesn't settle actual or intended audience with those manuals, either, but their authors weren't fiendishly clever. Surely some servants were literate: Baxter remembered learning to read from some tracts owned by a family servant; I assume the servant could read them himself.[124]

We learn something about Swift's text's reception from a later plug, that it has "never failed to produce entertainment to all those who have the least relish for picturesque diction."[125] While the footman says he's writing for gentlemen, he also assumes the cook won't be able to read his instructions but

121. "Causes," in *Prose Works*, 9:203.

122. David Cressy, *Literacy and the Social Order: Reading and Writing in Tudor and Stuart England* (Cambridge: Cambridge University Press, 1980), 119.

123. Keith Thomas thinks that this approach understates the number of readers: see his "The Meaning of Literacy in Early Modern England," in *The Written Word: Literacy in Transition*, ed. Gerd Baumann (Oxford: Clarendon, 1986). Ian Michael, *The Teaching of English: From the Sixteenth Century to 1870* (Cambridge: Cambridge University Press, 1987), has a wealth of information on how literacy was taught. Margaret Spufford, *Small Books and Pleasant Histories: Popular Fiction and Its Readership in Seventeenth-Century England* (Cambridge: Cambridge University Press, 1981), remains the best account of its kind.

124. Baxter, *Reliquiae Baxterianae*, lib. 1, pt. 1, p. 4.

125. [James Smith], *The Art of Living in London: A Poem, in Two Cantos* (London, 1768), [preface], n.p.

says she can get some other servant to do it for her. But my claim, that the text is only formally addressed to servants and its intended audience is their superiors, hangs finally on the claim that it works much better that way. It's a searing satiric frame: let's eavesdrop, Swift invites his real readers, on the advice a benevolent footman might deliver to his fellow servants. Then, as it turns out, the eavesdroppers don't enjoy the mawkish pleasures of condescending superiority. They find themselves rudely surprised.

How so? From the start, the footman's advice is astounding, but delivered in a deadpan voice becoming increasingly droll—and disquieting. "Give no Person any Liquor till he has called for it thrice at least," he instructs the butler on the opening page; "by which means, some out of Modesty, and others out of Forgetfulness, will call the seldomer, and thus your Master's Liquor be saved." Soon after:

> If any one calls for Small-beer towards the end of Dinner, do not give yourself the Pains of going down to the Cellar, but gather the Droppings and Leavings out of the several Cups, and Glasses, and Salvers into one; but turn your Back to the Company, for Fear of being observed: On the contrary, if any one calls for Ale towards the end of Dinner, fill the largest Tankard top-full, by which you will have the greatest Part left to oblige your Fellow-servants without the Sin of stealing from your Master.

It's tempting to think that Swift is trading on the difference between an evaluative norm, what people ought to do, and a statistical or descriptive norm, what in fact people tend to do. So the butler should dutifully pour when asked, but he's lazy, distracted, unresponsive. On this reading, the comic thrust of the text is pretending that the dismal facts of everyday practice are ideal.

This won't do. Not because of any rarefied worries about the fact / value distinction: even us vulgar pragmatists can tell the difference between "The cat is on the mat" and "The cat should be on the mat." Rather because Swift's terse advice shows that the butler is caught in a maze of conflicting imperatives. This example is an unremarkable and thus paradigm case of how, below the lofty horizon of consensus or even love, norms generate conflict. One might think the butler should promptly respond to the guests' orders for more drink: he should be polite and he should show that his master can afford generous entertainment. But the butler is also supposed to be thrifty and never waste his master's assets. It's glib to pretend that there is no real conflict here because we can demarcate a frontier on one side of which generosity rules, on the other thrift. There will be endless controversy over the location of the frontier. Picture the butler morosely forecasting his master's vexation when the guests leave their glasses mostly full. Worse, the frontier in this little normative space might have width, so that over some range of actions both norms officially control.

The advice on ale exploits two conflicts. Pouring a great tankard late in the dinner means the inevitable leftover goes to the servants. So the butler would be redistributing assets from the master to his fellow servants. The prior servants' manuals obsess about this conflict endlessly, especially in their strictures against "purloining," which they read broadly.[126] Paul's epistle was ready to hand: "Exhort servants to be obedient unto their own masters, and to please them well in all things; not answering again; Not purloining, but shewing all good fidelity; that they may adorn the doctrine of God our Saviour in all things."[127] (Henry Fielding offered a housekeeper indignant that her master hadn't singled her out in his will. "I'd have his Worship know I am no beggar. I have saved five hundred Pound in his Service, and after all to be used in this Manner. It is a fine Encouragement to Servants to be honest; and to be sure, if I have taken a little Something now and then, others have taken ten times as much; and now we are all put in a Lump together.")[128] But if Swift's butler pours more stingily, he threatens to violate the dictate that he supply the guests warm hospitality. Damned if he does, damned if he doesn't?

What about the alarming advice that the butler combine beer from others' glasses but conceal what he's doing? The servants' manuals seem never to notice this conflict between master and guest. Would—should—a master whose servants deceive the guests without their knowing it deplore his servants' duplicity or salute their savvy? Yes, this advice is comically over the top. It triggers the hasty thought, "Surely no master wants his butler to do *that*." But—you don't need a butler of your own to appreciate this point—the arts of entertaining still include gambits for making the spread look more lavish than it is. Are all such arts out of bounds? So too for this caustic advice

126. Burton, *Apprentices Companion*, 58–59; [Lucas], *Duty*, 53–57; [Zinzano], *Servants Calling*, 35–37.

127. Titus 2:9–10. See too Thomas Vincent, *Words of Advice to Young Men* (London, 1668), 101; [Hannah Woolley], *The Compleat Servant-Maid: or, The Young Maidens Tutor* (London, 1677), 2, 35–36, 63; Matthew Poole [et al.], *Annotations upon the Holy Bible*, 2 vols. (London, 1683–85), vol. 2, n.p.; Fleetwood, *Relative Duties*, 290–91; Waugh, *Duty of Apprentices*, 17–18; Wheatland, *Manual*, 14.

128. Fielding, *Tom Jones*, 1:245–46.

to the footman: "When you are ordered to call a Coach, although it be Midnight, go no further than the Door, for Fear of being out of the Way when you are wanted; and there stand bawling, Coach, Coach, for half an Hour." This putative conflict is absurd. But surely the footman often faces genuine dilemmas about when to carry out an order and when to remain available, let alone when mechanical obedience is properly overridden. The idea of spelling out exhaustive rules to govern all such situations is mad. The idea that love or devotion would resolve such quandaries is intoxicated.

Take this advice to the cook: "You can give a good Bit or a good Sop to the little Masters and Misses, and gain their Affections." That reveals a wedge between parents and children that could profitably be driven by a strategic cook. The master might not appreciate her dispensing goodies to his children. But the cook can use them as allies—or as an insurance policy. A master will think twice about firing or disciplining a cook whom his children adore. After all, as the footman continues wryly, "A Quarrel between you is very dangerous to you both, and will probably end in one of you being turned off." Or take this advice: "If you live in a rich Family, roasting and boiling are below the Dignity of your Office, and which it becomes you to be ignorant of; therefore leave that Work wholly to the Kitchen Wench, for fear of disgracing the Family you live in."[129] The cook has a pretext for avoiding unpleasant work—and the pretext is plausible. Rich households with a fine-grained division of labor among the domestic staff are engaged in conspicuous consumption. One servant's taking on another's duties indicates that the master is less wealthy than he might wish to advertise. He wants his food to be deliciously cooked and the cook is defter than the kitchen wench. But he also wants to make a symbolic statement about his status. Could the division of labor here be as exhaustively laid out as the rules of chess, this problem would evaporate. But that's a fantasy. The same kind of analysis shows the footman how he vindicates not just his own interest in shirking unpleasant duty, but also his master's interest in not appearing "poor or covetous," by getting the master to hire a lantern boy instead of doing the grungy job himself. It shows why the groom and others are right to drink liberally when traveling with the master, to publicly vindicate his generosity: "what is a Gallon of Ale, or a Pint of Brandy in his Worship's Pocket?"

Watch what happens when the servants throw the master's health into the

---

129. See too Fielding, *Tom Jones*, 1:393.

mix of conflicting considerations. "When you send up Butter for Sauce, be so thrifty as to let it be half Water; which is also much wholesomer." This dubious mixture will save the master money and be good for his health. But it will be less tasty and discerning guests will downgrade his status. Again, it's too easy to respond that no reasonable servant would ever act on this advice. Even if it's over the top, other versions of this conflict aren't. If the footman lets the coffee boil over, he should serve it anyway. "This I would have you do from a Principle of Conscience, for Coffee is very unwholesome; and out of Affection to your Lady, you ought to give it to her as weak as possible." Should servants promote their masters' welfare or respect their autonomy?

What about relations among the servants? Earlier prayers designed for servants offer more tributes to loving consensus. From 1612: "Send peace and quietnesse betweene mee and my fellowes, that in loue and kindnesse wee may all with one heart, and one minde, constantly & chearfully ioyne together, to follow our Masters businesse."[130] From 1713: "O thou Lover of Peace and Concord, enable me to live in Brotherly Affection, Unity and Concord with my Fellow-Servants; and grant that we may be a mutual Comfort and Assistance to one another, as well in our spiritual as temporal Concerns."[131] The manuals are laced with similar sentiments: the chambermaid must be "loving to her fellow-servants."[132]

Swift is less euphoric. "Let there always be a strict Friendship between you and the Butler," the footman urges the cook, "for it is both your Interests to be united." The two can swap food and alcohol. "However, be cautious of him," continues the footman, "for he is sometimes an inconstant Lover": he can "allure the Maids" with alcohol, too. If you're abstemious about the concept of interest, you might think the cook could maintain a purely businesslike relationship with the butler and not worry if he's off flirting with other women. She might reason that he'll want the food, so still she'll get the alcohol. But the butler might well surmise that he can exploit a threat advantage if the cook is more intent on alcohol than he is on extra food—or even if she just wants it badly enough, regardless of his own desperation. He might hold out for sexual favors and it is a businesslike cook indeed who will think that's just part of the bargain.

130. [Thomas Sorocold], *Supplications of Saints: A Booke of Prayers*, 3rd ed. enlarged (London, 1612), 336–37.

131. *A New Manual of Devotions*, 2nd ed. corr. (London, 1713), pt. 1, p. 124. Compare *The True Church of England-Man's Companion in the Closet*, 6th ed. corr. (London, 1731), 401.

132. [Shirley], *Accomplished Ladies Rich Closet*, 91.

Or again: Swift urges the cook to save time by combing her hair as she cooks. "If some of the Combings happen to be sent up with the Victuals, you may safely lay the Fault upon any of the Footmen that hath vexed you." Unable to observe for himself, the master has to rely on trust. The cook's bravado might see her through—to the unfair disadvantage of the footmen.

Or watch what the groom can do by asserting a solidarity of interests with others' servants when the master is traveling. He should urge those servants to line up to collect their tips and insist that his master not trust the butler to disburse the tips properly. "This will force your Master to be more generous," as will wildly exaggerating the tips the groom's former employer used to hand out. Then "be sure to tell the Servants what a good Office you did them: This will gain you Love, and your Master Honour." So too the groom should always prevail on the other house's staff, even if they have no groom, to hold the horse while the master mounts: "For Brother-servants must always befriend one another, and this also concerns your Master's Honour, because he cannot do less than give a Piece of Money to him who holds his Horse."

For all its blather about loving consensus, the prior genre of servants' manuals gets one conflict in sharp focus. Suppose a servant wrongs his master and another servant notices.

> How is a *Servant* to behave himself towards his guilty Fellow-servant, that he may, in such a case as this, acquit himself with a good Conscience towards GOD and Man? If he conceal his Fault, he is unfaithful to his Master; if he discover it, he is unkind to his Fellow-servant: He must betray the one or the other; if he do not reveal the Wrong he sees, his Master suffers, and, what is more, his Conscience must suffer too; if he do, he shall be hated and persecuted by his Fellow-servants, as an Informer; nay, per-adventure, what is worse than this, he that is accused shall out-wit him, or shall be able to form a Combination against him, and so find more Credit with the Master, and by consequence the good *Servant* shall by his Integrity and Justice forfeit his Place, and it may be, his Reputation, or at least live uneasily, persecuted by the vexatious Calumnies, Affronts and Unkind-nesses of those others that are combined against him.

Moving as that description is, the author saw no problem here. "Whence should spring this Question, Whether you should support and cherish a wicked Fellow-Servant in his Vice, or whether you should preserve a Master, (to whom you owe Fidelity, Truth and Love) from Injuries and Wrongs?" "I know," he burbled, "there may be some little strugglings of good Nature and Interest, in opposition to your Duty in this point," but duty must rule. Reprove the fellow servant—"acquaint him with the beauty and pleasure, the security and advantage of Virtue and the Fear of God"—or get someone else to reprove him. If that fails, "go directly to your Master or Mistress."[133] Robert Dodsley, that footman turned poet, set the sentiment to verse:

> 'Tis not enough that we ourselves are true,
> We must take Care that others are so too;
> For should we be unmindful of our Trust,
> 'Tis much the same, as if we were unjust:
> If others cheat, embezzle, and purloin,
> Through my Neglect, the Fault as much is mine,
> As if I actually with them combine.
> For Masters on our Care as much rely,
> As on our Justice and Integrity:
> Therefore to them it is the self-same Cheat,
> Or done by Carelessness, or by Deceit.[134]

Contrast Swift's brisker treatment of this problem:

> If you see your Master wronged by any of your Fellow-servants, be sure to conceal it, for fear of being called a Tell-tale: However, there is one Exception, in case of a favourite Servant, who is justly hated by the whole Family; who therefore are bound in Prudence to lay all the Faults they can upon the Favourite.

No cloying high-mindedness here! I suppose Swift would chortle at the vision of one servant reading another a sermon on the rewards of virtue. Here the *Directions'* first impulse is to present the likely course of affairs as the desirable one. The next sentence, though, is more interesting. The "whole Family" who hate the favorite are the other servants. Like any Stakhanovite

133. [Lucas], *Duty*, 57–60. Compare [Gother], *Instructions for Apprentices*, 34–35. Contrast [Walter Darell], *A Short Discourse of the Life of Seruingmen Plainly Expressing the Way That Is Best to Be Followed* (London, 1578), sig. C.ii recto: "Delight not to complaine of any of thy fellowes, to currie fauour and disquiet thy maister: but after a friendly manner vse gentle persuasions, that if any of thy fellowes haue neglected his duetie, tell him secreatly that it may be reformed." See too [Gervase Markham], *A Health to the Gentlemanly Profession of Servingmen: or, The Servingmans Comfort* (London, 1598), sig. G2 recto–G3 verso.

134. D[odsley], *Footman's Friendly Advice*, 17–18. See too Brathwait, *Times Treasury*, supplement, 35–36; Seaton, *Conduct of Servants*, 136. But contrast [Eliza Haywood], *A Present for a Servant-Maid: or, The Sure Means of Gaining Love and Esteem* (London, 1743), 10.

or rate-buster of later labor history, this favorite earns the derision of his peers, who must see him as an overbearing prig. So the unfaithful servants rat out the faithful servant for offenses he never committed. No doubt they report to the master with countenances radiating doleful duty. How's he to know they're betraying not just their fellow servant but also him?

The servants' manual and Swift both notice that servants might collude in false accusation. The manual produces this disheartening fact to steel the resolve of the righteous servant: report your fellow's misdeed quickly, before he manages to turn you in. It's reassuring, even an everyday theodicy: prompt moral action secures the interests of master and righteous servant alike and leads to the richly deserved discipline of the wrongdoer. Swift notices that the pursuit of interest might not yield such happy outcomes. Writing after starry-eyed Shaftesbury and Hutcheson tried to show how deeply interest and morality cohere,[135] Swift will have none of it.

We are (too) familiar with arguments that appeals to principle are nothing but pretexts for self-interest. Sometimes that's true. But so too self-interest can serve as a pretext for principle. If you're embarrassed that your friends will scoff at you as a tree hugger if you buy a hybrid, you might boast about the money you'll save on gasoline even if you're motivated by your carbon footprint. Principle can't always be a pretext, else no one would ever bother invoking it. Swift's dissection depends crucially on the claim that norms have genuine justificatory and motivational force. So he isn't what we call a realist. (Why do lunatics get to command the rhetoric of realism? Everything is motivated by self-interest; nations care only for geopolitical advantage; legal doctrine is endlessly pliable. Yeah, sure.) It's good that Swift's strategy isn't our familiar one, because that one is bankrupt.

A steady stream of maidservants reported illegitimate children to the authorities.[136] The fathers could be other servants—or masters or their sons.

135. [Anthony Ashley Cooper, Earl of Shaftesbury], *Characteristicks of Men, Manners, Opinions, Times*, 3 vols. ([London], 1711), vol. 2; [Francis Hutcheson], *An Inquiry into the Original of Our Ideas of Beauty and Virtue; in Two Treatises* (London, 1725), treatise 2.

136. For instance St. Martin's in the Fields Pauper Biographies Project, Settlement Examinations, Elizabeth Price, 15 May 1732, *London Lives, 1690–1800*, smdsset_17_1805 (www.londonlives.org); see too in St. Martin's Biographies: smdsset_116_59032, Sarah Stratford, 15 December 1739; smdsset_112_58691, Isabella Atkinson, 31 January 1740; smdsset_112_58670, Isabella Bartheston, 5 March 1740; smdsset_109_58404, Catherine Halden, 6 December 1740; smdsset_109_58410, Isabella Thompson, 12 December 1740; smdsset_110_58482, Jane Burden, 3 February 1741; smdsset_111_58629, Isabella Brotherston, 12 August 1741; smdsset_112_58655, Isabella Atkinson, 2 December 1741; smdsset_108_58250, Jane Tinkerson, 12 January 1742; smdsset_106_58069, Mary Beaver, 9 August 1743; smdsset_102_57692, Elizabeth Cockin, 2 August 1746; smdsset_102_57704, Mary Kingdom, 11 September 1746;

Eliza Haywood took for granted that a servant maid should resist the sexual advances of her master and his son. She knew that would be hard to do. But she insisted that the maid would appeal to her mistress in vain: the master would probably lie and wreck her reputation. Even if he didn't, she'd be guilty of disturbing marital harmony. Even if she had the extraordinary luck to marry the son, she should blame herself for his marrying beneath his station, being ill treated by his friends, and suffering remorse for his generosity.[137] Haywood's allocation of responsibility is breathtaking. That aside, the maid who marries the master, made a cultural icon in Richardson's *Pamela*, was also, now and again, a real figure, at least if we can trust the newspapers. One seventeen-year-old with an inheritance of £20,000 married his forty-year-old servant maid.[138]

Swift didn't think that servants could always run circles around masters. Consider this advice to the chambermaid:

> If you are in a great Family, and my Lady's Woman, my Lord may probably like you, although you are not half so handsome as his own Lady. In this Case, take Care to get as much out of him as you can; and never allow him the smallest Liberty, not the squeezing of your Hand, unless he puts a Guinea into it; so, by degrees, make him pay accordingly for every new Attempt, doubling upon him in proportion to the Concessions you allow, and always struggling, and threatening to cry out, or tell your Lady, although you receive his Money: Five Guineas for handling your Breast is a cheap Pennyworth, although you seem to resist with all your Might; but never allow him the last Favour under a hundred Guineas, or a Settlement of twenty Pounds a Year for Life.

The chambermaid can't stop the master's harassment.[139] She can only profit from it on terms that don't begin to show the transaction is voluntary. (It can't be voluntary unless she has a reasonable alternative. Does she?) Swift's

smdsset_103–57734, Sarah Oxley, 9 November 1746; smdsset_103–57771, Mary Ford, 8 January 1747; smdsset_98–57272, Margaret Loch, 10 February 1748; smdsset_96–57109, Elizabeth Carr, 17 June 1748; smdsset_97–57163, Grace Wilson, 24 September 1748; smdsset_95–57012, Margaret Morrison, 3 February 1750.

137. [Haywood], *Present*, 46–48.

138. *London Morning Advertiser*, 14 March 1743.

139. For the chambermaid as sexually available, see Rich[ard] Fleckno[e], *Enigmaticall Characters, All Taken to the Life* (London, 1658), 38–39; or, despite the title, the version in Rich[ard] Flecknoe, *Ænigmatical Characters: Being Rather a New Work, Then New Impression of the Old* (London, 1665), 38–39.

footman thinks the chambermaid can shrug off the persistent attentions of the master's eldest son. Maybe the maid will be skillful enough to get him to marry her. Then she'll be a lady. But if he's a rogue, warns the footman, "you will get nothing from him, but a big Belly, or a Clap, and probably both together." Well, one wants to respond, and from the master too. The servant who bore children twice in 1649, once to her master and once to his son, might have found baffling the claim that she was powerless against one but not the other.[140] Yet again, you might be tempted to brand Swift a misogynist with a cavalier attitude about sexual exploitation. Before you leap to smug conclusions, consider this: he blocked a pardon for a man convicted of rape. "'Tis true, the fellow had lain with her a hundred times before; but what care I for that? What! must a woman be ravished because she is a whore?"[141]

Here's another caution. Yes, often masters were sexually exploiting helpless female servants.[142] Or trying to: one servant maid testified that her master "would often kiss me and put his tongue into my mouth and has several times thrown me down on the bed and endeavoured to debauch me," that another time he said, "God damn you for a bitch, I will fuck you," but she managed to get away when the butler came in.[143] Often they got away with it. (But sometimes servants found bargaining leverage.)[144] Occasionally they didn't: Francis Chartres was convicted of raping his servant maid.[145] But sometimes male servants were sleeping with their mistresses. "A Servant whiles he keeps his place is a comely necessary help, but if he begin to control his Master, to usurp his Masters Chair, to woo his Mistris, &c. its intollerable," as one scriptural commentary had it.[146] No wonder we find successful tort actions for adultery brought by masters against servants: "Yesterday in the Afternoon

140. Laura Gowing, "The Haunting of Susan Lay: Servants and Mistresses in Seventeenth-Century England," *Gender and History* 14, no. 2 (2002): 183–85. Virtuous Amanda remains faithful to her husband, most recently sleeping with her lovely servant Berinthia, in [Sir John Vanbrugh], *The Relapse: or, Virtue in Danger* (London, 1698). Fans of melodrama should consult *The Unnatural Mother and Ungrateful Wife, a Narrative* (London, [1735?]).

141. Swift, *Journal to Stella*, 1:320 (25 July 1711).

142. For a tale with an unhappy legal twist, see Lawrence Stone, *Uncertain Unions: Marriage in England, 1660–1753* (Oxford: Oxford University Press, 1992), 92–95.

143. Lawrence Stone, *Broken Lives: Separation and Divorce in England, 1660–1857* (Oxford: Oxford University Press, 1993), 72.

144. Bernard Capp, "The Double Standard Revisited: Plebeian Women and Male Sexual Reputation in Early Modern England," *Past & Present*, no. 162 (1999): 80–83.

145. *The Tryal of Colonel Francis Chartres, for a Rape Committed by Him on the Body of Mrs. Anne Bond, His Servant-Maid* (London, 1730).

146. Rogers, *Godly & Fruitful Exposition*, 551.

there was a Trial at Guildhall between a Mercer at Aldgate, Plaintiff, and his Servant, Defendant, for criminal Conversation with his Wife: The Jury gave the Plaintiff 500 l. Damages."[147] No, a servant wouldn't have had £500 to pay in damages. Perhaps the master wanted him in debtors' prison. Perhaps he wanted to humiliate his wife and was willing to swallow the public humiliation himself.[148] Ben Agar's sexually dissatisfied wife slept with her husband's clerk and finally ran off with him.[149] The point is not that sex in domestic service wasn't all about power and exploitation, nor that there aren't nefarious gender dynamics in play. (No duh.) The point is that we find more than household heads with patriarchal authority molesting women without it.[150]

Before we round on Swift's suggestion that the chambermaid sell sexual favors with our own incensed retorts, let's also remember my suggestion that his real reading audience isn't the servants. So the advice to the chambermaid to charge money for sexual favors confronts his polite readers with the actual terms of trade their households operate on—with who's groping whom and how they're getting away with it. So too for the terse advice to the wet nurse: "Contrive to be with Child, as soon as you can, while you are giving Suck, that you may be ready for another Service, when the Child you nurse dies, or is weaned." Readers previously inclined to condemn the wet nurse for such frivolous or self-destructive behavior might now have to wonder, how else is she to fend for herself? Lucky ducks aside, polite readers already knew their servants weren't all that loving. But—the usual manuals to the rescue—they blamed their servants. Swift's text invites them to think instead about the structure of domestic service.

Let's back up for an overview. Swift punctures long-standing exhortations to servants to revere and even love their masters, bombastic advice that

147. *London Evening-Post*, 21 May 1728. See too *General Evening Post*, 25 December 1735; and for a successful action against an apprentice, *Tryal before the Lord Chief Justice R——y——d at Guild Hall between Mr. J—— C—— a Mercer at Aldgate, and Mr. J. E—— for Criminal Conversation with His Wife* (London, 1730?). See more generally on the complicated issues surrounding a husband's suing over his wife's adultery Elizabeth A. Foyster, *Manhood in Early Modern England: Honour, Sex and Marriage* (London: Longman, 1999), 164–72.

148. I was puzzled by these actions: thanks to Steve Pincus and Alan Houston for helping me see what was going on.

149. [Ben Agar], *The Lost Sheepe Is Found, under a New Disguisement of a Young-raw-scull'd Wit, &c.* (London, 1642), 6–7, 12.

150. For a facetious take on these matters, see *The Ladies Remonstrance: or, A Declaration of the Waiting-Gentlewomen, Chamber-Maids, and Servant-Maids, of the City of London, and within the Loyns of Copulation; to All Gentlemen, London-Apprentices, and Others Whom It May Concern* (London, 1659). For a woman sexually assaulting her maidservant in 1699, see David M. Turner, *Fashioning Adultery: Gender, Sex and Civility in England, 1660–1740* (Cambridge: Cambridge University Press, 2002), 154.

holds out consensus as the key to an orderly household. With his eye stead-
fastly trained on the nitty-gritty terrain of everyday life, he shows that the
household is shot through with conflicts of interest. But principles or norms
don't magically solve or dissolve these conflicts. Often further conflict is
created by shared norms: servants should be thrifty, they should honor their
masters, and so on. All these are what I've called the grounds of conflict.
Again, sometimes we call them conflict itself and it's entirely predictable that
they will give rise to further conflict. So it's confused to imagine that conflict
and social order are antonyms. If you fear that the household Swift portrays is
terribly disorderly, then yes, I agree, something is wrong. Not with that
household, though. Rather with your criteria for order—and your fevered
imagination of what is possible.

Again, Swift wasn't inclined to underplay the dangers of domestic service. Here's more from the "Causes":

> IF we consider the many Misfortunes that befal private Families, it will
> be found that Servants are the Causes and Instruments of them all: Are
> our Goods embezzled, wasted, and destroyed? Is our House burnt down to
> the Ground? It is by the Sloth, the Drunkenness or the Villainy of Ser-
> vants. Are we robbed and murdered in our Beds? It is by Confederacy with
> our Servants. Are we engaged in Quarrels and Misunderstandings with our
> Neighbours? These were all begun and inflamed by the false, malicious
> Tongues of our Servants. Are the Secrets of our Family betrayed, and
> evil Repute spread of us? Our Servants were the Authors. Do false Ac-
> cusers rise up against us? (an Evil too frequent in this Country) they
> have been tampering with our Servants. Do our Children discover Folly,
> Malice, Pride, Cruelty, Revenge, Undutifulness in their Words and Ac-
> tions? Are they seduced to Lewdness or scandalous Marriages? It is all
> by our Servants. Nay, the very Mistakes, Follies, Blunders, and Absurdities
> of those in our Service, are able to ruffle and discompose the mildest
> Nature, and are often of such Consequence, as to put whole Families into
> Confusion.[151]

Some of these evils could perhaps be mitigated by the assiduous moral education Swift recommends in the "Causes."[152] Yet it's absurd to pretend that
cloying tributes to harmony and love can dissolve conflict.

151. "Causes of the Wretched Condition of Ireland," in *Prose Works*, 9:204.
152. See too R[ogers], *Matrimoniall Honovr*, 142; [Edmund Calamy], *A Serious Advice to the Citizens
of London* (n.p., [1657]), n.p.: "*Catechize* your children and servants; instruct them in the fundamentals of
religion; would you keep them from error in the Head, from loosness in the life, make conscience of this
duty"; Owen Stockton, *A Treatise of Family Instruction: Wherein It Is Proved to Be the Duty of Parents and*

Swift's keen analysis didn't dam the flood of moralistic advice. Nor did it persuade everyone that bids for sweet consensus as the opposite of social conflict were bankrupt. This pearl could have been secreted decades, centuries, before Swift. Or centuries after: it looks sadly like a dress rehearsal for the sociologistic theorem, missing only the unutterable jargon.

> That family is disorderly, and cannot be prosperous and happy, where it is not evident that the interest of the servants is intimately connected with that of the master; and that servant cannot really and truly prosper, who doth not make his master's interest his own. For all good families have one common interest; and all the members of them, even their lowest animals, feel the effects of that affectionate regard to it, which governs the whole.[153]

But it happens to be from 1779, a few decades after the publication of Swift's text. Worse, its anonymous author adopts Swift's title, *Directions to Servants*. There's no artful subversion of Swift's artful subversion here, just a bland reassertion of the traditional unwisdom, as if Swift's text had been airbrushed out of the historical record.[154] Apparently paeans to consensus and harmony of interests are hypnotic.

Meanwhile, as the World Turns . . .

In February 1745, a servant named John How quit. We have his resignation letter:

> SIR,
>
> I shall take your warning from this day; I think it is proper to speak to those that dress your victuals, and not to them as have nothing to do with it.

Masters of Families to Train up Their Children and Servants in the Knowledge of the Scriptures (London, 1672); H. C., *The Country-Curate's Advice to His Parishioners* (London, 1693), chap. 4. John Locke recommended keeping children "as much out of the servants company as you can espetialy the eldest of them": Locke to Mrs. Mary Clarke, 22 March [1695?], in *Correspondence of Locke*, 5:296.

153. *Directions to Servants; Particularly Those Who Have the Care of Children* (London, 1779), 8. For a servant mockingly offering advice to an aristocratic master, see *Directions to Lords, and Ladies, Masters and Mistresses, for the Improvement of Their Conduct to Servants and Tenants, Tradesmen, and Humble Friends and Cousins: Design'd as a Return for Their Impertinent Directions to Servants* (London, 1766), esp. 27–28, on how to avoid paying servants their wages.

154. For the same sort of conventional wisdom after Swift, see for instance *The New Whole Duty of Man, Containing the Faith as Well as Practice of a Christian*, 16th ed. (London, [1759]), 236–41. But see the endlessly facetious Lemuel Gulliver, *The Pleasures and Felicity of Marriage, Display'd in Ten Books*, 2nd ed. (London, 1745), 21, on the servants' escapades.

I see there is no such thing as pleasing you, I knew what business was before I came to you and more than what you have to do, and though I cant please you, I dont doubt but I shall please other people very well, I never had the uneasiness anywhere, as I have here, & I hope never shall, again; for you are never easy nor * * * * [torn] let one do never so much for you, and you can get Mrs. Buck or any body else as may do your work better for I will not stay with you, to be found fault with for nothing; when I am in a fault, I desire to be told of it, but not to be told of other peoples, Betty is too good a servant for you, you neve[r] had a better, nor will have again; she understands business, better than you can teach her; And I expect to be paid for the half year I have been without cloaths;

I am your

Servant

JNO HOW[155]

You have to admire the ritual closing: How was indeed Dr. Lardner's servant, but he offered not deference but icy defiance and hot anger. The frustrations of working for an ingrate, being blamed without deserving it, and finally not being paid properly—servants' wages routinely included clothing[156]—were too much for him. This servant judged his master, found him wanting, and moved on. But I suppose Dr. Lardner hired a replacement. I'm not confident they embraced in loving harmony.

The year continued unsurprisingly with servants attracting the attention of the criminal law. In September 1745, Susanna Hall, a London servant, was sentenced to transportation for stealing some cloth goods and silver from her mistress.[157] In October, James Davis, a Bedson servant, was sentenced to transportation for stealing a waistcoat and shirt from a fellow servant.[158] On 28 November 1745, the *St. James's Evening Post* announced the publication of Swift's *Directions to Servants*. It also reprinted a private letter revealing that "Lord Kilmartin's Servant ran away with his Master's two best Horses" and

155. Jno How to [Dr. Lardner], 1 February 1745, in Mary Adelaide, Lady Jennings, *A Kentish Country House: or, Records of the Hall House, Hawkhurst, and Its Inhabitants, from the Great Plague of London to the Jubilee of Queen Victoria, 1665–1887* (Guildford, 1894), 73. I owe the reference to J. Jean Hecht, *The Domestic Servant Class in Eighteenth-Century England* (London: Routledge & Kegan Paul, 1956), 78.

156. See Constantia Comb-brush's lament in *Spectator*, no. 366 (30 April 1712), in Bond, *The Spectator*, 3:378–79.

157. *OBP*, 11 September 1745, Susanna Hall (t17450911–16).

158. *OBP*, 16 October 1745, James Davis (t17451016–8).

hadn't been found.[159] Probably he had joined the abortive uprising for bonnie Prince Charlie and the restoration of the Stuarts. So it went, along with feasts of misrule not severe enough to warrant the attention of newspapers or the criminal law. The authors of the servants' manuals still had plenty to deplore —and plenty of rhapsodies to love to deliver. 1745 also saw this tribute to virtuous Marcia:

> Where-e'er she rules, so justly mild's her Sway,
> Her Servants love, and from that Source obey:
> No dire Contention, no domestic Strife,
> No baneful Discord, the worst Plagues of Life,
> Disturb her candid Soul's serene Repose.[160]

If this blather were a snapshot of everyday life, we could embellish the thesis that the master's authority was naturalized or essentialized. We could marvel at the false consciousness of the servants. But now we know there's no call to pursue such fantasies.

Whatever Marcia's admirers longed for, life had other refrains. The next March, the *London Magazine* printed this alarming snippet of news:

> This Morning the Lady of Capt. *Dalrymple*, of *Wigmore Street, Cavendish Square*, was found murder'd in her Bed, and the House robb'd: The Murder was executed in a most barbarous and shocking Manner, by *Matthew Henderson*, the Foot-Boy (about 17 Years old) who had been brought up in the Family from 5 Years of Age. He was apprehended, and had a long Examination before Sir *Thomas de Veil*, who sent him to the *Gatehouse* to be secur'd for farther Examination: On *Thursday, Robert Wright*, Esq; the Coroner, finish'd his Enquiry on this Shocking Affair: After which the following Account was made publick. The Servant Maid, one *Mary Platt*, gave a very circumstantial Evidence, so as to clear herself of the least Imputation in being concerned in the Murder.—*Matthew Henderson*, the Foot-boy, at first said nothing material; but the Coroner ordering an Iron Cleaver to be laid before him on the Table (which Cleaver was found in the Bog-House) he instantly turned about, wept bitterly, and declared he knew it very well; for it was with that he had murdered his Mistress when she was asleep. He said he gave her several Blows with it before she awakened, and the Words she then used, were, *Oh, Lord, what is that?* But he pursued his

159. *St. James's Evening Post*, 28 November 1745.
160. A Norfolk Gentleman [James Poole], *Advice to the Ladies: A Poem* (London, 1745), 9.

Blows, and, in struggling, the Lady tumbled out of Bed, where he also repeated his Blows.—*Mrs. Dalrymple* had six prodigious Wounds upon her Head, one of her Eyes cut out, both the Cheek Bones cut thro,' and in two Places of the Head cut into the Brain.—He acknowledged no Person was concerned with him in the Act, and the other Persons he had sworn against were innocent, which the other accused People sufficiently proved.—The other Wounds the Lady had upon her Body were, as near as could be computed, about forty.[161]

The *London Magazine* also published a "Solemn Declaration" from Henderson while he was awaiting execution. Like many another gallows speech, this one was doctored or even created from whole cloth, probably by some learned divine: the vocabulary is ludicrously elevated for a seventeen-year-old catch fart. So what did the puppet masters of his speech find it useful to have him say? "No Servant could be better used than I was, and I never had the least Dislike to my deceased Lady; for she was a Lady of great Humanity, and greatly respected by all her Servants, and my Master a most worthy Gentleman." Yet he found himself thinking of killing his mistress. Clutching the cleaver, he "sat down upon my Bed, about 20 or 30 Minutes, considering whether I should commit the murder. My Heart relented, and I thought I could not do it, because I never had received any Affront." In this account, Henderson hadn't suffered even a single beating. Or perhaps if he had, he thought it well deserved and so no affront at all. "However, I concluded to do it; for there was no one in the House but the Deceased and myself." Up the stairs, down the stairs, more hesitation, back up, another bit of hesitation, but this time because of the watchman's passing by: then he slipped into the room. "When I was in the Room I could not kill her: I was in great Fear and Terror; and I went out of the Room as far as the Stair Head, not above two or three Yards from her Chamber-Door, but immediately returned with a full Resolution to murder her." So he did. Only then did it occur to him to rob the house. Then he stopped off at his wife's lodgings to stash his loot. She had been the Dalrymples' servant herself. Henderson had married her nine months before.

---

161. *London Magazine*, March 1746, 153–54. The ordinary of Newgate thought Henderson "about nineteen years of age": *The Ordinary of Newgate His Account of the Behaviour, Confession, and Dying Words of Matthew Henderson*, no. 2 (London, 1746), 20. The substance of the ordinary's narration is reprinted in [John Villette], *The Annals of Newgate: or, Malefactors Register*, 4 vols. (London, 1776), 4:270–74; and, more loosely, *The Malefactor's Register: or, New Newgate and Tyburn Calendar*, 5 vols. (London, [1779]), 3:90–94; William Jackson, *The New and Complete Newgate Calendar: or, Villany Displayed in All Its Branches*, 6 vols. (London, [1795]), 3:90–94.

She was now "big with Child" and he was intent on rebutting the allegation that she was in on the murder plot. More treachery from the underlings: the jewelry Henderson stole ended up in the custody of the jail's turnkey, who sold it. He was convicted and transported.[162]

Mary Platt returned at about 6:00 a.m. and Henderson feigned surprise when the two of them found the corpse. His remorse is exquisite: "It is not possible to express the Sorrow and Terror I am under." Story had it that Henderson had callously responded to the rumor that he'd hang in chains, "*I hope not, for if they hang me in Chains, I shall catch Cold.*" I bet that when print-Henderson denies he's ever said such a thing, we are seeing the censorious hand of whoever is editing or telling the tale not quite erasing a glimpse of the bloodthirsty young scamp.[163]

The *Gentleman's Magazine* saluted the murder as "one of the most horrid and aggravated that perhaps ever happened." They found Henderson's solemn declaration mystifying. If he was only pretending to be repentant, he wasn't going to avoid hanging and the lie wasn't going to please God. But if he was repentant, how could he have done it "in opposition to his nature, his conscience, and his interest with respect to both worlds, and all this without gratifying any passion, without obtaining any present enjoyment, in short, for no reason, and to no end"? Both alternatives seemed "repugnant, and indeed absolutely impossible."[164] The case captivated the popular imagination. Walpole snarled, "one hears of nothing else wherever one goes."[165]

Henderson's deed looks like enmity, not conflict. Not because of the brute fact of violence: all those stripes showered down on servants were thought permissible. Not even because of the brute fact of killing: most contemporaries didn't doubt it was permissible for the state to put Henderson to death. Rather because it looks as though the rules of the game, however construed, don't make this murder an even vaguely permissible move. It was neither predictable nor particularly intelligible, either. But what matters in distinguishing conflict from enmity is whether it was permissible: recall the suggestion that there are permissible ways of misbehaving. So Henderson

162. *OBP*, 5 December 1746, John Poulter and Elizabeth Bradbury (t17461205–11).

163. *London Magazine*, April 1746, 186–89. See too *The Solemn Declaration of Matthew Henderson, Now under Sentence of Death in Newgate, for the Inhuman Murder of His Lady, Elizabeth Dalrymple* (London, [1746]).

164. *Gentleman's Magazine*, April 1746, 175–76, italics reversed.

165. Horace Walpole to Horace Mann, 28 March 1746, in *The Yale Edition of Horace Walpole's Correspondence*, ed. W. S. Lewis, 48 vols. (New Haven, CT: Yale University Press, 1937–83), 19:235.

doesn't belong with many of my other servants, caught up in more pedestrian conflicts. That distinction didn't stop one Thomas Broughton from seizing the occasion to offer more advice to servants.[166] (Henry Fielding seized the occasion, too, but "Tom Skipton," the footman he ventriloquized, avoided the facts of the case and preached the merits of honesty.)[167] In a curious deadpan tone, opening his pamphlet by addressing masters, Broughton acknowledged, "THE many *robberies* and *murders* which have been committed of late years by *Servants,* may justly alarm you; and raise some uneasy apprehensions in your breasts." His "little piece," he explains, "points out a remedy for those fears, by attempting to instill such principles into the minds of your *Dependents,* as may, by the blessing of GOD, secure their *fidelity* to you." What were those principles?

We might all be God's servants, "yet in the course of his providence he has thought good to appoint various orders and degrees of men here upon earth." "THE principal duty required in Servants is *Faithfulness;* which consists in your being strictly *just* and *honest* in your service. . . . You should . . . tremble at the approach of every temptation that may offer to wrong your Master," lest the devil pounce and the gallows await.[168] The hypocrisy, the ingratitude, the deceptiveness of servants eager to betray their masters shocked Broughton. He thought it should shock servants, too. He warned against drunkenness, against "*keeping bad company,* especially that of lewd women"—one would think Judith Brown and other women servants never committed murder themselves—and against gambling. If only servants knew "what happiness it yields to read the holy Scriptures," they would "let no opportunity slip," especially on the Sabbath, of immersing themselves. "Always begin and end the day with GOD." "To your daily and devout use of the means of grace, you must be careful to add the beauties and ornaments of a holy life." Broughton helpfully supplied some prayers for servants to recite.

Broughton added that Henderson was "neither a *Drunkard, Whoremon-*

---

166. Thomas Broughton, *A Serious and Affectionate Warning to Servants, More Especially Those of Our Nobility and Gentry; Occasioned by the Shameful and Untimely Death of Matthew Henderson: Who Was Executed on Friday, 25th April, 1746 for the Murder of His Lady, Mrs. Dalrymple* (London, 1746).

167. *True Patriot,* no. 28 (6–13 May 1746), in Henry Fielding, *"The True Patriot" and Related Writings,* ed. W. B. Coley (Middletown, CT: Wesleyan University Press, 1987), 284–89. For more on Fielding's use of the case, see Claude E. Jones, "Fielding's *True Patriot* and the Henderson Murder," *Modern Language Review* 52, no. 4 (1957): 498–503.

168. Ephesians 6:5 is in the background: see William Gouge, *Of Domesticall Dvties: Eight Treatises* (London, 1622), 163.

ger, or *Gamester,*" at least if one could believe what he said while awaiting his execution. Henderson, he acknowledged, had the decency not to try to implicate Mary Platt. He pled guilty, too.[169] This time we learn that Henderson's sole grievance against Dalrymple was a beating after "he accidentally trod upon his lady's toes"[170] and he admitted that Mrs. Dalrymple had been especially good-natured before he killed her. He blamed his crime on the devil. Yet he also recalled that his aunt was "often out of her senses" and reported that he himself was "at times in such excess of mirth, that he was like one intoxicated with liquor; at other times so melancholy and gloomy that he could not bear any one to speak to him." It would be wrong to imagine observers missed the significance of this report in the rush to the devil. The same report added, "if we can credit him, surely it must be the effect only of madness."[171] Broughton "found him stored with religious principles, and melted into tenderness and contrition." It's a puzzling pamphlet, then. After Henderson's execution for murder, Broughton conjectures that servants spurn God because of their pursuit of wine, women, and lucre. Then he nonchalantly remarks that Henderson didn't pursue wine, women, and lucre and was devoted to God. In fact, "he gave a good account from the Scriptures of the general Judgement." No matter. Servants should still pray, "Give me grace to behave myself with sobriety, diligence, and honesty, in the business of my station, and with duty and submission to those whom thou hath set over me; and to desire and endeavour to live in peace and love with my fellow servants." Worried that your servant might become a murderer? Apply a liberal dose of blather; rinse and repeat.

A Congregationalist prepared a scripture-studded letter to Henderson, hoping the criminal would repent and win salvation before his death. He claimed that the ordinary of Newgate thought it a Methodist text (shudder) and a dissenting minister snatched it away when Henderson asked for an explanation.[172] The ordinary, though, reported that Henderson "complained at the officiousness of a certain Methodist, who sent him a letter . . . the

---

169. *The Proceedings on the King's Commission of the Peace, Oyer and Terminer, and Gaol Delivery for the City of London,* pt. 2, no. 4 (London, 1746), 140.

170. *Ordinary of Newgate,* 25.

171. *Ordinary of Newgate,* 22. For studied ambivalence about the devil in another setting, see *The Devil and the Strumpet: or, The Old Bawd Tormented* (London, [1700?]), esp. 8.

172. [Robert Fowler], *The Copy of a Letter Sent to Matthew Henderson, while under Sentence of Death in Newgate, for the Barbarous Murder of His Mistress, the Lady Dalrymple* (London, [1746?]), 12, title page. This piece is reprinted in *Christ Alone Exalted, in the Following Tracts* (London, 1747).

contents of which, when he began to read them, gave him so much dislike, that he had not the patience to go through with it."[173] John Wesley himself visited Henderson in jail. "At the earnest request of a friend," wrote the great Methodist, "I visited Matthew Henderson, condemned for murdering his mistress. A real, deep work of God seemed to be already begun in his soul. Perhaps by driving him too fast, Satan has driven him to God; to that repentance which shall never be repented of."[174]

Here Swift was prophetic: he'd warned his footman that he'd probably face the gallows for robbery, murder, or the like. But he could sail off with casual elegance:

> Some of your kind Wenches will provide you with a *Holland* Shirt, and white Cap crowned with a crimson or black Ribbon: Take Leave cheerfully of all your Friends in *Newgate:* Mount the Cart with Courage: Fall on your Knees: Lift up your Eyes: Hold a Book in your Hands although you cannot read a Word: Deny the Fact at the Gallows: Kiss and forgive the Hangman, and so Farewel: You shall be buried in Pomp, at the Charge of the Fraternity: The Surgeon shall not touch a Limb of you; and your Fame shall continue until a Successor of equal Renown succeeds in your Place.

(The incongruous humor of writing to a man who "cannot read a Word" underlines my suggestion that Swift's real audience is polite society.) Later writers domesticated even that acerbic gesture. One 1767 writer bewailed the plight of modest families abandoned by domestic help in search of bigger tips.

> As soon as they get a tolerable Servant, and have been at much Pains to qualify him for his Place, that Servant hearing from others how much more Vails are got elsewhere, must needs try his Fortune in a large Family, there he too often gets so totally spoiled by the other Servants, and becomes so abominably wicked, as to be absolutely unfit for every Thing, but to practice Dean *Swift*'s Directions for Servants, and to follow his Advice for the Behaviour of Footmen at the Place of Execution.[175]

I don't know if love makes the world go 'round, but it sure does make certain commentators dizzy. Or if not love, more austere versions of unity.

---

173. *Ordinary of Newgate*, 25.

174. *An Extract of the Rev. Mr. John Wesley's Journal, from Oct. 27, 1743, to Nov. 17, 1746, VI* (London, 1779), 130 (23 April 1746).

175. *A Letter from a Gentleman to His Friend, concerning the Custom of Giving and Taking Vails* (London, 1767), 19.

Even today, the charm of unity shows up in unexpected quarters: we find one rational-choice theorist positing "the deep and basic need of each individual to conform to community standards,"[176] two economists arguing that tastes don't "differ importantly between people."[177] Such views lighten explanatory burdens at the price of suspending disbelief, something we're supposed to do reading fiction, not hardheaded social science.

Not love, not consensus, but conflict glued the domestic household together. Cohabiting couples not under the spell of bad social theory or for that matter of tawdry romantic fantasies should know that, even if they're not themselves locked in combat. Master against servant, master against mistress, servant against servant, and more: these were not falls from some prior state of grace, not lamentable departures from consensus and harmony of interests, not evidence of unraveling social practices. They were business as usual for centuries on end. Their sheer persistence suggests that it's screwy to cast conflict as the enemy of social order.

Conflict is an everyday fact of life. Paeans to consensus blink reality. I want to emphasize again that it's not a matter of conflicting preferences and interests, all to be resolved happily by principles or norms. Ordinarily, we grapple with many norms. There are endless controversies over which of them apply, how they apply, and how to adjudicate conflicts among them. What I've dubbed the grounds of conflict are here to stay, even for people acting in good faith. No surprise that we so often see outright conflict. No need to introduce any skulking villains to see it.

I don't mean that conflict enables parties to sort out their disagreements and arrive at some compromise or adopt a better view. That sort of view—it's a causal claim—is a venerable staple of liberal and democratic theory, worth insisting on against those who worry that tense debates or milling crowds signal incipient or full-blown social disorder. But it casts conflict as a preliminary state to the deeper consensus we hope to arrive at. By contrast, the view I'm pressing here—it's a constitutive claim—is not that conflict might produce consensus. It's that conflict itself qualifies as social order.

Have I stacked the deck by stipulating that conflict, unlike enmity, depends on some shared background? No, because that shared background can

176. Michael Suk-Young Chwe, *Rational Ritual: Culture, Coordination, and Common Knowledge* (Princeton, NJ: Princeton University Press, 2001), 41.

177. George J. Stigler and Gary S. Becker, "De Gustibus Non Est Disputandum," *American Economic Review* 67, no. 2 (1977): 76.

be quite minimal, not the sort of thing fans of consensus seem to have in mind. When the servants' manuals pay tribute to love, when they tell us that servants should revere their masters, that they should be pleased to leap into action at their masters' beckoning, that they should patiently suffer even undeserved physical blows, they are invoking a much thicker consensus than the sort of shared background I have in mind. Some of what they say can be interpreted as the attractive suggestion that we should peacefully resolve the grounds of conflict. Much of it can't be. A relatively thin shared background is all it takes to get Swift's puzzles up and running. Recall the further suggestion that the sharing needn't be complete. Swift is exploring the terrain the servants' manuals indict as dreadful disorder and his portrait is affectionate, if wryly so.

Have I played on a verbal equivocation? My opponents might respond, "Stop ridiculing us for fretting about incipient disorder. In your lingo, we'll repackage our view this way. There are two kinds of social order. One features fundamental agreement. The other relies on a relatively thin shared background that licenses or even generates all kinds of conflict—but right, it isn't like living in Hobbes's state of nature. We think the first kind of social order is better." I have a couple of rejoinders. One: it isn't in the cards. Look where you will—families, friendships, monasteries—and you'll find ongoing conflict. Two, in case you were about to say that still, the nearer we approach consensus, the better off we are: it isn't desirable. Instead of longing for unity, we should see it as deadening monotony. Here I would lean on the causal claim: it takes conflict to explore problems, air competing views, hash out a plan of action, and move forward. A community where everyone purrs in sweet agreement is in no position to notice what it's doing wrong—or to grapple with the inevitable new problems thrown up by social change. Consider here the liberal democratic category *loyal opposition*. It's no oxymoron. It means that parties sharing a background commitment to the government's legitimacy are then free to disagree about policy. No one should accuse dissidents of being traitors, though more or less that happens all the time.

My critique is directed at wholesale defenses of consensus or worries about conflict. So I'm happy to concede that if we go retail, sometimes we could do with less conflict or, more micro yet, less of a particular kind of conflict. But that too invites a riposte: sometimes we could do with more conflict or more of a particular kind of conflict. If you like the concession but shrink from the riposte, a plausible diagnosis is that you're suffering a galloping case of conflict aversion. Time to wake up and smell the skunk cabbage.

What shall we say about the endlessly seductive vision of modeling social order on deep consensus and imagining that conflict is the opposite of order? "A *picture* held us captive," as Wittgenstein said in another context. "And we could not get outside it, for it lay in our language and language seemed to repeat it to us inexorably." My strategy too has been "Back to the rough ground!" (Though alas, "don't think, but look!" isn't great advice. Look, sure, but think about what you see.)[178] Here I've chosen the ground of domestic service in early modern England. But I calmly confess to harboring a much broader suspicion: the vision isn't any more sensible in other settings. Happily, though, it's possible to see it for the confused cartoon it is.

One last thought. Theorists fond of unmasking naturalized or essentialized authority, of exploding false consciousness, imagine themselves as the staunch opponents of those blathering on about consensus. But in a crucial way, they're co-conspirators. The first denounce as pernicious ideology what the second embrace as social order. Appraisals aside, they think they've found the same thing. Sometimes—one thinks of Marx's brief and dreamy comments about communism—even the first look forward to their own ideal consensus. Both are looking for love in all the wrong places—looking for all the wrong things in love, too. Actual social orders are riven by conflict. Often it's self-consciously controversy about legitimate authority, so it's robustly political conflict, too.

As far as patriarchal control over women and servants goes, those in early modern England knew that. They weren't staggering through life in a daze, weren't narcoleptics afflicted with a big sleep. Remember, they're the ones who could read a casual quip about its being blasphemous to invoke patriarchal authority outside church. They're the ones who chafed even in the pews hearing about it. They're the ones who lit upon the helpful term *catch fart* to describe a footboy.

But some do need to be roused from their dogmatic slumbers. They're our sophisticated social critics, obsessed with naturalized authority. Their quest to emancipate us is pleasing (in congratulating us on how much progress we've made), daunting (in underlining how much work remains), scary (in exhibiting everyday life as the scene of domination both ruthless and unnoticed), but finally a quixotic fantasy.

178. Ludwig Wittgenstein, *Philosophical Investigations*, trans. G. E. M. Anscombe, 3rd ed. (Malden, MA: Blackwell, 2001), §§ 115, 107, 66 (pp. 41e, 40e, 27e).

Conclusion

So we're in no position to congratulate ourselves on the allegedly new insight that the household is political. We shouldn't imagine that the early modern English naturalized or essentialized patriarchal authority: they didn't. We shouldn't imagine that an insidiously gendered public/private distinction made the political subordination of women invisible: it didn't. We shouldn't imagine that it was virtually impossible for the early modern English—men and women alike—to confidently adopt and act on feminist views: it wasn't. Such portraits don't need to be painted with more subtlety, nuance, or shading to acquire historical and theoretical verisimilitude. They need to be discarded. Conflict was the order of the day. Conflict over legitimate authority—politics—pervaded the household. The early modern English weren't oblivious to prominent features of their lives.

I launched this exploration with some lines from John Fletcher's 1626 play, *The Noble Gentleman*. Remember that impotent husband, Marine, whose harrumphing about ruling his wife, liberally peppered with asides underlining the fatuity of his pose, gives way in short order to his urging her to wear the breeches. The visual gag, his literally dropping his pants, makes for a suitably cute and vulgar moment. But there's nothing even slightly novel about the substance of what Fletcher is up to.

That same year, Apollo noticed that many women were unfaithful to their husbands, who were then saddled with the proverbial cuckold's horns. So he instructed Sir Philip Sidney, Orpheus Junior, and a few others "to set downe some wholesome remedies for married men to gouerne their Wiues, that they *horne* them not"—and for husbands not to be tempted by other women. That added thought did not, as you'll see, lead to egalitarian proposals. Apollo's instruction was the setup of one of the chapters of William Vaughan's *Golden Fleece*,[1] an odd pastiche of verse and prose, some recycled, some misattributed. I won't pretend this late in the day to find Apollo's invocation of government surprising. I will remind you that the routine use of such language militates against the big sleep thesis.

Sidney obligingly spun out some verse with the usual tangled combination of equality, inferiority, and superiority:

> If thou wilt haue her loue and honour thee,
> First, let her thine Affections largely see.
> What shee doth for thee kindly that respect,
> And shew how thou her loue dost well affect.
> Remember she is neighbour to thy heart,
> And not thy slaue: shee is thy better part.
> Thinke tis enough that her thou migh[t]st command:
> Whilest she in Marriage bonds doth loyall stand,
> Although thy power thou neuer doe approue,
> For thats the way to make her leaue to loue.

The sense of *approve* in that last couplet, courtesy of the *OED*, must be *prove* or *demonstrate*, and *leave to love* is *stop loving*. The ideal husband commands a wife, who's his superior, gently enough that he never has to produce the iron fist from his velvet glove. The lines aren't actually from Sidney. They're plucked, not consecutively, from a translation of Ariosto's *Seven Satires*.[2] Vaughan's Sidney delicately skips over some of the translation's other lines:

> Many will boast what wonders they haue wrought
> By blowes, and how their wishes they haue caught.
> How they haue tam'd their shrewes & puld them downe,
> Making them vaile euen to the smallest frowne.

The *OED* also helps with *vail*: "to lower in sign of submission or respect." These boors invite Ariosto's scathing sneer:

---

1. Orpheus Junior [William Vaughan], *The Golden Fleece: Divided into Three Parts* (London, 1626), pt. 2, pp. 62–69.

2. *Ariosto's Satyres, in Seven Famovs Discourses,* trans. Garuis Markham [Robert Tofte], 2nd ed. (London, 1608), 62–63.

> But let those Gyants which such boastings loue,
> Tell me what they haue got and it will proue,
> Their wiues their blowes, on hands & face do beare,
> And they their wiues marks on their foreheads weare.

If battered wives festoon their husbands' brows with cuckolds' horns, physical blows make for imprudent governance. Sidney doesn't quite airbrush the point out of his picture, but he does soften it.

Master Whately conceded that Sidney had sketched the duties of virtuous husbands and wives. "But what," he demanded,

> if the wife exceed in wilfull repugnancie or rather rebellion against her Husband, who is her Lord and Head, as *Christ* is the Head and Crowne of the Husband according to *S. Paul*, and as I haue punctually proued in my Worke called the *Bridebush*, shall the Man degenerate from his virilitie and Christian vigour, as to suffer his *Subiect* and vnderling to waxe proud and to weare the Breeches? Shall he like *Sardanapalus*, or effeminated *Hercules* sit spinning in a Petticoate among her Maides, whiles shee flaunts it, like an vntamed Gallant, and iadishly kicks vp her heeles with a knaue, making her Lord accessarie to capitall baudry?

The real William Whately's *Bridebush* first appeared as a slim volume of fifty-some pages in 1617; the second edition of 1623 was swollen to four times that length. Like Vaughan, the real Whately cordially embraced male dominance: "The man must be taken for Gods immediate officer in the house, and as it were the King in the family; the woman must account her selfe his deputie, an officer substituted to him, not as equall, but as subordinate: and in this order they must gouerne; he, by the authoritie deriued vnto him from God immediatly, she, by authority deriued to her from her husband."[3]

Scant pages later, Whately returned to the husband's authority over his wife. A husband, he explained, had a "speciall" duty to "gouerne his wife," a duty requiring "two things": "one, that he keepe his authoritie; the other, that he doe vse it." Nature and God had the same inspiring design. Whately shuddered in contemplating its earthly "deformitie":

> That house is a misshapen house, and is (wee may vse that terme) a crump-shouldered, or hutch-backt house, where the husband hath made himself

---

3. William Whately, *A Bride-bvsh: or, A Direction for Married Persons* (London, 1623), 89. For the wife's duty to "carry her selfe as an inferiour," see 193.

and vnderling to his wife, and giuen away his power and regiment to his
inferior: without question it is a sinne for a man to come lower, than God
hath set him. It is not humilitie, but basenesse, to be ruled by her, whom he
should rule.[4]

No doubt, he conceded, many women battled for authority in the household.
But husbands were solely to blame if they ceded it. Not that they should be
harsh about their assigned role. Like Vaughan's fictional Sidney, Whately
wanted that fist well concealed: "Know yee therefore all yee husbands, that
the way to maintain authoritie in this societie, is not to vse violence, but
skill." Husbands should inspire obedience with their superior "goodnesse . . .
humilitie, godlinesse, wisdom." "Take paines to make thy selfe good, and that
is the most compendious way to make thy selfe reuerenced."[5]

Whately was reluctant to let husbands strike their wives. "It is most
intollerable for a man in anger to strike his wife for those weaknesses which
are incident euen to vertuous women." Still—now we tiptoe back toward the
role Vaughan enlisted Whately to play in his own text—what was a husband
to do with a wife who will use "vnwomanly words"? Or who will dish out
"bold and impudent resistances" or even "flie in his face with violence"? Or
who "will tell him to his teeth, that she cares not for him, and that she will as
she lusts for all him"? (That is, that she'll do what she wants whatever he
makes of it.) If "reproofs and perswasion" failed, the poor husband could try
to enlist his father-in-law "to fight." (So the joke about the battered wife who
complains to her father, who responds by battering her too, isn't only a joke.)
If that wouldn't do the trick, "I thinke the husband shall not offend, in vsing a
foole according to her folly; a child in vnderstanding, like a child in yeeres;
and a woman of base and seruile condition, in base and seruile manner."[6] To
be socially inferior is to be exposed to beatings; to be exposed to beatings is to
be socially inferior. Even then, emphasized Whately, the husband's blows
should rain down in a spirit of mild reproof, not anger. He should have
"teares in his eies" and grieve over what duty requires of him. After all, a
surgeon driven to burn a man's flesh with a hot iron takes no pleasure in
the deed.[7]

Back to Vaughan, who faithfully transcribed Whately's sentiments, even
the bit about the surgeon, all in more colorful wording. His Whately an-

4. Whately, *Bride-bvsh*, 97, 98.
5. Whately, *Bride-bvsh*, 99–101; and see 162–63.
6. Whately, *Bride-bvsh*, 106–8.
7. Whately, *Bride-bvsh*, 169–73.

swered his own defiant questions to Sidney: "he must shew his manly pre-
rogatiue, and rebuke her for such ridiculous carriage. . . . Hee must let her
know the wise mans sentence, that a *Rod becomes the back of a Foole.*" That
last is pulled from Proverbs 26:3. Orpheus Junior promptly sniffed that
Whately didn't need scripture "to verifie the prophane Prouerbe, that an
Asse, a Nut, and a Woman will neuer be good without beating." If men wish
to avoid being cuckolded, he added, they should stay faithful to their own
wives. Then he squirted out a condensed list of what men can expect from
women, anyway: "you shall not finde one among a thousand women, specially after Marriage, but shee is diseased, either with vnnaturall heat, a
stinking breath, rotten teeth, a withered face, with a windie mattrie stomack,
casting vp whole gobbets of snottie flegme, like rotten oysters, with the
dropsie, or lothsome issue in her legs." We are vanishingly close to the
images of sexual disgust in Swift's *Lady's Dressing Room*. Even if that poem
mocks men's romantic illusions, Orpheus's language reminds us that such
images could fuel cruelty.

From Sidney's lofty sentiments to (ventriloquized) Whately's after-
thought that still a particular wife might need beating to Orpheus's jaunty
suggestion that all women need beating and they're repulsive anyway: quite
the downhill slalom. But Apollo isn't drawing any distinctions. He professes
himself well pleased with the men's advice. Do they embrace inequality?
Sure. Misogyny? Sure. Have they "naturalized" or "essentialized" patriarchy? Not at all. Petticoat government is horribly wrong but all too possible,
and women have the effrontery to back it up with arguments. Apollo's ad-
visers' occasional appeals to nature are appeals to a normative standard, not
to any alleged necessity putting male dominion outside the realm of criticism
and justification. No wonder they talk effortlessly about men governing their
wives. No wonder they worry that their authority so readily crumbles.

The introduction of wife beating doesn't move us from conflict to enmity
—at least not in (real and ventriloquized) Whately's case. We're still in the
realm of rule-governed activity, where the rules aren't mere maxims of prudence but have some claim to legitimacy, however disputed that claim may be.
The law permitted men to beat their wives, with a due sense of proportion.
Plenty of men used and abused the privilege. Controversy about those rules,
the stuff of politics, was pervasive.[8] Tobias Cage ruefully detailed the long

---

8. Consider the jaundiced take from Joseph Swetnam, *The Arraignment of Lewd, Idle Froward, and
Unconstant Women: or, The Vanities of Them; (Chuse You Whether) with a Commendation of the Wise,*

train of abuses that finally led him to beat his wife: he understood that others might look askance.[9] Defenders of male supremacy knew that wife beating was controversial, not innocuous; attention grabbing, not sleep inducing.[10] So did the women who were battered, sometimes killed, and the women who lived in fear that they were next. Instead of dwelling on Vaughan's polyphonic intertextuality—and I'm no foe of basking in the pleasures of the text—let's turn unflinchingly to the world.

Goodbye, Margaret Kief

A century later, gruesome news wound its dilatory way from Dublin to London. Newspapers grabbing the hot story could reprint the original. But some offered new scoops, perhaps from their own Irish sources, perhaps from their own sales-hungry imaginations. Probably the Dublin paper's reports are more trustworthy, but some of the key issues seem not to have survived.

John Andovin was charged with murdering his servant maid. That spelling of his name soon gave way to Audouin. It took longer for his servant to gain any name in the prints. It turned out to be Margaret Kief—and her murder was especially savage: "her Throat was cut, insomuch that the Head hung only by a Bit of Flesh, stabb'd in the Body, wounded in the Head, her Hand and Arm hacked to Pieces (supposed in Defence of her Throat.)"[11] Audouin had told contradictory stories. Kief had murdered herself. No, she'd been murdered. He'd been robbed. But his cupboard seemed amply furnished and he claimed only trifling losses. He hadn't handled the corpse. So why was

---

Vertuous, and Honest Women (London, 1733), 15–16: "if thou go about to master a Woman, hoping to bring her to Humility; there is no way to make her good with Stripes, except thou beat her to Death; for do thou what thou wilt, yet a forward Woman in her frantick Mood will pull, hawl, swear, scratch, [and] tear all that stands in her Way." This text was endlessly reprinted; apparently the first edition is [Joseph Swetnam], *The Araignment of Levvd, Idle, Froward, and Vnconstant Women: or, The Vanitie of Them, Choose You Whether* (London, 1615).

9. Tobias Cage, *A Letter to a Person of Quality, Occasioned by a Printed Libel, Entituled, "The Cause of the Difference between Tobias Cage Esquire, and Mary His Wife Stated by the Said Mary in a Letter to a Gentleman"* ([London? 1678]).

10. For more debates on its appropriateness, see Elizabeth A. Foyster, *Manhood in Early Modern England: Honour, Sex and Marriage* (London: Longman, 1999), 184–91. Generally see Frances E. Dolan, *Dangerous Familiars: Representations of Domestic Crime in England, 1550–1700* (Ithaca, NY: Cornell University Press, 1994).

11. *Country Journal: or, The Craftsman*, 18 May 1728, with trifling variations in the *British Journal: or, The Censor*, 18 May 1728, and *Weekly Journal: or, The British Gazetteer*, 18 May 1728.

his shirt bloody? Oh, right, actually he had handled it. No wonder he was soon held for murder. Fourteen swore affidavits against him.

The trial, reported several London newspapers, surfaced a motive:

> The chief Evidence against Mr. Audouin was one John Turner, a Shoe-Boy, who swore that on the Night the Murder was committed, he was in Mr. Audouin's House, and Margaret Kief said to him, *Go and hide yourself, for my Master is in an ill Humour, and will beat you if he finds you here;* upon which, he, the said Boy, hid himself in the Coal-Hole, where he had not been long before the Prisoner at the Bar came into the Kitchen, and asked the Deceased, Margaret Kief, if she was not going to be married: The Maid desired to know the Reason for asking her that Question; to which he (the Prisoner) replied, *I must have your Maidenhead before you are marry'd;* and that then he attempted to force her, but she resisted; upon which he took one of his Pistols and knock'd her down: And the above Turner further saith, That Mr. Audouin afterwards brought a Knife with a Wooden Handle, and cut and mangled her in a most barbarous, bloody and inhuman Manner.[12]

The motive makes the murder intelligible. It fits Weber's criteria for social action: Audouin would have attached subjective meaning to it and his actions were oriented toward others' behavior. But it is enmity, not conflict. Yes, we've seen that upper-class men claimed rights of sexual access to lower-class women, especially servants. Recall Pepys caught by his wife with his hand in his servant Deb's vagina, the visitors slobbering over their friends' servant maids. Yet however elastic contemporaries' understandings of consent and rape in these settings, no one thought it legitimate to murder a servant who refused sex. With no toehold for disputes about legitimacy, we can't call this conflict. We can instead think about this violence as the continuation of politics by other means, but construe *other* in the way Clausewitz disavowed and say that now we're outside the bounds of politics. I say this violence, not violence more generally, because certain violence can be deemed perfectly legitimate. The law permitted masters to beat their servants. Plenty of servants were whipped, thanks not least to Jesus's apparent approval of stripes, and plenty of others lived in fear.

Audouin was convicted. The sentence, underlining how dramatically his

---

12. *London Evening-Post,* 30 May 1728; see too *Daily Journal,* 1 June 1728; *Glouccester Journal,* 4 June 1728; and, for a one-sentence version of the story, *Mist's Weekly Journal,* 1 June 1728.

act had exceeded the boundaries of conflict, was graphic enough to merit its own publication in a broadside:

> *John Audouin,* you must go to the place from whence you came, your Irons must be knock'd off, you must be brought to the place of Execution which is the common Gallows, and there you must Hang by the Neck until you are half Dead, your Members to be cut off and thrown in your Face, your Bowels to be cut out and Burn'd, your Head to be separated from your Body, and your Body to be devided into four Quarters and left to the Kings Mercy.[13]

While he waited in jail, a leering broadside purporting to be from his French-Irish compatriots appeared. It picked up on Turner's story or something very like it: "Why did you not keep de pretty *Girl,* and give her two Tirteen every week, she make de Mis-triss for you, when you have de-Inclination, *Futre* if you Dance you must pay de *Pi-per.*"[14] Ariosto-cum-Sidney's husband doesn't beat his wife when he can find more gentle and insidious ways of asserting his will. Similarly, why was Audouin resorting to attempted rape and then murder when money could have closed the deal?

The longest surviving published account of Audouin's trial is a modest eight pages; it has no testimony about Kief refusing sex and enraging him.[15] We have outright denials that any such testimony was offered. "There was no such Evidence against him, as that of Turner a Shoe Boy, as mention'd in some Advices from Dublin," insisted the *Weekly Journal.*[16] The *Dublin Intelligence,* at the scene, also rejected the tale.[17]

At the scaffold, Audouin was resolute: "But as to the fact for which I am to Dye for, the Murdering my Maid *Margaret Keef,* I solemnly Declare in the presence of God, I am entirely Innocent."[18] *Solemn Declaration*—we saw the same phrase in Matthew Henderson's case—was the conventional label for a gallows speech. It reminds us of the heavy pressure exerted on these texts by churchmen and other benevolent authorities. No repentance here, though: I

---

13. *The Whole Sentence of Death Pronounced This Present Wednesday Being the 29th of This Instant May, 1728 against Doctor John Audouin, for the Barbarous and Bloody Murder of Margret Kief the 20th of April Last* (Dublin, [1728]). Contrast the wording in the *Dublin Intelligence,* 1 June 1728.

14. *A Letter of Advice from the French Gentlemen of Ireland, to Doctor John Audouin Prisoner in Newgate, How to Procure His Pardon or Make off with His Life* (Dublin, 1728).

15. *A True and Exact Account of the Tryal of Mr. John Audouin, Surgeon* (Dublin, 1728). So too for a densely packed single sheet: *An Account of the Tryal and Examination of Mr. John Audowin* (Dublin, 1728).

16. *Weekly Journal: or, The British Gazetteer,* 22 June 1728.

17. *Dublin Intelligence,* 8 June 1728.

18. *The Last Speech Confession and Dying Words of Surgeon John Odwin* (Dublin, 1728), 1; compare *The Last Speech and Dying Words, of Mr. John Audouin* (Edinburgh, 1728).

don't doubt Audouin denied he'd killed Kief. There are intimations that public sympathy swung Audouin's way. One broadside praises his "modest behavior when in Confinement" and adds that his gallows demeanor "extorted Tears" from the executioner;[19] the *Dublin Intelligence* reports that after his execution, friends surfaced witnesses who could have helped.[20] A century later, we find the repeated claim that someone else had confessed to the murder. He was already in the house to rob it, the story went, when Audouin returned. The robber tried to get away; Kief tried to stop him; he bashed her head with a candlestick and fled. I've found no contemporary support for such a story, which anyway wouldn't make sense of the uncontroverted testimony about her gruesome wounds. Still, Audouin's execution became a somber warning of the dangers of relying on circumstantial evidence and ammunition against the death penalty.[21]

I'd bet long odds that Audouin murdered Margaret Kief. He wouldn't be the first or last to meet his maker right after a bold public lie. Whatever cultural and political work his execution was enlisted to do a century after, at the time it stood for a man who grotesquely abused his authority. The allegation that Audouin killed Kief because she rejected his sexual advance would make the story different from that of Elizabeth Branch and her daughter's murdering their fourteen-year-old servant. But the latter serves as a caution: we don't need male sexual dominance for servants to be murdered. Now ask: what could Audouin's execution, or the Branches', have taught contemporaries about the proper use of authority over servants? and what political controversies would it have sparked? And ask: with women and servants taking it on the chin, sometimes literally, sometimes worse than that, how much loving harmony could anyone in his right mind expect?

Kiss Me, Kate; Rape Me, England

In the closing jollities of Shakespeare's *Taming of the Shrew,*[22] Petruchio flaunts his command of the newly docile Katherina: "I charge thee, tell these headstrong women / What duty they do owe their lords and husbands."

19. *The Life Actions Birth, Parentage, and Education, of Doctor John Audouin* (Dublin, 1728).

20. *Dublin Intelligence,* 15 June 1728.

21. *Gentleman's Magazine,* March 1824, 202–3; Charles Spear, *Essays on the Punishment of Death* (Boston, 1844), 108–9; *Prisoner's Friend* 1 (1849): 389–90. For a somewhat earlier published claim of his innocence, see John Trusler, *The Tablet of Memory: or, Historian's Guide* (Dublin, 1782), 10.

22. *The Taming of the Shrew,* act 5, sc. 2.

Those headstrong women, one of whom is her beautiful sister Bianca, the one all the men have been lusting after, scoff. But Katherina obligingly recites a lesson of just the sort the blathering conduct manuals constantly proposed:

> Fie, fie! unknit that threatening unkind brow,
> And dart not scornful glances from those eyes,
> To wound thy lord, thy king, thy governor. . . .
> Thy husband is thy lord, thy life, thy keeper,
> Thy head, thy sovereign. . . .
> Such duty as the subject owes the prince
> Even such a woman oweth to her husband;
> And when she is froward, peevish, sullen, sour,
> And not obedient to his honest will,
> What is she but a foul contending rebel
> And graceless traitor to her loving lord?
> I am ashamed that women are so simple
> To offer war where they should kneel for peace;
> Or seek for rule, supremacy and sway,
> When they are bound to serve, love and obey.

Katherina couldn't be more emphatic that husbands govern wives. She doesn't naturalize or essentialize that authority, doesn't make it invisible or part of the fabric of the universe. She goes on to try to justify it by appealing to the facts of women's bodies: they're "soft and weak and smooth," so their hearts should be deferential, too. This appeal to nature offers a putative justification for male authority, the sort we saw from Halifax, Cavendish, and others. It doesn't suggest that justification and criticism are somehow off the table.

"Such duty as the subject owes the prince / Even such a woman oweth to her husband": Petruchio's triumph is precisely that Katherina grasps her subordination as explicitly political. Overjoyed by her recitation, Petruchio exclaims, "Why, there's a wench! Come on, and kiss me, Kate." That kiss, whether perfunctory, affectionate, or erotic, won't represent a realm of private affection removed from politics, and not only because outsiders are watching. Neither Kate nor Petruchio imagines that the household is (choose your prefix) prepolitical or unpolitical or apolitical. It's political just as the realm is. If the kiss isn't perfunctory, its affectionate or sexual charge is enabled by the acknowledgment of Petruchio's governance: here the personal is political with a vengeance. Notoriously there's room to argue that she's ironically parroting a script to stop his endless campaign of cruelty. I don't doubt that the play can be produced that way. Nor that contemporaries could have read or seen it that way: she wouldn't be the first wife whose verbal submission helped mollify her husband. For my purposes, it doesn't matter what Shakespeare intended. Realizing that her blather was endlessly echoed and endlessly challenged should make it impossible to see this effusion of poetic splendor as an innocent portrait of early modern marriage. We should see it instead as a contentious campaign slogan in sometimes internecine warfare.

Fast-forward over a century to *The Story of the Injured Lady*, Jonathan Swift's barbed lament for the 1707 Act of Union between England and Scotland.[23] The injured lady is Ireland, more or less raped by the alleged gentleman, England—"I must confess with Shame, that I was undone by the common Arts practiced upon all easy credulous Virgins, half by Force, and half by Consent, after solemn Vows and Protestations of Marriage"—who's now decided to ditch her, marry Scotland, and go on exploiting her to boot. England so contemns Ireland that "whenever he imagines the smallest Advantage will redound to one of his Foot-boys by any new Oppression of me and my whole Family and Estate, he never disputeth it a Moment." Poor Ireland is assigned "the Office of being Sempstress to his Grooms and Footmen, which I am forced to accept or starve." From eager fiancée to servant to base footmen: quite the wretched fall. So too England strips poor Ireland of "the Government of my Family"; "I must not . . . give any Directions for the well-governing of my Family, but what he countermands whenever he pleaseth." Eager to limn political treachery, the last thing Swift wants to do is pretend that the Act of Union is "merely" a matter of premarital sex gone wrong. The pamphlet's conceit depends on the thought that international diplomacy is recondite. To grasp the outrage, Swift thinks, his readers can model England's treatment of Ireland on sordid political scenes they know all too well.

It's not just that contemporaries found causal links between household and state, though they did that, too. Clarendon linked civil war, regicide, and the horrors of the interregnum to a breakdown of authority in the household: women, children, and servants were unloosed.[24] It's also that household and state are each fully political, so the way is clear to use either to illuminate the other. Husbands are sovereign: so some insisted, triggering others' defiance.

---

23. In *The Prose Works of Jonathan Swift*, ed. Herbert Davis, 14 vols. (Oxford: Basil Blackwell, 1939–68), 9:3–9.

24. *Continuation of the Life*, in *The Life of Edward Earl of Clarendon* (Oxford, 1759), 21–22.

The king is father of his people: insistence triggered defiance. In both cases, defiance triggered insistence, too. Again, people insist on principles when they think others reject them. The language is ever more intricate, even dizzying: sometimes Parliament is the king's "political wife,"[25] sometimes the General Council of the New Model Army is,[26] sometimes the people are. The possibilities careen ever on: in one print, the state plays henpecked husband to the church.[27] In a typically unfortunate spurt of excess, Dryden voiced the loyal subjects' longing for Charles II's restoration: "Our cross Stars deny'd us *Charles* his Bed / Whom Our first Flames and Virgin Love did wed."[28] There's a lot to say about the merits of all this language. But suggesting that it naturalizes the state's authority is a howler. Surmising that only much later did feminist insights become available is inadvertently hilarious. Nor did the language of family lock anyone into any political view. We've canvassed wide-ranging possibilities.[29]

Shakespeare and Swift are aligned with one faceless publication—joke, song, pamphlet, sermon, play, you name it—after another. They claim that the household is political. Or, we could say, they know it is. They can know it, not just claim it, because it's true. The household is not sort of vaguely political or a causal antecedent of politics. The household is shot through with controversies about legitimate authority, richly political, full stop. The early modern English couldn't have been clearer in articulating and pursuing the stakes.

25. Roger Acherley, *The Britannic Constitution: or, The Fundamental Form of Government in Britain* (London, 1727), 507; Eustace Budgell, *Liberty and Property: A Pamphlet Highly Necessary to Be Read by Every Englishman* (London, 1732), 152.

26. E[lizabeth] Pool[e], *A Vision: Wherein Is Manifested the Disease and Cure of the Kingdome* (London, 1648), [4].

27. *The Hierarchical Skimington: or, A Representation of the Ambitious and Arbitrary Views of a Party* (London, 1735).

28. *Astraea Redux* [1660], in *The Works of John Dryden*, ed. Edward Niles Hooker et al., 20 vols. (Berkeley: University of California Press, 1956–89), 1:22.

29. Similarly, see Rachel Weil, *Political Passions: Gender, the Family, and Political Argument in England, 1680–1714* (Manchester: Manchester University Press, 1999); Su Fang Ng, *Literature and the Politics of the Family in Seventeenth-Century England* (Cambridge: Cambridge University Press, 2007). Lynn Hunt, *The Family Romance of the French Revolution* (Berkeley: University of California Press, 1992), agrees that the invocation of family "could take many different forms and serve many different political ends," but I sharply dissent from her claim that "The family romance was a kind of prepolitical category for organizing political experience" (196).

Index